Praise for *Horizontalism*

"To read this book is to join the crucial conversation taking place within its pages: the inspiring, maddening, joyful cacophony of debate among movements building a genuinely new politics. Through her deeply respectful documentary editing, Marina Sitrin has produced a work that embodies the values and practices it portrays."—Avi Lewis and Naomi Klein, co-creators of *The Take*

"This book is really excellent. It goes straight to the important issues and gets people to talk about them in their own words. The result is a fascinating and important account of what is fresh and new about the Argentinian uprising."—John Holloway, author of *Change the World Without Taking Power*

"'Another world is possible' was the catch-phrase of the World Social Forum, but it wasn't just possible; while the north was dreaming, that world was and is being built and lived in many parts of the global south. With the analytical insight of a political philosopher, the investigative zeal of a reporter, and the heart of a sister, Marina Sitrin has immersed herself in one of the most radical and important of these other worlds and brought us back stories, voices, and possibilities. This book on the many facets, phases and possibilities of the insurrections in Argentina since the economic implosion of December 2001 is riveting, moving, and profoundly important for those who want to know what revolution in our time might look like."—Rebecca Solnit, author of *Savage Dreams* and *Hope in the Dark*

"This is the story of how people at the bottom turned Argentina upside down—told by those who did the overturning. Workers, community residents, and the unemployed drove out four national governments in two weeks; blocked highways and forced public officials to negotiate with them on the spot; formed hundreds of new participatory neighborhood assemblies; and occupied factories, hotels, and other enterprises and ran them under their workers' own control. Beyond that, this is the story of how they developed an emerging practice of '*horizontalidad*' that is now transforming Argentine social relations day by day. This is a book for anyone who wants to understand what it's really like to change society from below."—Jeremy Brecher, author of *Strike!* and *Globalization from Below*

"The movements in Argentina have been among the most creative and inspirational in recent years. Marina Sitrin's collection allows us to learn from the activists themselves and continue the experiments in autonomy and democracy they have begun."—Michael Hardt, co-author of *Empire*

"Marina Sitrin has provided an invaluable service to scholars and activists around the world by compiling the testimonies of the participants in some of the most prominent and original Argentine popular movements. These activists speak of political passion, determination, solidarity, and new forms of horizontal organization. They also speak of frustration, obstacles, and repression. Overall, their voices show in startling detail the stubborn hope of a new generation of sufferers and fighters. Sitrin should be commended for all the hard work that went into producing the book, a work of political love and compañerismo."—Javier Auyero, author of *Contentious Lives*

"This book is like a musical instrument, as we learn from the prologue, on which the reader chooses what music to play. This chorus of voices, recorded with such sensibility, echoes the diversity that gives life to the Argentine social movements. Taken each in their own right, they represent individual battles freed from the heat of a collective one. Taken together, they represent resistance on a human scale. The sound of this instrument is simple, but its echo profound."—Claudia Acuña, lavaca.org, editor of *Sin Patron*

"This book contains much more than the voices and ideas of the on-the-ground) architects of horizontalidad. It offers a comprehensive analysis of the ideological and material dynamics of the movement, presented by the participants themselves, as they respond to the insightful analytic probing of scholar/activist Marina Sitrin."—Michael Schwartz, author of *Radical Protest and Social Structure*

"These are the voices of Argentina's grassroots activists, captured amidst the most important burst of democratic innovation the world has seen in the last decade. Listen, and learn how to make history from the bottom up!"—Marie Kennedy, co-editor of *Radical Politics of Place in America*, and Chris Tilly, co-author of *Glass Ceilings and Bottomless Pits*

HORIZONTALISM

VOICES OF POPULAR POWER IN ARGENTINA

EDITED BY MARINA SITRIN

AK PRESS

EDINBURGH • OAKLAND • WEST VIRGINIA

Horizontalism: Voices of Popular Power in Argentina
© 2006 Marina Sitrin

ISBN 1-904859-58-5
ISBN-13 978-1-904859-58-1
Library of Congress Control Number: 2006920972

AK Press   AK Press
674-A 23rd Street   PO Box 12766
Oakland, CA 94612-1163   Edinburgh EH8 9YE
USA   Scotland

akpress@akpress.org   ak@akedin.demon.co.uk
www.akpress.org   www.akuk.com

The addresses above would be delighted to provide you with the latest complete AK catalog, featuring several thousand books, pamphlets, zines, audio and video products, and stylish apparel published and distributed by AK Press. Alternately, please visit our websites for the complete catalog, latest news and updates, events and secure ordering.

Printed in Canada on acid-free, 100% recycled paper.

Front cover photo by Nicolás Pousthomis/www.sub.coop
Cover design by John Yates/www.stealworks.com

Contents

Translating we walk

Horizontalidad: Voces de Poder Popular, the original Spanish version of this book, was published in 2005 at Chilavert, a recuperated printing press in Argentina. The printing process was collaborative, filled with *compañerismo* and love. As Candido (one of the compañeros from Chilavert you will meet in the book) often says: with solidarity and love all is possible. I am forever indebted to my friends at Chilavert for reminding me of all that is possible.

This is not a conventionally translated or edited book. It has its own methodology, one from which I am never absent. I have attempted to work in the spirit of the new politics of affectivity. My aim as a translator and editor was, first and foremost, to facilitate the fullest meanings and sentiments of people in the social movements. Methodologically, I've done this through participation in those movements. The new politics taking shape in Argentina require new forms of translation, new ways of communicating political experiences. For a translator this poses a serious challenge.

What I've chosen to do with this translation is to retain certain words that don't make immediate sense in English, leaving room for new meanings and significations. This process requires the patience of an understanding reader. As many of the people I interview remind us, old words cannot define new things—a new language is necessary. However, a dilemma arises when that new language is developing in Spanish and we, who speak English, generally do not yet share the experiences that are creating a new vocabulary. This is where the patience comes in. We must try to listen to the experience before attempting to translate it into the language of our own experience.

In traditional debates about translation, there are two options: one can try to be faithful to the literal wording of the original or one can create a new work entirely. The choice is between being loyal to the language or to the experience. This new translation should be neither. It is first and foremost a participatory political process. New movements put new demands and expectations on translators and editors. They demand participation. Language is one of the most delicate, and tricky, political tools. Words and expressions are filled with previously held emotions and meanings. They have histories. Their meanings change over time. The tricky thing about this oral history is that, not only have new words been created in Spanish to describe new experiences, but the meanings of older, fairly common words have evolved. Patience and openness is required on both counts. One must simultaneously be open to a new, unfamiliar vocabulary and also understand that familiar words might signify in new ways.

As Emilio, a seventeen-year-old activist in Argentina at the time of our conversations, puts it:

> So, today we're constructing something different. And, in the process, a whole new language and new forms of expression come into being. *Horizontalidad*, direct democracy, sharing and effecting one another's movements, contamination, articulation, organizing in networks—these expressions are not often heard from the traditional left... There are many words from the past that could define today's situation, but since they're old words used to define new things, they create confusion.

Below are a few examples of such words and expressions. It's neither meant to be an exhaustive list, nor a thorough explanation of the new meanings, but rather a brief guide.

Horizontalidad

This word and it's meaning are discussed in the introduction. By far it is one of the most widely used words coming from the new movements in Argentina. I have occasionally translated it as horizontality or horizontalism, but these are translations that miss the full sense of the word. *Horizontalidad* does not just imply a flat plane for organizing, or non-hierarchical relationships in which people no longer make decisions for others. It is a positive word that implies the use of direct democracy and the striving for consensus, processes in which everyone is heard and new relationships are created. *Horizontalidad* is a new way of relating, based in affective politics, and against all of the implications of "isms."

Protagonism and Subjectivity

Many people in the movements speak of themselves as protagonists, of a new subjectivity, and of social protagonism. This reflects not only people's sense of self-activity, but of a social phenomenon in which people are deciding for themselves, breaking from a past of political party brokerage and silence. It also refers to a new collective sense of being, where, through direct democracy, new individuals and collectives are being born.

Dignity

On the surface, dignity is a word that is easily understood in English, but it has taken on important connotations in the movements in Argentina. Under Peronism, dignity referred to the good worker, who went to work, came home, returned to work the next day, and felt pride in this relationship as a worker with a boss. This word now, especially for those in the occupied and recuperated factories, as well as the unemployed workers' movements, represents the self-organization and autonomy of working without bosses or hierarchy. Dignity is now created by individuals and collectives.

Autogestión

Autogestión is a word that has no exact English translation. Historically, the anarchist idea of self-management comes closest to its current use in Argentina's movements. *Autogestión* is based not in the *what*, but in the *how*. It is the relationships among people that create a particular project, not simply the project itself. It is a word reflecting an autonomous and collective practice. When people in the movements in Argentina speak of *autogestión* they usually are implying directly democratic decision-making processes and the creation of new subjectivities along the way. I have sometimes left this word in Spanish to emphasize these many meanings.

Política Afectiva

One way people in the movements describe the territory they are creating is through the idea of *política afectiva*, or affective politics. They are affective in the sense of creating affection, creating a base that is loving and supportive, the only base from which one can create politics. It is a politics of social relationships and love. To translate this term as "love-based politics" would miss many of the social relationships it implies.

The Politics of Walking

Similar to the Zapatistas and other movements, many in Argentina speak in terms of process and walking. The Zapatistas often refer to the importance of the walk, and not the goal or destination per se. Without much initial contact between the two movements, the Argentines are speaking similarly.

For the reader, this reference to actions and ideas as processes, rather than something done, may be frustrating at times. One may want the speaker to just say that something is a certain way, but in fact the "way" that it is, is a walk, a process. I've consciously used the progressive tense a great deal in my translation. People will say, "we are creating," rather than "we have created." This is a part of the new politics. Similarly, many people introduce ideas by saying that they believe certain things, not that they think them. This may seem like a minor issue, but believing something implies an emotional commitment in an ongoing process, while thinking can imply that the process is over.

Many people helped me translate sections of this book, and I am deeply grateful. Millions of gracias go to: Abby Anzalone, Mike McGuire, Irene Peña, Jodi Zisow, George Ciccariello Maher, and my mother, Carol Cositore Sitrin. I did, however, edit and re-edit, so any mistakes are mine.

Acknowledgements

I have learned the meaning of affective politics through practice. The process of creating this book over the past few years was filled with trust, love, support, and *compañerismo*. I received so much love and support from people in the various movements in Argentina that, truly, this book could not have happened otherwise. Paula H. and Martín K. welcomed me into their homes and movements before I even arrived in Argentina—at the World Social Forum in Brazil, where the idea for this book was born. The love from Claudia A. and her family, who housed me, helped orient me, argued and always collaborated is something that goes beyond words. And Neka, one of the most inspiring, loving, and free people I have the privilege of knowing, who always helps me to listen beyond what I hear. And of course, Candido, a friend, compañero, and the definition of solidarity in human form. Thank you to the compañeros of the MTDs Solano, Allen, and Chipolleti, the recuperated factory Chilavert, and the Asamblea Colegiales—some of the most transformative spaces for me as a revolutionary person, and as the editor of this book.

My family, especially my mother and father, played a huge role in helping me though every phase of the process—they believed in me from the beginning, and helped every step of the way. I am grateful to Michael Schwartz, a wonderful mentor, who provided support for the method and the content of these pages. To David Solnit, my dear friend Robin Hood, who continues to be an inspiration in action and words, and has always been there to encourage, and remind me that this book is an important tool for others. Thanks to the Institute for Anarchist Studies who gave me my first grant at the inception of the book. And thanks to AK Press who believed in the vision even before reading the book, and Lorna in particular, an ever supportive and clear editor. Also big thanks to Rachel Lockman and Charles Weigl for editorial support. And, to my island, my half of the apple, and my dream, Andrej Grubacic. *Zauvek*!

A draft of this book was circulated among a number of people in the movements. Due to geographic and time limitations, this process was not as collective as I would have liked. Thank you to the many compañeros who were able to give me such valuable input.

introduction

This book is the story of a changing society told by people who are taking their lives and communities into their own hands. It is told in their own voices. It is a story of cooperation, vision, creation, and discovery.

Over the past ten years, the world has been witnessing an upsurge in prefigurative revolutionary movements; movements, that create the future in the present. These new movements are not creating party platforms or programs. They do not look to one leader, but make space for all to be leaders. They place more importance on asking the right questions than on providing the correct answers. They do not adhere to dogma and hierarchy, instead they build direct democracy and consensus. They are movements based in trust and love.

Where are these movements? They are everywhere. They are in the autonomous Zapatista communities of Chiapas, Mexico, where indigenous communities are organizing autonomously from the state to meet their basic needs, while using consensus-based decision-making to create themselves anew. They are in the massive organizations in rural Brazil, where the landless movement (MST) has been reclaiming the land, creating the future in their daily activities and interactions. They are in the shanty-towns of South Africa, where women and men, "the poors," use direct democracy and action to take back electricity, housing, water, and other things stolen by corporations and government. They are in India, where many thousands of people are coming together to protect the environment and prevent the construction of dams, using mass action and participatory decision-making. They are in Ecuador and Bolivia, where indigenous groups are stopping privatization and preventing the destruction of the earth through mass blockades and mass democracy. They are in Italy, where new social centers are providing direct services as well as space to gather for those involved in direct democracy projects. They are in the many groups in Eastern Europe, organizing against national borders, while asserting the principal that no person can be illegal. They are in the US and Canada, where autonomous groupings are being built on the basis of consensus decision-making, anti-hierarchy, and anti-capitalism.

The autonomous social movements in Argentina are one part of this global phenomenon. Within Argentina, they are also a "movement of movements." They are working class people taking over factories and running them collectively. They are the urban middle class, many recently declassed, working to meet their needs in solidarity with those around them. They are the unemployed, like so many unemployed around the globe, facing the prospect of never finding regular work, yet collectively finding ways to survive and become self-sufficient, using mutual-aid and love. They are autonomous indigenous communities struggling to liberate stolen land.

In Argentina, these active movements are now communicating, assisting, and learning from one another, and thus constructing new types of networks that reject the hierarchical template bequeathed to them by established politics. A core part of this rejection includes a break with the idea of "power-over." People are attempting, instead, to organize on a flatter plane, with the goal of creating "power-with" one another. Embedded in these efforts is a commitment to value both the individual and the collective. Simultaneously, separately, and together, these groups are organizing in the direction of a more meaningful and deeper freedom, using the tools of direct democracy and direct action. They are constructing a new form of popular power.

Horizontalidad is a word that has come to embody the new social arrangements and principles of organization of these movements in Argentina. As its name suggests, *horizontalidad* implies democratic communication on a level plane and involves—or at least intentionally strives towards—non-hierarchical and anti-authoritarian creation rather than reaction. It is a break

The banging of a pot in protest.

with vertical ways of organizing and relating.

Horizontalidad is a living word that reflects an ever-changing experience. Months after the popular rebellion in December of 2001, many movement participants began speaking of their relationships as horizontal in order to describe the new forms of decision-making. Years after the rebellion, those continuing to build new movements speak of *horizontalidad* as a goal, as well as a tool.

Our relationships are deeply affected by the power dynamics of capitalism and hierarchy, which operate in our collective and creative spaces, especially in how we relate to one another in terms of economic resources, gender, race, access to information and experience. We see this arise often in our meetings, assemblies, activities, and actions. While usually not intentional, power based in various sorts of privileges often comes up and can silence others in a group or movement. As a result, until these fundamental social dynamics are overcome, the goal of *horizontalidad* cannot be achieved. Simply desiring egalitarian relationships does not make them so. But the process of *horizontalidad* is also a tool to achieve this goal. Thus *horizontalidad* is desired and is a goal, but it is also the means—the tool—for achieving this end. In the second chapter, "*Horizontalidad*," dozens of movement participants discuss their experiences and reflections on this new social relationship.

The social movements in Argentina describe themselves as autonomous in order to distinguish themselves from the state and other hierarchical institutions. Autonomy also describes a politics of self-organization, *autogestión*, and direct, democratic participation. This use of the word "autonomous" is not meant to address, or reflect, any direct relationship to the autonomous Marxist currents, which have their origins in Italy. While the autonomous movements in Argentina are not the largest numerically, I believe they are the most interesting in terms of what they are creating. The effect of these movements is much larger than their physical size would suggest. This is true in part because of the new social relationships and articulations of these relationships that these movements are creating—relationships and institutions that can be emulated. "Autonomy," the fourth section of the book, will clarify this choice of political identification.

The movements described in this book are prefigurative movements; movements, that is, that are creating the future in their present social relationships. Unlike past movements, social change isn't deferred to a later date by demanding reforms from the state, or by taking state power and eventually, instituting these reforms. As the interviews reflect, most in the autonomous movements are placing their energies in how and what they organize in the present. Most of the movements are anti-capitalist, and some anti-state, but their strategy for the creation of a new society is not grounded in either state dependency or the taking of power to create another state. Their intention is, to borrow John Holloway's phrase, to change the world without taking power.

Over the past five years, in particular, the autonomous social movements in Argentina have begun to articulate a new and revolutionary politics, embodied in various new practices and in language used to describe these practices. Some participants say that they are not political, or that they are anti-political. Often this is related to their experiences with "old" ways of doing politics, with the use of hierarchy and political parties that make decisions for people, taking away their agency. Today, they are engaged in the more immediate politics of everyday life, creating the future in their present. They reject hierarchy, bosses, managers, party brokers, and *punteros*. Simply put, they reject the very idea of anyone having power over someone else. They organize themselves in every aspect of their lives, both independently and in solidarity with others: *autogestiónandose* in communities, neighborhoods, workplaces, schools, and universities. What is the name of this revolutionary process: *Horizontalidad*? *Autogestión*? Socialism? Anarchism? Autonomy? *Politica afectiva*? None of these? All of them? Certainly, no single word can describe it. It is a process of continuous creation, constant growth, and the development of new relations, with ideas flowing from these changing practices.

Historical context

Argentina has a long rich history of rebellions, resistance, and self-organization. The movements discussed in this book are the most recent of these, and developed in two cumulative waves. The first wave represented a movement of unemployed workers, which emerged in the 1990s. It had little support from, and in some cases was violently opposed by, the still relatively prosperous Argentine middle class. However, the collapse of the Argentine economy and the declassing of much of the middle class as a result of the coercive policies of the IMF, sparked a second wave of popular rebellion, during which the now declassed Argentine middle class linked up with unemployed and underemployed workers.

The people of Argentina have endured a long history of domination of their communities and neighborhoods by those who, while claiming to represent them, make huge profits from this alleged representation. This concept of "representation" was seen most notably under Peronism, particularly with its reliance on "*punteros*," local neighborhood Party bureaucrats or brokers. This system resulted in a politics of "clientelism" where, particularly in poor neighborhoods, nothing could be accomplished without the mediation of the *punteros*, and people were forced to exchange their autonomy for basic necessities. The new autonomous social movements are a conscious break with this form of politics. They reject the hierarchy inherent in the clientelist system and replace it with direct democracy, and in public gatherings, discuss alternative plans, deciding openly and collectively what to do. Chapter 1, "Context and Rupture," discusses this new form of direct democracy. Clientelism still exists in many neighborhoods and is discussed in parts of chapter 3, "Challenges to *Autogestión*."

Olivia, a woman in her eighties living in Ledesma, Jujuy, in the far north of the country, explained how things today are different from how they were for most of her life. She spoke with tremendous pride about being a part of an unemployed workers' movement in her neighborhood—one of thirty-three neighborhoods organized in Ledesma. As a part of that movement, she now participates in the decisions that affect her life, as well as the life of her community. One of the ways this is done is through weekly neighborhood assemblies that use direct democracy and synthesis as a means of making decisions. Decisions are made on a town-wide basis once a month, when over 3,000 people come together in a mass assembly. Everyone has a voice. Discussions range from direct action planning, to the coordination of bakeries, childcare centers, and beauty salons, all self-organized by the neighborhood movements.

The creation of directly democratic organizations, such as those in Ledesma, are clear rejections of, and decisive ruptures with, past vertical organizational structures of clientelism, as well as concepts of "representation."

Unemployed workers' movements

The emerging rejection of old political ways became publicly visible in the north and south of the country in the 1990s, when unemployed workers' movements, as well as other popular movements, began organizing against local governments and corporations. Generally led by unemployed women workers in the provinces of Salta, Jujuy, and Neuquen, they took to the streets by the thousands, blocking major transportation arteries to demand subsidies from the government. In a decisive break with the past, this organizing was not led or brokered by elected leaders. Instead, those in the streets decided day-by-day and moment-to-moment what to do next.

Front of a road blockade.

During the road blockades, people used direct forms of decision-making, and began creating new social relationships, which, in many places, evolved into what are now known formally as unemployed workers' movements (MTDs), Unions of unemployed workers (UTDs), or the Movement for Work and Dignity (MTD). They are referred to informally as *piqueteros* (both the people and the movement), a name taken from "*piquete*," the tactic of blockading roads.

In some places, as is described by participants in the Unemployed Workers' Movement in the Solano neighborhood, people came together, tried to discover what needs existed in the neighborhood, formed a community with common interests and desires, and together decided to blockade roads as one of their many tactics. In other areas, the movements began with a group of neighbors meeting in the street to demand something. They would form a road blockade, and then use democratic forms of decision-making to collectively decide their demands, and then negotiate with representatives of government. From these points of collective action and decision-making, the movements were born. Distinct from previous forms of organizing, where there was always a person speaking for the group (most often without consent), in these early *piquetes*, people decided they would negotiate at the blockade itself. There are some cases of government officials being helicoptered onto the road to negotiate directly with the assembly at the blockade. The *piqueteros'* initial actions forced the government to give the first (small) unemployment subsidies in the history of Latin America. The confidence that this victory inspired lead to the creation of many projects and visions, opening many people's imaginations to what more might be possible. The chapters "Autogestión" and "Creation" describe the specifics of what the various movements are doing. Projects range from bakeries and organic gardens, to alternative medicine clinics, education and schools, to raising animals and taking over land for housing and food production.

The relationship of various movements to one another continues to evolve. Soon after the popular rebellion of 2001, the dozens of autonomous unemployed workers' movements, which reflected the participation of tens of thousands, created a loose network called Anibal Veron, after a *piquetero* who was murdered by the police in northern Argentina. This network had regular gatherings to share information, experiences, and to plan collective direct actions. The various movements in the network organized around the principles of *horizontalidad,* autonomy, dignity, and social change. Over time, this network stopped functioning, and some movements continued to coordinate actions through the Frente Dario Santillan, named after another young *piquetero* murdered by police at a road blockade. Others formed a loose network that focused on an exchange of information and support. These changes reflect friction over the question of autonomy, and how it is understood in practice by the various movements. Around 2003, a number of the MTDs decided—some of them after these interviews were conducted—that they no longer wanted to fight for the government unemployment subsidy. They felt this maintained a relationship with the state, rather than focusing their energy on self-organization, *autogestión*, and attempts at self-sufficiency. Organizing a road blockade creates a contentious relationship to the state, when many would prefer no relationship at all. It also entails a sophisticated level of organizing, which takes a great deal of time to develop. These questions of time and political priorities pushed a number of movements to stop using the road blockade as a frequent tactic. Other movements that continue organizing regular *piquetes* are critical of those that do not, both for theoretical reasons—they don't see the relationship to the state being overly determined—but there is also a sense of frustration because they believe support is needed from everyone in the movements to make the blockades successful. This is an ongoing discussion and debate.

Rebellions

While the *piquetero* movement was still growing, the increasing economic crisis pushed thousands into the streets in the northern town of Santiago del Estero. As one of the first contemporary urban uprisings, this rebellion looms large in the imagination of millions of Argentines. It involved protests against government, as well as the creation of libratory spaces where people together began to feel their collective power. Government buildings were destroyed—as were the homes of government officials. "Representatives" were forced to leave office, due to their fear of the rebelling population. These early rebellions remain significant because they represent, in the memory and imagination of Argentines, the rejection of systems of representation, in favor of direct action and other forms of democracy.

The definitive rupture with past practice, however, occurred in the popular rebellion of the 19th and 20th of December of 2001, often referred to as the "nineteenth and twentieth." Millions spontaneously took to the streets across Argentina and, without leaders or hierarchies, forced the government to resign, and then, through continuous mobilizations, proceeded to expel four more governments in less than two weeks. The precipitating incident was the government's freezing of people's bank accounts, and converting their money, once pegged to the US dollar, into a financial asset that would be held by the banks and used to secure payments to foreign investors, but that could not be accessed by the depositers.

This was the spark dropped on a long smoldering fire. The government of Argentina had taken out huge loans with the IMF in the 1990s, and in the late 90s began to pay these loans back through privitization and severe austerity measures. Thousands of people were laid off, wages and pensions were cut, and social services degraded. These measures eminated from the IMF as part of the contract for yet another loan of billions of dollars. As with most of Latin America (and the world) the results were disasterous for most people. Working and middle class Argentines experienced no direct relief from the new loans, and by 2001 industrial production had fallen by over 25 percent. The official poverty level grew to 44 percent, with the unofficial level substantially higher. For many Argentines the popular rebellion was no surprise.

The weekly march of the Mothers of the Plaza de Mayo. "No to the payment of the external debt."

As with the previous experiences in the north and south, the experience of the rebellion was one of direct democracy and direct action. The government quickly responded by declaring a state of emergency, ordering citizens to stay at home, and attempting to disperse the people in the street. In response to this repression by the state that killed dozens and wounded many hundreds of others, and was witnessed on television by the general population, hundreds of thousands poured onto the streets of Buenos Aires.

These protesters were not demanding something new, but were creating it. As pointed out by a number of those interviewed in this book, this massive outpouring into the streets, despite the state of emergency and repression witnessed by all, is hugely significant. These days, many refer to this moment as a rupture with the past, a break from the deeply instilled fear and silence that was a legacy of the most brutal dictatorship in Argentine history—a dictatorship that "disappeared" 30,000 people, torturing them in the most horrific ways. Some see the nineteenth and twentieth as a break in collective memory. In chapter 1, "Context and Rupture" many reflect upon this simultaneous break and opening.

Neighborhood assemblies

The popular rebellion was comprised of workers and unemployed, of the middle class, and of those recently de-classed. It was a rebellion without leadership, either by established parties or by a newly emerged elite. Its strength was measured in the fall of four consecutive national governments in two weeks. It precipitated the birth of hundreds of neighborhood assemblies involving many tens of thousands of active participants.

People in the neighborhood assemblies first met to try and discover new ways of supporting one another and ways to meet their basic needs. Many explain the organization of the first assemblies as an encounter, as finding one another. People were in the streets, they began talking to one another, they saw the need to gather, and they did so, street corner by street corner, park by park. In many cases, someone would write on a wall or street, "neighbors, let's meet Tuesday at 9PM" and an assembly was begun.

In each neighborhood, the assemblies work on a variety of projects, from helping facilitate barter networks, creating popular kitchens, planting organic gardens, and sometimes taking over buildings—including the highly symbolic take-over of abandoned banks, which they turn into community centers. These occupied spaces can house any number of things, including kitchens, small print shops, day care areas, they may offer after-school help for kids, free internet access and computer usage, and one even has a small movie theater.

The assemblies change form...

The years after the rebellion have witnessed a significant decrease in the organization of, and participation in, neighborhood assemblies. Many dozens are still active, but this is much less than the hundreds that instantly emerged. While we will explore the reasons in the interviews ahead, some recurring themes are: the intrusion of left political parties, a lack of concreteness in activity, and interference from the state.

After the first months of self-organizing, a number of political parties saw an opportunity for recruitment and control. Party members entered neighborhood assemblies, and attempted to take them over. Many neighborhood assembly participants recounted stories of political party members coming to their assemblies and attempting to dominate discussions by speaking at great length, as well as by raising political demands that the assembly must adhere to—such as an end to all imperialism and the creation of a workers' state. Many people described to me a high level of frustration about this. The nature of the assemblies, which were based on trust and listening with respect, many say, opened the space for this problem. Party members used this to enter the assembly and talk or shout endlessly until many neighbors left out of frustration. Many explained that it was not that they were against the political demands raised per se, but that this was not what the neighborhood assembly was organized for.

Similar attempts to dominate the assemblies occurred in the *inter-barrial* assemblies, where hundreds of assemblies would come together in a park in the center of Buenos Aires, and exchange ideas and experiences in order to create networks of mutual support. As has also occurred around the world historically, political parties created front groups— false neighborhood assemblies, in this case—so that they would have the right to speak at the *inter-barrial* assemblies. They then used this time to push their political line and program, and again participants in the real neighborhood assemblies decided to remove themselves from this experience. There is a great deal of hostility toward the political parties for this disruption. Many neighborhood assemblies' participants saw the *inter-barrial* as a potential place to begin to generalize the local neighborhood experience into a city-wide phenomenon of direct democracy and new politics.

Many of the assemblies lacked concrete projects and ended up talking a great deal more than doing. While one of the lasting effects of the assembly movement is the change in the participant's sense of self, community, and collectivity (a process many refer to as the creation of new subjectivities), without concrete projects to ground the assemblies, many people drifted away. Of the assemblies that continue to exist, almost all are involved in a variety of neighborhood-based projects, and some continue to function in occupied buildings.

The neighborhood assemblies quickly became one of the focal points of the government's attempts to regain control of society. These efforts generally involved, on the one hand, overt repression (such as violent evictions of occupied buildings and police harassment), and on the other hand, covert repression, with the government using cooptation and other means to destabilize movements in an attempt to regain legitimacy. The choice to run the notorious Carlos Menem as a candidate for president made many feel they had no alternative but to vote against him, for example. Menem, with good reason, was seen as the person most responsible for privatizing Argentina. This privatization was profound, and included everything from natural resources to the zoo. He ran his campaign on a "Law and Order" ticket, promising to "clean" the country of its disrupters, referring to people in the social movements. Because of this, many people in the neighborhood assemblies decided that they had to vote—not for Menem, but against him. The result was that focus was once again on the state, conferring legitimacy onto the process of elections, and the state itself.

Another sometimes successful tactic the government used was to offer services, goods, and sometimes even physical space to the neighborhood assemblies. Most assemblies self-organized all of their popular kitchens and projects, including the occupation of buildings for community use. The government saw this as an opportunity to gain credibility, and began to offer assemblies boxes of food and even buildings where they could hold their assemblies, rather than conducting them on the street corner. These offers were sometimes debated for months in the various assemblies, and created huge distractions from projects that were already underway.

Many of those interviewed in this book imagined a potential decline in the participation in the neighborhood assemblies, and some even reflected that this would not have a huge impact, since something had changed in them as people, as well as in how they relate to each other. These changes could not be undone, even if the structures of organization changed. This change would then be reflected and infused into new organizations and relationships.

This may be true. I returned to Argentina several times in 2005, after this book was published in Spanish. I witnessed and participated in the emergence of a number of groups, including political prisoner support groups, anti-repression organizations, new assemblies in parks, collectives of street artisans, and high school student groups. All of these began with the basic consensus that they would organize based on *horizontalidad* and autonomy. They referred to the neighborhood assemblies or MTDs when discussing their conceptions of *horizontalidad* and direct democracy. Like earlier groups, these new formations absolutely rejected political parties and hierarchical organization. I was fortunate enough to witness a number of meetings and assemblies where political parties that tried to dominate were kicked out, sometimes with people even referencing previous experience. The experience of the neighborhood assemblies continues as a living part of an overall continuity from the days of the rebellion and the social creation that followed. This is something that many participants imagined would take place as early as 2002. Some even said explicitly that if the neighborhood assemblies no longer existed as a structure it would not be that big a deal, since something had changed in people and their social relationships.

Relationships among autonomous movements

Just as the popular rebellion sparked the growth of neighborhood assemblies, it also inspired the unemployed workers' movements. As they grew to include tens of thousands of participants, these groups developed an even more sophisticated theoretical framework. A network formation grew among those in the various autonomous movements—a network that crossed class lines and class identification. One of the most significant relationships in this network was that between the *piqueteros* and neighborhood assemblies. Before the 2001 rebellion, the middle class (or at least those who identified themselves as such) considered the *piqueteros'* use of road blockades more than an annoyance. There was a general, social consensus that the unemployed were to blame for their own economic and social condition, and that drastic methods were justified in suppressing them. After the rebellion, a relationship of words and deeds developed between the *piqueteros* and the neighborhood assemblies. Joint actions with middle class groups

Madre and Piquetero in a march.

were organized, including bridge and road blockades. The same middle class people who had hated the *piqueteros* for disrupting daily life were now supporting blockades as a necessary action for re-establishing economic viability. At the same time, many *piqueteros* who, in the past, had seen the middle class as partly responsible for the dire economic situation (or at least culpable through their inactivity), were now organizing side by side with them.

A "space for autonomous thought and reflection," as the bi-weekly autonomous gatherings were called, began taking place on land occupied by unemployed workers' movements, with participants from neighborhood assemblies, unemployed workers' movements, indigenous communities, arts and media collectives, and various other social actors. For a time the slogan *"Piquete y cacerola, la lucha es una sola"* [The road blockade and the banging of pots and pans is one struggle], was widely used.

Recuperated workplaces

The dozen or so occupied factories that existed at the start of the 2001 rebellion grew in only two years to include hundreds of workplaces, taken over and run directly by workers, without bosses or hierarchy. Many in the new movements gathered inspiration from the occupation and recuperation of workplaces, and those workplaces received much support from the movements, particularly the neighborhood assemblies and new arts and media collectives. In most instances of occupation, it is the immediate neighbors and various collectives and assemblies that physically come to support and defend the occupied workplace. In the example of the printing press, Chilavert, it was the retirement home across the street that came out, and not only defended the factory from the police, but insisted on being the front line of defense. In many other workplaces, the neighborhood assemblies cook lunch and bring it to the workers, and then sit down with them to eat. There is also often a relationship with media and arts collectives who collaborate on the use of space in the factories, who open art galleries, venues for live music for the neighborhood at night, as well as cafés, and after-school programs. Almost every workplace sees itself as an integral part of the community, and the community sees the workplace in the same way. As the workers of Zanon, a ceramic factory say, "Zanon is of the people."

Workplaces range widely: from printing presses and metal shops to medical clinics, from cookie, shoe, and balloon factories to a four-star hotel and a daily newspaper. Throughout this book, participants in the recuperated workplaces say that what they are doing conceptually is not very complicated despite the challenges, and quote the slogan: "Occupy, Resist, and Produce." The third chapter, *"Autogestión,"* is where these stories are discussed in the most detail. *Autogestión*—meaning self-organization and self-management—is how most in the recuperated movements describe what they are creating and how.

This movement—now generally calling itself a movement of recuperated workplaces (though some use the terms "occupied factories" and "recovered factories")—continues to grow and gather support throughout Argentina, despite threats of eviction. Thus far, each threat has been met with sufficient mobilization to thwart the government's efforts. The government does not seem to know what to do with the recuperated workplaces, and acts in contradictory ways. The recuperations are hugely popular, and many outside the movements explained them to me quite simply, saying that there is a lack of work and these people want to work. Based in part on this support, the government will sometimes give start up loans to recovered workplaces. However this is only temporary, and the government has also aided attempts to evict countless workplaces. Each eviction is met with an outpouring of support from neighbors and other participants in the factory movement. The help includes food, money, and other physical manifestations of support, to hundreds and sometimes thousands of people organizing (as was the case with Zanon and Brukman) to physically defend the factories. Battles including slingshots and molotov cocktails are not uncommon as a part of these defenses of the factories.

Over time, recuperated workplaces have begun to link with one another, creating barter relationships for their products. For example, a local medical clinic will service members of a printing factory in exchange for the free printing of all of their material. This has happened on globally, as well. A number of workplaces now have international relationships, including relationships for the exchange or purchase of products. In November 2005, the "First Gathering of Recuperated Workplaces" took place in Caracas, Venezuela. There were 263 recuperated workplaces represented, from eight Latin American countries. All participants agreed in a final document that they distributed that this was, "the first step in the creating of a network of workplaces and factories without bosses or owners." The recuperated workplaces gathered there, signed seventy-five agreements. Some were for the exchange of material goods, while others were more creative. A tourist agency in Venezuela, for example, agreed to provide yearly vacations to the families of workers at a recuperated newspaper in Argentina, in exchange for advertising.

New movements' internationalism

The particular movements discussed in this book may be new, but some of the goals and methods of achieving them, are familiar historically. While movements of such rapid growth, diversity, and popularity are not unprecedented, the most significant innovation in Argentina may be that disparate groups are aware of one other, that they are interrelated, and that they can make use of (or create) many more networks of exchange and communication around the globe. Argentine movements, for example, have made significant connections to the MST in Brazil, trading experiences and strategies for land take-overs, forms of traditional medicine, and tools for democratic practices. The Zapatistas have also consistently engaged in exchanges, visiting and being visited by people in other movements. Since the 2001 rebellion, a number of people from various unemployed workers' movements have been invited by the Zapatistas to spend time in the autonomous communities in Chiapas, exchanging ideas and experiences. Also,

Piquetero scarecrow holding a Brazilian MST flag, and the plants are from seeds exchanged with the MST.

participants in the then Frente Zapatista spent time with movements in Argentina discussing a range of things, including how the election of a so-called progressive president affects the movements. Despite limited resources, dialogue between various movements has been long and varied.

During the past three years in Buenos Aires, autonomous movements have held an annual gathering called *Enero Autonomo* (Autonomous January). Groups came from all over Latin America and Europe—including Mujeres Creando from Bolivia, and autonomous groups from Brazil. Participants also included various collectives and community-based organizations in Europe and the United States. This linking process has gained momentum over the past few years and all signs indicate that this growth is accelerating.

A number of networks, conferences, and connections between the various autonomous movements around the globe have been created over the past decade—groups and gatherings including Peoples' Global Action (PGA), the World Social Forum, Via Campesina, and Indymedia, to name just a few. Many of these new global networks, such as PGA and Via Campesina, for example, were created and facilitated by participants in the global movement of movements. The relationships of the movement of movements in Argentina, is one piece of a much larger global phenomenon of networking and horizontal relationships.

Intention of and approach to this book

There is a growing body of Spanish literature analyzing the social movements of the last decade in Argentina. A brief list would include: Colectivo Situaciones, *Mas Alla de los Piquetes,* and *19 y 20: Apuntes para el Nuevo protagonismo Social*; MTD la Matanza, *De la Culpa a la Autogestión*; Sebastian Pereyra y Maristella Svampa, *Entre la Ruta y El Barrio*; Raúl Zibechi, *Genealogía de la Revuelta.* This book however, is not another analysis. Instead, it offers the direct testimony of the participants themselves, through interviews conducted during 2003 and 2004.

These interviews allow the activists themselves to speak about what they are creating, why they are creating it in the ways that they are, what it feels like, what their dreams and desires are, and what it all might mean.

One caveat is in order here. While it may appear that you are looking through a transparent window at the person speaking, this is a window that I have constructed. I initiated and participated in all the conversations in this book. After choosing what topics were to be addressed, and deciding which communities were fully explored, I selected the passages to be included in the final manuscript. For this reason, I think it is important to situate myself for you. I am not from Argentina, although I have spent a good deal of time there. I do not ascribe to any one ideology or practice, but partake in many, and feel that it is only through the practice of individual and collective social creation that we will invent, as the Zapatistas discuss, many new worlds. I am part of the global movement of movements, and I am not neutral towards the movements described in these pages. On the contrary, I traveled to Argentina because I had heard of them and felt that sharing this experience in whatever way I could would be important and useful to people who are committed to social change.

The texts are full of depth, emotion, intellect, and passion, but they also require patient readers. Some voices will sound familiar, others less so. Some of the narratives may seem redundant, however, it is often the similarity of the tales that is most fascinating. The ideas of a factory worker take on new meaning when echoed by a middle-class assembly participant, a *piquetara*, and a university student. Similarly, it is remarkable that an unemployed worker in the south speaks of autonomy in almost the same terms as someone from an indigenous Guaraní community in the north. *Horizontalidad,* as a goal and tool of the autonomous movements, spans a great deal of physical and experiential geography. Both the similarities and differences make the movements in Argentina especially unique and the interviews I conducted so exciting. It is not just what is said, but the diversity of the voices speaking.

Rather than a contextualized history, this book reflects and explains what people are doing, what motivates them, how they are relating to one another, and how they have changed individually and collectively in the creation process. It is not so much a movement of actions, but rather a movement of new social actors, new subjects, new protagonists.

In my opinion, *horizontalidad* and direct democracy are important for building a new society. One basis for this new society is the creation of loving and trusting spaces. From this same space of trust and love, using the tools of *horizontalidad,* a new person—who is a protagonist in her or his own life—begins to be created. This is not random, it is a conscious process of social creation, as discussed in chapter nine. Women, in particular, have created new roles for themselves (addressed specifically in chapter eight). Based on this new individual protagonist, a new collective protagonism appears, which changes the sense of the individual, and then the sense of the collective. From this relationship arises the need for new ways of speaking, a new language (as discussed is in chapter five).

Ideas and relationships cannot occur in a vacuum. They take place in real places, in "territories" that are liberated from hierarchical structures, and involve real people. These territories are laboratories of social creation. What is being created, and how, is discussed in the chapters "Autogestión," "Creation, " and "Power." These chapters also address some of the challenges being faced.

As I write in July of 2006, the government of Argentina has been increasing its repression of the new social movements. This repression, while not as violent as that practiced by earlier regimes—in that tens of thousands are not "disappearing" or being tortured—is nevertheless daunting. Thousands of people are being forced through the legal system, many without formal charges, and many awaiting trial while in jail—some for years. Their crime? Trying to create a new world. What offence did they commit? They protested the lack of jobs and their children's hunger. In some cases, they took back their ancestral land, which had been stolen by corporations and the government. Or they worked in the street in order to feed their family. Chapter seven, "Repression," which is based on conversations in 2006, reflects on this current situation, and suggests some responses.

"Dreams," the last chapter of the book, gives a glimpse of what some of us dream. It is from dreams that we begin the creation of new worlds.

context and rupture

December 19 and 20, 2001

Pablo, Asamblea Colegiales (a neighborhood assembly)

It was the night of the nineteenth. The middle class sat at home watching the news on television—seeing poor people crying, women crying in front of supermarkets, begging for or taking food—and the state of Siege was declared. That's when the sound of the *cacerola* (the banging of pots and pans) began. From one window and then another, from one house and then another, came the noise of the *cacerola*. Television newscasters reported that there were *cacerolas* in one neighborhood and another and another until people realized that their individual reactions were forming part of a collective reaction. The mass media functioned as a kind of mirror, multiplying the protest—involuntarily I suppose, but it functioned like that.

The first person began to bang a pot and saw the neighbor across the street banging one, and the neighbor downstairs too, and soon there were four, five, fifteen, twenty. People moved to their doorways and saw other people banging pots in theirs. They saw on television that this was happening in more and more neighborhoods, and soon they went to the main corner of their neighborhood—for example, in this neighborhood it's this one [pointing outside to an intersection], this is a very important corner—and hundreds of people gathered banging pots until one point, when the people banging pots began to walk. Newscasters reported that groups of *cacerolas* were marching to the house of the Minister of the Economy, because Cavallo had resigned. Then others began walking to the Plaza de Mayo, downtown, and more people headed there, without really understanding why, but going anyway. You could see them arriving on television and calling, "Come, come, everyone come." The Minister of the Economy had resigned. He'd resigned, but they began to say it wasn't enough. "The rest of them must go. They must all go. We want them all to go. *Que se vayan todos.*" And it was born there—that was the first time those words were spoken and it's important to know that, until that moment, they'd never been spoken before.

That's how it was. The movement of the nineteenth and twentieth began with a sound—the sound of someone banging on a pot. That sound grew, and then bodies began to move from their houses to the corner, and then to the center of the city, and finally to the Plaza de Mayo. Bodies moved and pots banged, and finally that new phrase was spoken—not speeches, not explanations, not political party placards. No one knew exactly who was there, whether people were from the left, right, or center. There were housewives, young people—everyone was there—and they said with a common voice, "They all must go."

They were saying that all the leaders must go, that by extension everyone in a position of power—all the politicians, all the representatives, all the judges—they all must go. This belief, combined with our knowledge of government scandal, corruption, and fraud, made us realize that the minority with financial power was making decisions every day while the rest of the population felt they were unable to do anything about it... That was the explosion of the nineteenth and twentieth. They all must go. And the government of De La Rúa fell, and the improvised governments lasted a week and also fell. There was a strong offensive against the Supreme Court for corruption... It didn't fall, but it was powerfully threatened. There were important mobilizations by the *ahorristas* (those who had savings)—the ones who had deposited their money in international banks. Suddenly the banks were not returning their savings in pesos or dollars. These people had deposited their money in dollars with guarantees from the international banks and the banks wouldn't...Citibank, the huge banks, wouldn't return their money. There were huge mobilizations by people who felt robbed of their money, and who had been left in total uncertainty. In many cases the savings were small—those of retired people, people saving to buy a home, or simply people with a little bit of money put aside. The financiers didn't have their money in those banks anymore—theirs was outside the country or invested somewhere. It's possible that some fortunes were trapped, but most were small savings. People went out and demonstrated—sixty- or seventy-year-old women, sick people—they went to the banks to demand their money and then to vandalize the banks. The banks put up walls to protect themselves, but were trashed nonetheless. The Congressional Building had to put up fences and walls. Congresspeople couldn't go out on the street because they knew they were an insult to the population, and wherever they went and they were, in turn, insulted.

There was a general reaction against, and rejection of, the political sectors, against financial power, and against judicial power. It was like a demonstration, the feeling in the neighborhoods, the middle class that went out in the *cacerolazo*, mostly those in Buenos Aires. The unemployed were not as active that day, and it was unorganized sectors that began to meet on many neighborhood corners in the form of assemblies—neighborhood assemblies. That was the beginning of the assemblies meeting to express their opinions—the end of December, the beginning of January.

In one month in urban Buenos Aires, there were about 200 assemblies that met weekly with 200 or 300 neighbors in each assembly.

Paloma, Asamblea Palermo Viejo (a neighborhood assembly)

I believe what detonated the explosion of the nineteenth and twentieth was seeing the lootings, followed by the declaration of the state of Seige. It was like something in our collective memory said, "No, I'm not going to put up with it, I'm not going to take it." It began with some *cacerolazos,* and I remember...boom! People lost their fear—the fear we had from the military era, when we had to be silent for fear that the government would bring out the tanks. And now we're advancing. Our advances, although small, go...little by little, but they go well.

Those of us who were here can't forget what happened in the 1970s: 30,000 people disappeared. This has touched us. It isn't just the 30,000, but also all of the fear that remained, as if people couldn't be political... and well, this is like waking up. I don't know, it's a vision I have, but it seems much more than that, as well. It's extremely complex.

Paula, feminist and GLTTB (Gays, Lesbians, Transvestites, Transsexuals, and Bisexuals) collectives

No one expected what happened on the nineteenth and twentieth. It was a complete surprise. I remember that on the nineteenth, I went to my department at the university to hand in my students' grades, and when I left, the front of the supermarket in my neighborhood of *Paternal* was full of police. So I asked them, "What happened here?" That was the day of the looting. It was that night that everyone went out in the street—the nineteenth. And well, the twentieth we know what happened, right?

For me, the twentieth was very strange. It was as if something took hold of me. I'm not a person who is very... I don't know, really I don't have much courage; I'm not very brave. When I see the police, I run away in terror. Repression is something I've always been very afraid of. I see a policeman and I split. The police terrify me. Early on the night of the twentieth, I was at home watching television with my sister, where we saw the police repressing the Madres of the Plaza de Mayo—using horses and everything. Despite my fear of police, I was seized with such a powerful indignation that I said, "Come on, we're going." It was crazy because we knew they could kill us—they had killed someone the night before. We headed first to the Congreso area, downtown, but police were using teargas nearby, so along with another friend, we took a different street to get to the Plaza de Mayo. We could see what was happening. We saw the police kill someone right in front of us. I can't tell you how horrible that was, but it still didn't deter us. It was something unconscious, you know? We needed to be there.

Toto, MTD la Plata (an unemployed workers' movement)

So many things took place in my neighborhood on the nineteenth and twentieth. The nineteenth was more meaningful for us because it was the day of the lootings. The twentieth was more distant, since it was something that happened farther away—downtown, which is a few hours away from us here. It also didn't seem to have much to do with the everyday politics of the neighborhood; we weren't used to direct confrontation with the government. The nineteenth was unusual. I remember the heat, in particular. We were watching the 11 o'clock news, which we rarely do, and while we watched the looting on TV, we began to wonder what we could do. We asked each other, half joking, "Do we go or don't we?"

There wasn't anything formally organized— nothing like a looting movement—but it was in the air. It was like that for at least ten days. We felt closer to the people who were killed while looting than the people who were killed in the Plaza de Mayo. We had more in common.

Mural with a list of those killed by the police.

We had been organizing many different types of activities in the neighborhood for a while before the nineteenth and twentieth. For example, we took over some land where families in the movement could build homes. We also organized a library where we held activities for children and seniors from the neighborhood. Because we wanted to evaluate the neighborhood's material needs and also share our collective fear, we organized a meeting to discuss the lootings specifically. A lot of people who usually didn't participate in the activities of the center, came to that meeting.

We decided we wanted to go and get food, because we needed it. Since many people died as a result of the lootings, we wanted to make sure we were peaceful, and asked the supermarket's owners for food. We mobilized fifty or sixty people, and together we walked to the store to ask for food. The neighborhoods we walked through to get there were more middle class than ours. I remember walking the ten or fifteen blocks to the market and passing many people who looked scared and thought our group of sixty people was going to loot. But we were calm—too calm, perhaps.

As we were walking to the supermarket, I remember chatting with my friends about how we felt ashamed to ask for food. We felt like going to ask for food was crossing some sort of line. I think that's why more people didn't come with us, for this same feeling of shame. Our mobilization for food was important for a number of reasons.

The store gave us food, marking the first of many of these mobilizations. It was also the beginning of actions for other purposes, including *planes de trabajo* [unemployment subsidies].

Ezequiel, Asamblea Cid Campeador (a neighborhood assembly)

I was very angry at my country and neighbors before this rebellion. I saw that the whole economic situation had deteriorated a great deal, and the population hadn't responded. Take me, for example—I'm one of the many people whose salary was cut by 13 percent before the rebellion. I couldn't understand why people weren't doing anything. I was very resentful and very angry... And so people's reactions on the nineteenth and twentieth were particularly unexpected. As soon as President De La Rua gave his State of the Nation speech, people began taking to the streets. I was talking on the phone with my brother at the time—he lives in Once, a neighborhood near downtown—and we were having a long conversation about nothing, nothing to do politics, and then he heard the *cacerolazo*... It was like a wave that began to cover the whole city, and he said to me, "There's a strange noise and I don't know what it is." That minute, right then, I began to hear it as well, here in my neighborhood, so I hung up immediately and went out to the street. It was hard to believe what was happening.

People were coming down *en masse* from buildings and making bonfires on street corners. What began angrily, with people coming out on the street in a rage, quickly turned joyful. People smiled and mutually recognized that something had changed. Later came euphoria. It was a very intense feeling that I'll never forget.

The next day I woke up a little late because I went to bed so late after the *cacerolazo*. I turned on the radio and heard that people had gone to the Plaza de Mayo and that the police were repressing the Madres of the Plaza de Mayo. I felt an urgent need to go there and left immediately. Later—it was funny—I went to the plaza and participated in everything... I was dressed like this, I wasn't prepared. I knew everything one brings to a demonstration—the vinegar, bandana, and all that—but I didn't bring anything. I just went as I was. I was at the North Diagonal where we spent many hours advancing and retreating, fighting with police on horseback and everything. There were moments of great euphoria, in spite of the stress and difficulty of the situation—with the teargas all the time, for example. The police would knock you down with the gas and you would feel horrible for five minutes—but at the same time you'd feel euphoric, because adrenaline took over. Everyone felt united against the police.

It was very moving how those people who were not participating in the rebellion helped those who were. For example, all the employees of one café, who of course weren't working, set up a table and gave us water to wash our faces, and were sympathetic even though during the revolt, their windows had been broken. They could easily have been very angry with us, but instead they helped us. I saw many similar things—doormen giving refuge to people who were injured, and so many other things. I never felt anything like it before. For a time—for a few hours—those of us who were in the street were in control of what happened—just for a while, because the next day was different. But then, we felt we were able to exert pressure and accomplish a great deal. In those few hours we were in control of the situation—at least that's how I felt, and it seemed to me that everyone felt the same way. When the fall of De La Rua was announced, it was already irrelevant—at least where I was, people didn't rejoice, didn't erupt in joy. At this point it was an annoyance, a little thing that was not so important. I also remember the feeling of walking back after everything was over. That feeling of returning with so many people, walking openly on Corrientes, a main avenue in Buenos Aires, with the satisfaction of having played a part; feeling that we were in charge of ourselves.

There were people of all ages in the streets—everyone was there, including families. The *cacerolazo* was great because people went out as they were—some in pajamas. They went out as they were. It was very authentic and purely spontaneous.

Alberto, Clínica Medrano (a recuperated clinic)

December 19th and 20th marked a change in the country. Many sectors of society began to fight in a different way. It was the detonation of something that couldn't be held back anymore—the nineteenth and twentieth were very spontaneous. Later came the organization—from the recuperated businesses to the unemployed, and from state to private workers. Everyone began to organize differently. Many unions and associations were reclaimed from the union bureaucracy. For example, many sections of the teachers union in Greater Buenos Aires, which was in the hands of the union bureaucracy, were recuperated, as were several sections of the railroad workers union.

This was a revolution in every sense. It was a revolution from the viewpoint of, "I can't take it anymore," and without thinking about it, workers together, including us, began to look for a solution. Both state and private workers began to learn how to resolve their problem. And what was their problem? Their problem was corrupt leaders who didn't fight for them, who didn't work to make things improve. The workers began to get rid of these leaders that didn't allow struggle. In our case, we didn't have a way out and we decided: okay, we're going to put our energy into this health clinic. We were also struggling against the government and against the union bureaucracy. The union bureaucrats told us that if we formed a cooperative, they were going to abandon us since they would consider us owners… And that's exactly what they did. Without our having a part in the decision—without a vote—they simply announced it to us at a meeting.

Carina, Argentine World Social Forum mobilizing committee

There is an important distinction: on the one hand, I met my neighbors in our neighborhood park or on X corner and we talked about our problems, and on the other hand, this idea of direct democracy, *horizontalidad*… It's different and not so different. It's partly a reclaiming of the old social spaces that had been lost—because we suffered a similar fragmentation though it was greater, stronger, more palpable in the 1990s—but we had been suffering it since the last military dictatorship. What we lost was meeting face to face with our neighbors.

When you went out with the *cacerola* on the nineteenth, you saw your neighbors also *cacerolando*. And you said, how crazy! Because I never speak to this person, or we see that one in the street and only say good morning, or not, and here my neighbor is also banging a pot! Or, my neighborhood butcher is *cacerolando*! The neighborhood pharmacist! How strange, and we're all meeting on this corner and now we're in the street! And it was strange, and it was a reconnection with something that was lost. Many ways of being social had been lost—like the neighborhood club, the neighborhood library, the unions as a place to meet. Due to the economic and labor reforms, every one of us was running, trying to get the problems under control... One of the first things we regained with the nineteenth and twentieth was face-to-face interaction. We regained our community.

There's always something new and something old. It feels like the collective memory is always at work. I remember the first meeting of the assembly in my neighborhood, where we all got together to talk about our problems.

Something that was fundamental for the middle class was the *corralito* [the freezing of bank accounts], and all the running around in December because no one had a cent. People had to go from bank to bank to see how to make do with the little money each had. It sounds crazy, but some of the social interaction began in banks. I went to the bank with my mother and she started talking to a neighbor who said, "My daughter left the country because the economic situation leaves no opportunities." My mama answered, "My daughter is also thinking of doing the same thing." And they exchanged phone numbers. Because of the situation, they were suddenly friends. A multitude of people went to the banks and became at least acquaintances. The feeling of community began with this: let's share our problems.

Ariel, Partido Obrero (Trotskyist Party)

For me in my life—like the life of the country—there's a before and after. December 19th and 20th marked the end of an era of working class defeat. It ended the epoch that began in 1975 and 1976. It was the downfall of an attempt to radically transform Argentine society. The most significant part, on the most personal level, was that you felt like a protagonist in history—like you played a role in history. Sometimes you have the opportunity to share struggles—often from a distance of time or place, through photos or television—but this time the struggle was immediate, and you could choose to be a protagonist or watch it from afar.

Eluney, Etcétera (a militant art collective)

For me, the nineteenth and twentieth were alive—effervescent with expectation, surprise, and fear. Fear was inevitable when listening to the mainstream media's broadcasts about the massive number of people in the street and about the police repression. I remember I was at a friend's house when everything began, when the news came over the radio. I immediately called home to see how everyone was. It all happened spontaneously. My father told me that he was with my little brothers when they heard a "chin-chin-chin," and they went downstairs and joined the *cacerola*. My father was in slippers and shorts—he'd just come from work—and he brought my three-year-old brother with him from the Flores neighborhood all the way to Congreso, downtown—a really long way, walking, and *cacerolando*.

I believe that the nineteenth and twentieth brought things out into the open. Some collectives began on these important dates, but also the work people had been doing for years became more visible. I believe there are many very good things that came from this. There are movements—people working on collective documentaries like Arde Arte [Art on Fire], el Grupo de Arte Callejero [Group of Street Art], Etcétera, and other militant art collectives that are doing a lot of very good work. I also think there are many people that are trying to join and having a hard time. It's difficult in the beginning to be able to understand a new group and new social dynamics, as well as become a part of things. It's a lot of work. There are also many, many people that were never part of any group or movement before, who are now a part of this. And there are even those who have put aside their criticism and participate enthusiastically. There are a lot of people who are now beginning to be much more politically active.

Christian, Attac Autónomo (an anti-capitalist collective)

December 19th and 20th was a historic process. I was there, with everyone, combating a system. I believe no other country in the world had four presidents—and one day without a president—in just one week. I don't believe this has ever happened in any other part of the world. And it was the people that got rid of them. Clearly, when the people unite no one can bring them down. The government had weapons, missiles, rifles, but the people, united, are an incredible force. I couldn't believe it. I saw the middle class fighting alongside me. We were everyone, all different types of people, but we were all fighting against the system, against the way things were, against those who taxed us, against the type of things done by the military dictatorship—we were all together.

On the nineteenth and twentieth the people took to the streets. It wasn't expected—the demonstrations multiplied from one second to the next. People didn't know where they were marching or why they were marching, they were just so fed up with this typically neoliberal system that Menem implemented—that we lived under because of US imperialism—we were so very fed up with everything. It was if at the moment we took to the streets, we were saying: what are we doing? Where are we going? They're all going there, so we're going there. There was no communication, no organization. We were absolutely cut off from one another as far as communication went, but took to the street nonetheless and began the *cacerolazos*. We overthrew many presidents in a short time, and were strong.

Martín K., Asamblea Colegiales (a neighborhood assembly)

Creation, that's what I believe came first. The events of the nineteenth and twentieth weren't mobilizations of the masses behind some leader—nobody orchestrated it. At first, it wasn't a reaction against an idea, it was a sound. [Singing] *Oh, que se vayan todos* [they all must go] was the only thing said. There was no program or formed political position. It wasn't planned. It was something innate.

And then the sensation—particularly by those that lived near the neighborhood assemblies—was, this is good, we're in the street, now what do we do? It was like as long as we were in the street, we would accomplish something together. Of course, not everyone who was part of the nineteenth and twentieth is still participating. We're talking about a year and five months later, and those who have remained are the most militant. A lot of things have happened that show that suddenly this other world is possible... The difference is that it is not a revolution in the 1970s sense, where what they saw was the future. This is a revolution that's seen in flashes, and one where worlds come together. It's like it's not necessary to wait for the revolution—we can begin now, but that also implies that what we're doing now isn't so visible.

Yes, it's revolutionary. To give you an idea, it's like what happened to me on the nineteenth and twentieth. The sensation I had was that society was a kind of desert, marginalized, even culturally, and out shopping. Everything related to the market and this marginalization expressed itself in social relations as well.

Social interactions were pretty much limited to going out to eat in noisy bars and restaurants, and even that wasn't so common. After what happened, people began to meet in more intimate places. Argentina—or at least Buenos Aires—has a tradition, almost a culture, of meeting a friend to talk over a coffee, which had not been happening very much. After the nineteenth and twentieth people began to socialize again. For example, my neighbor Pablo, who lives in my building...he and I met for the first time in the assembly. It was incredible, it was like, where have we been? That was the first surprise.

So in this way it has been a revolutionary epoch. It's changed everyone's lives. I believe that even if the assemblies disappear, people will continue to act differently. This experience has left a marvelous memory within us.

The 1990s

Paloma, Asamblea Palermo Viejo (a neighborhood assembly)

There was great disillusionment in everything—in all the formal institutions, whether parties or unions, really everything that represented the system in those ten or twelve years. What provoked this was savage liberalism. It seems to me that we hit bottom, and the revolution began because people had no work. The unemployed, in particular, reached a point where they said, okay, we organize or we'll die. It was a question of survival. I think they discovered that they had nothing, and they had no one to trust except themselves. Gradually, but powerfully, they escaped. It seems to me that the organizations, like the assemblies, were a result of the nineteenth and twentieth, but the *piqueteros* came from a history of at least seven years—at least since 1997.

Carina, Argentine World Social Forum mobilizing committee

The economic conditions changed a great deal from when I was eighteen, in my first year at the university. Later, not even drinking a cup of coffee was the same. Our economic situation changed significantly. This was a time of massive economic failure—of the first large-scale privatizations and closures of factories. Later, the *piquetero* groups began to organize, and other workers began to take over the factories.

The economic crisis of the 1990s was also when the first new social movements began. The first highway blockades started in the interior of the country: Jujuy, Cutral-có, General Moscóni. Entire towns that once had good economies became ghost towns with the privatization of state companies such as YPF [Repsol-Yacimientos Petrolíferos Fiscales, a petroleum company]. Whole towns became unemployed.

A strong criticism of politics and politicians also developed in the 1990s. People from across the political spectrum were critical of official politics—primarily the political parties and their leaders, but also the political parties as institutions, the way the leaders made policy, and the system of representation itself. That was the moment of crisis both within Argentina and internationally, when economic policy had changed so much that the relationship between Argentina and the rest of the world was affected.

Traditional and non-traditional ideas changed when it came time to vote. The political system wasn't producing new responses or confronting the growing dissatisfaction. People felt like, this guy, who says he represents me, doesn't, and I have to do something about it! The typical 1990s middle class response was reactive, not revolutionary: They are all sons of bitches, only worried about themselves. After the nineteenth and twentieth, the assemblies organized themselves. They are part of a politic that doesn't end when everyone votes. If we want anything to change, we have to constantly participate in public affairs.

Ezequiel, Asamblea Cid Campeador (a neighborhood assembly)

The protagonists of the *cacerolazo* were the type of people that had never gone out into the street to protest, or at least not since before the dictatorship. During part of the 1990s, we had strikes and active *piquetero* groups—mostly in the country's interior—but generally there was a great deal of passivity in the more urban groups, you could say the middle class. This decade was very dreary—at least for me—in the sense that everyone seemed to be enthusiastically buying cell phones and believing in individual salvation. It was all about the individual. During the 1990s, horrible things were happening in this country and no one wanted to see them. There was a brutal blindness. And I was understandably surprised when these people... I imagine they didn't expect

"Wake Up."

that so many of them would join us in the streets, but on the night of the nineteenth, the people filled the streets all over the city. Everyone was in the streets...so many people, and no one had predicted anything like it.

Compañeros, Chilavert (a recuperated workplace)

COMPAÑERO 1: Everything stems from 1998, from the sudden recession that began to drown Argentina, the closing of workplaces and the growing unemployment. It's sad for a father to come home and not even have bread to give to his child. What can the unemployed do? What can their children do? If they're teenagers, they dropped out of school and began to act out, they caused trouble for themselves, and became a delinquent or drug user. Fathers practically abandoned their families because they couldn't stand the situation, and families broke apart. If we hadn't stopped this, if we didn't say no, if we had accepted the closing of the factories, accepted our government's 150 pesos handout, if we'd accepted that our children would leave school, eat what they could find, I think that would have been a disgrace. Not only on a personal level, but on an organizational and social level. If we hadn't stopped this, we were headed for destruction.

We're trying to demonstrate to those who have power that they have to act in our interest, not for the International Monetary Fund or the huge corporations.

COMPAÑERO 2: In a country in crisis, as Argentina was, we had a twenty-page list of printing presses alone that shut down, claiming bankruptcy. Tons of workplaces...

Paula, feminist and GLTTB collectives

Political participation was nonexistent in Argentina before the nineteenth and twentieth. We came from a decade of Menem, a horrifying situation. In a way we're trying to take charge of our own history.

Neka, MTD Solano (an unemployed workers' movement)

When we started the MTD Solano, it was a little quirky, partly because it was one of the first movements around this urban area to block highways. It's interesting to look at this in historical context...how this developed in a time of political extremism, sparked by an era of military dictatorship beginning in the 1970s, when many *compañeros* disappeared, and when there was intense state terrorism. People were coming from a society that was totally squashed, they were totally terrified, and it was very difficult to rebuild solidarity, especially among neighbors. On the other hand, according to the government, we also came from a democracy. They had us believe we had a democracy, so why should we continue to struggle if now we had democratic presidents elected by the people, presidents who would govern according to the people's interests? All of this was combined with the privatization campaign and the propaganda in the press, which said that things were getting better because our resources were being given to the wealthy, who were going to create change. A lot of these expectations were generated during Menem's tenure, and the same people who supported Menem's government, who supported the military coup—the middle class—they were the same people who took to the streets later over the closing of bank accounts. That's heavy, isn't it?

It was very difficult in these neighborhoods where hunger hit us so hard, where unemployment hit so hard. It was very difficult to begin to organize and have confidence that if we organized we could improve our situation. The first steps were really difficult. At that time there was a kind of clientalism [political consumerism] organized by the Justicialista Party, when the Duhalde governed in Buenos Aires Province. They exercised social control by handing out bread crumbs, and they made the people dependent on them with this little bit of money. They responded to real hunger and misery with a little box of food to get people to support their political agenda. I believe that one of the greatest things we were able to do in the MTD is break from this clientalism. That was one of the first things we focused on, trying to reject this type of submission. This was especially true with women who were looking for ways to feed their hungry children. When we began, the MTD was 90 percent women, pressured by the hunger and illness of their children. It was a very, very powerful experience.

In the beginning it wasn't easy at all. We had to struggle against many systems and apparatuses. We began in a church, but after two months, the church hierarchy started to give us problems. The bishop even asked the priest to evict the unemployed from the parish. Our neighborhood assembly then decided to occupy a church that had been empty for ten years. The priest and the community okayed it, but the police evicted us. The struggle was against the church structure, the state, everyone—every clientalist organization in our neighborhoods.

I believe we got our confidence from meeting and working through issues and winning battles together. I wouldn't belong to an organization where two or three directed and gave orders. I don't know if that would even have been possible because there are so many differences among people's relationships and experiences. If anything allowed us to move forward, it was that we accepted each other as equals with the same needs and abilities. We were equal in participation, decision-making, and opinions.

horizontalidad

Emilio, Tierra del Sur (a neighborhood assembly, occupied building, and community center)

Horizontalidad is a new process of construction in Argentina that appeared practically overnight. For me, the theories that are valid—that last and really matter—are those that come into practice out of necessity. For example, the concepts of *horizontalidad, autogestión,* and direct democracy, are in no way new. They existed a long time before the uprising of the nineteenth and twentieth. The anarchist movement has been talking about these ideas for years. Indigenous communities have practiced these ideas in their lives and philosophies from the beginning. What's new in Argentina is that, just as rapidly as groups formed, they formed with horizontal practices.

An economic and social crisis existed as far back as 1998 in Argentina, but what is taking place now is really the culmination of many things. People had to start resolving their own problems—not because of political conviction, or because all of a sudden they realized they were anti-capitalist, but for the simple reason that no one else had done it before. The state was in retreat, factories were being occupied, and looting was happening all over the country. People took it upon themselves to resolve their problems.

The crisis that began in 1998, and a ton of political questions that followed, caused a deep disbelief in formal institutions. A concentration of hate and helplessness in society brought the events of the nineteenth about. So between all of the people who went out in the street and everything else that happened during those days, people were overjoyed to realize that it was finally time. We woke up. This new enthusiasm for change wasn't simply based on desire, but also necessity. So we began to gather on corners and form assemblies. We organized collectives, and the collectives that existed before the nineteenth and twentieth became stronger. Each of the spaces that emerged had horizontal practices.

Horizontalism begins when people begin to solve problems themselves, without turning to the institutions that caused the problems in the first place. The neighborhood assemblies are an example. For the people that began to organize themselves on the street corners, there was an intense hatred of everything from politicians to the representative system, and a ton of other things. So when they began to get together, the first thing that came out was the rejection of old practices and, consequently, the development of new ones. Before, we elected people to make decisions for us, but now we will make our own decisions. If they talk a lot but don't do anything, we'll take action ourselves.

Yes, the politics of reaction were first. First was the shout/scream. First was *"Que se vayan todos"* (they all must go). First was the shout, a reaction to an unsustainable situation, and then the creation—almost at the same time. That's to say, and it's

"They all must go. Almagro Assembly. Thursday 8:30"

almost obvious, to break with something first you have to say "no" to it, and from there start building something new. That's how we begin to construct differently. *Horizontalidad* starts there. I believe that *horizontalidad*, like autonomy and *autogestión,* are momentary constructions and they are in themselves opening space for something more in Argentina.

Today we are horizontal, first because we broke with representatives, with the old, with concepts of delegation. But I don't believe that if things continue the way they are that the objective will be *horizontalidad* in itself, but it is, rather, a process that constructs and brings us to something more. It is dynamic. *Horizontalidad* as a practice is something amazing, because, for example, the middle class in Argentina wasn't used to direct participation in society. They were used to the traditional institutions of representative democracy—schools, political parties, elections. It isn't that people in Argentina elected the best candidate by reading all politicians' platforms. The vote is a lie. Here, we're not used to participation. There's a huge *mea culpa* in society.

It's really interesting to see how quickly a group that didn't use what little power they had, now want all of it—and fast. They'd only recently started to be political, and do politics in a different way. It's so interesting to see people of all ages joining in the discussion in an assembly and really being conscious of wanting something different. You can't build something new with old tools. These are the fantastic things you see today, because they didn't come from any book. They were in books, but they came from the *cacerolas,* from necessity. People obviously didn't learn just from the neighborhood assemblies—the *piquetero* groups also influenced them. Many of the *piquetero* groups organize and make decisions in assemblies. They are really similar to the neighborhood assemblies that I just talked about. So, for me, one of the things that gives me the most energy, excitement, and hope in Argentina are the new forms of construction that come from necessity. Out of necessity people come together, discuss in assemblies, and develop *horizontalidad*, look for *autogestión*, and take concepts of environmentalism and bring them into practice. It's important that the assembly isn't the only place where we're horizontal and relate like this. There are environmental, feminist, artistic, and other movements, and all of them have integrated nonpolitical people's lessons and experiences into their struggles. The current movements are everywhere.

Horizontalidad is a tool arising from necessity. And this tool is an opportunity, an opportunity for something better.

Pablo, Asamblea Colegiales (a neighborhood assembly)

No one was obeying some ideological command. People simply met on a street corner in their neighborhood, with other neighbors who had participated in the *cacerolazo*s. For example, in my assembly, in the neighborhood of Colegiales—and I know many other cases—someone simply wrote on the sidewalk, in chalk, "Neighbors let's meet here Thursday night." Period. Who wrote this? No one knows. In the first meeting there were maybe fifteen people, and by the next week it was triple that. Why did it increase in this way? It wasn't an ideological decision, or an intellectual, academic, or political one. It's like asking why people went out to *cacerolas*. It was the most spontaneous and elemental thing, to go out in

Street graffiti in Buenos Aires
"Assembly here, Wednesdays"

the street and meet others on the corner. It isn't that there was a decision to be horizontal—it's not that there was a decision to use direct democracy as if someone had just thought it up. It wasn't a decision. We simply came together with a powerful rejection of all we knew. A strong rejection of political parties and their structures, a strong rejection of all those who represented the state or who wanted to occupy positions in the state. We made a specific decision that we are going to do things for ourselves.

To understand this phenomenon requires more than calling it "direct democracy." Naming it is an interpretation. To call this new relationship direct democracy is technically correct, but "direct democracy" wasn't in people's vocabulary back then. The initial vocabulary was simply: Let's do things for ourselves, and do them right. Let's decide for ourselves. Let's decide democratically, and if we do, then let's explicitly agree that we're all equal here, that there are no bosses, that we don't want bosses, and that no one can lead us. We lead ourselves. We lead together. We lead and decide amongst ourselves. Someone said, this is horizontal, and well, yes this is horizontal because it's not vertical. We don't want bosses, and because of this it isn't vertical, but it isn't part of any theory of *horizontalidad* or direct democracy. Like the *cacerolazo*, no one invented it. That was a way to protest. It just happened. We met one another on the corner and decided, enough! Enough of this, let's start everything anew. Let's invent new organizational forms and reinvent society.

It was a huge challenge. Where would we begin with the assembly? How to begin? What would we need? These questions generated an agenda, a new agenda, an infinite agenda that was the same as a new agenda. It was really difficult to prioritize ideas. What should come first? Is one thing more important than another? Where should we concentrate our energy? On one thing? Three? Ten? All of them are important. It's really difficult to generate an agenda and to create a methodology. Beyond our saying, "Ok, there are no bosses and no leaders, there are no structures," there are questions. How are we going to function? Who speaks first? Who speaks next? Who decides who will speak? Are people asked to speak? Or, what happens if one person talks a lot? Some rules have to exist, like a speaking order, for example. From that realization, things began to get difficult. To transform the rejection, the *"que se vayan todos,"* into constructive practices, ones of new sociability and new forms of organization, not ones like the state, but new forms... This was really difficult.

Project-based groups soon began to form in the neighborhood assembly. One group planted a garden, another group figured out how to buy things directly from producers, another created a health project, another a group for political reflection and study, and still another planned cultural activities. These smaller groups depended not on an agenda, but on the initiatives, capacities, and skills of the individuals who decided to be involved.

Ximena, Asamblea Villa Pueyrredon and Hernán, Asamblea de Pompeya (neighborhood assemblies)

HERNÁN: The social structure of political parties is like a pyramid—it forces you to obey the person right above you, unless you're the boss. Here, when the police came to the building our neighborhood assembly occupied and asked who was responsible, we looked at each other and said everyone, everyone. I think this shows the main difference between us and vertical systems of control. We're all responsible for the decisions that we make in the assembly, even though some of us might not fully agree with them. We have to support the final decision of the assembly because the majority agreed, but the minority was also heard.

XIMENA: We have some idea of where we want to go strategically, though the daily operation of the collective is most important—that and getting more people involved. Every question is important, whether small or big. We see everything as a part of the political movement. It's not that the *Bible* comes into the picture, or the "Ten Commandments," and people feel they have to follow them. I think that this project has to do with the future...created every day. As we move along, we check to see if our path is effective or if we need to change it.

It has to do with the collective, with the day to day, with the experiences we have and conclusions we come to as a collective. All experiences—from those that some people see as steps forward to ones others perceive as steps backward. It is something that's very, very dynamic and cannot be predicted.

One can say that capitalism is fucked up and that change has to come. We can call it socialism, for example, and we see that theoretically there may be another path, but things are still missing. There are so many things to do, learn, overcome, and so many experiences that will bring us towards a change. Also, there can be 50,000 changes, and it will never be ideal—it's too volatile and complicated.

There are so many good things in these new relationships and phenomena. One challenge that comes up is time. For example, if someone is being evicted, or something urgent happens and we all have to run, we often don't have time to discuss or think much in the process. There are other questions that are not so urgent, like deciding what the assembly should do, seeing if we all agree, and what to do if some people don't follow through. We have this constant back-and-forth that sometimes makes people impatient to be done. Somehow we eventually finish.

Group of compañeras, MTD la Matanza (an unemployed workers' movement)

COMPAÑERA 1: It's about relationships. I can disagree with her, but we still cooperate. Why adopt another's ideas?

COMPAÑERA 2: It's about horizontal consensus.

COMPAÑERA 3: We make a lot of decisions using consensus.

COMPAÑERA 2: But positive consensus, where everyone shares their opinions, not the false consensus where silence is taken as agreement. No, here you have to speak.

COMPAÑERA 3: Generally decision-making takes a lot of time.

COMPAÑERA 4: Yeah, totally. [All smile, nodding agreement.]

Alberto, Clínica Medrano (a recuperated clinic)

There are tons of factories that aren't in any formal grouping. In this clinic we are also politically independent. Our politics are as a cooperative, where everything is resolved in assemblies—even the smallest things, like changing our hours. It might not seem necessary to decide these sorts of things in assemblies, but we want to be careful not to have only a few individuals making the decisions, so we all make them together. We feel that when more people participate in the decision, we're less likely to make mistakes. With this principle in mind, we meet about practical issues related to the functioning of the clinic—things like equipment questions, relationships with doctors, travel allowances—not just the work itself, but everything. We also meet to talk about all types of internal questions, like shift schedules, how to organize shifts, etc. Not to say that we don't make mistakes. Just because we're an assembly doesn't mean all of our decisions are written in stone. There's always room for error.

We really do discuss and resolve everything in the assembly. Today, for example, there were two *compañeras* having an intense discussion—no one holds anything back. I'm a fan of this way of relating, where no one holds things in. It all comes out in the assembly, because it's less likely that any of us will explode later from pent-up frustration. Today, the discussion was with one *compañera* who, well, wasn't doing all of her work, and the other *compañera* called her on it. She told her what she thought, and the other *compañera* defended herself, explaining her reasons. There were tense moments during the discussion—if you had seen it as an outsider you would think, "they really go at it here," and think it might break into a fight any second. But it's useful for us to clear the air of all the little work details so we can do things in the best possible way. And, well, this is how we self-organize.

Daniela and Marta, MTD Almirante Brown (an unemployed workers' movement)

DANIELA: We've learned a lot from history and experience. We're breaking from organizing in vertical ways, the way that the system and government work. We are basically starting from scratch. Our movement started because of concrete needs. I feel like we just got tired of people coming around and telling us what to do, unwilling to do things themselves. So, it's both breaking from that and starting new things, like collective decision-making, where everyone participates using direct democracy. Now each of us has a voice and a vote. What's important is that everyone can express their opinions; it's the participation of all the *compañeros*. We believe that everybody knows something, which is different from the old idea that nobody knows anything. Really what we're doing is breaking from the old to create the new. And it's not easy;

A vote in a neighborhood assembly

sometimes it's hard for *compañeros* to talk in the assemblies. Really, it's hard for all of us, but sometimes *compañeros* don't see that we're creating something totally new. More than anything, I think this is a new chapter in the history of Argentina, and what it's really about is confronting what's imposed on you and holding onto what's yours—the truth.

MARTA: We're taking a risk, which others have also done before us, and as Dani said, we're rejecting the old leadership-style. We're rejecting the system where we would go looking for work, and a leader would make a deal with the government that left us with nothing. The leaders I'm talking about aren't necessarily the president, who's supposedly elected by the people and speaks for us. It can be on a smaller scale, like a local neighborhood coordinator, *puntero*, who goes to the negotiating table with the government and then might sell us out, leaving us with nothing. We don't accept these sorts of power relationships anymore. The way it is now, we can focus on our day-to-day in the barrio, all of us, working together. We're not going to let anyone mediate for us or make a living from being a leader. It's the people who really have the knowledge, the ones that live this every day.

Paula, feminist and GLTTB collectives

I have been thinking about this for years, since I first read gender theory. It was then that I began to read feminist theory, but not just feminist, theories of social construction, and the rest of it—reflecting on relationships to or with other people without thinking about the differences between them. What is it that makes a person different from me? If I only think about difference, then I am sort of pigeon-holing them and making a separation. *Horizontalidad*, permits us to think not solely in terms of difference, but rather to live with other people and be able to have political discussions with them, without trying to define them. This is really important to me. I had a very powerful and important political experience in the GLTTB movement, which is pure *horizontalidad*. That's where I first experimented with *horizontalidad*, before my experience with the neighborhood assemblies. The GLTTB movement functioned horizontally, though they didn't use that term. It wasn't important if you were lesbian, transvestite, gay, heterosexual, or whatever. It wasn't important. The question was not asked, and that's interesting—no one asked, how do you identify yourself? The discussions were about people and politics, and this is fundamental for me. It was not about the creation of divisions.

In my opinion, horizontalist practices began developing in Argentina in December of 2001, because of the social demands that emerged at that time, demands that couldn't be resolved by either leftist political parties or the bourgeois parties. The left-parties' discourse is correct, but is very abstract for people. Abstract, in that it does not refer to new identities like gender, race, sexuality, or ethnicity. Abstract, in that the only problem the left sees is capitalism, and the only way to resolve problems is to get rid of capitalism.

Horizontalidad is a new way to think about political action, based in the acceptance of the other—of course in a democratic context. For example, if the "other" is Nazi, then no, we're not talking about *horizontalidad*. To have *horizontalidad* you need to have an emancipatory base.

In December, there were all sorts of conflicts—not just economic, but many types. People reacted against everything they knew. *Horizontalidad* appeared as a new and massive system because it addressed the very political necessities that the parties couldn't hear and weren't dealing with. Also, *horizontalidad* permitted the emergence and acceptance of differences. The party structures are very macho, and there's a division between manual and intellectual work. The parties reproduce the very things that they claim to be critical of. *Horizontalidad* gives voice to women, gays and lesbians, transvestites (here there are many), and immigrants. It permits the debate of ideas and the acceptance of differences.

Daniel, Argentina Arde and *Revista 19/20* (alternative media and art collective, and the magazine *19/20*)

Horizontalidad is something we're talking about a lot. I believe that, like a lot of things, we're talking about it more than practicing it. I believe that we continue learning as we walk. *Horizontalidad* is a tool, not an end in itself. Many of us, myself included, romanticize the idea of *horizontalidad*. In our concrete actions, in the moments when we meet each other in our everyday work and try to relate in a different way—within our collectives, our different educations, experiences, practices, personalities, and egos—we struggle with this. It's a challenge to reach a horizontal relationship. *Horizontalidad* isn't an end all, it has concrete limits that have to do with our various human characteristics. I think that at first it's sort of a utopia, which is a good place to begin the walk, the walk towards *horizontalidad*. I also believe going on this walk towards *horizontalidad* is one of the intentions of *horizontalidad*.

If you have a particular ability or skill and you do that thing well, that may become one of the things you do in your collective or group, but this doesn't mean that we have a hierarchy and that you're better than the rest of the group. Each person plays a different, agreed-upon role, often based on ability, but what is most important is that we're all equal in decision-making. It's this equality in decisions that is at the core of *horizontalidad*.

Within a collective, like the magazine, *19/20, horizontalidad* is basically unity in action. All decisions are consensual to or voted on. We're constantly trying to work without verticalisms, attempting to create a situation where there isn't a boss telling everyone else what to do. The objectives of a horizontal collective are decided by everyone in the group as they come to agreements through the most collective possible process. This can have its challenges and limitations, because we're not all coming from the same place. We don't all have the same education or abilities. There are people who don't have a lot of experience working within organizations, and while they might have a hard time completing certain tasks, they're good at planning and organizing. If that's how they're most effective, that might become one of their roles. This doesn't mean we have a hierarchy. Everyone has an equal role in decision-making. This, for me, is *horizontalidad*.

Group of compañeras, MTD Allen (an unemployed workers' movement)

COMPAÑERA 1: It isn't easy, partly because we don't all think the same way. Our ideas are often really different from one another. Sometimes we try to think alike. We talk and talk, but in the end, there's always someone who disagrees. It is a struggle, a difficult struggle.

COMPAÑERA 2: It's also in and through this process that the discussion can become richer. If we all agreed, our conversations wouldn't be so deep. When there's disagreement, we try to find out why, and that's important for real democracy. This is what the assemblies and direct democracy are all about: that all of us can share opinions about something, have a meeting, and work together to find a solution that everyone feels okay about, something that all of us can be a part of.

COMPAÑERA 1: Sometimes there are fights, discussions that are *puteadas*. And there's also silence. When the movement begins to be silent, it's because something isn't right.

COMPAÑERA 3: I believe that all of us are making a change in this society, in this corrupt country. I also believe that we're making a change in ourselves, in our very beings, especially through *autogestión*, acting in solidarity, organizing in assemblies and different workshops, and through everyone sharing opinions.

Ezequiel, Asamblea Cid Campeador (a neighborhood assembly)

The first thing I want to say is that I don't know where the idea of *horizontalidad* comes from. All I know is that before the 19th and 20th of December, that word wasn't really part of our political vocabulary, not at all. Maybe some people and small groups used it, but it wasn't common, and then it rapidly transformed into a concept that everyone uses, knows, debates, defends, or attacks. I suppose that, at first, *horizontalidad* was a type of defense against the old, and then later, through its practice, became something positive—something that one doesn't use only to defend oneself. For example, at first in the neighborhood assemblies, there were reactions that were almost instinctive. We were facing a feeling and experience of abandonment; the president was a total idiot, and none of the existing institutions were trustworthy. Congress had lost all credibility because they were all corrupt, the Supreme Court was questionable at best, and the trade unions in Argentina had been really corrupt for many years. The political parties were attacked as the ones responsible for the situation we were in, and the security forces and military were even less credible than them. In this context, you felt like you were in a sinking ship with no one to trust. The instinct was to come together with your neighbor—with your equal—and ask, "What happened? What's going on?" The reaction was to go out and ask each other what was happening, to turn off the television, to leave the solitary confinement of the house, and go out and talk to others—to speak with your neighbors. In this sense, the beginning was purely instinctive, as well as defensive.

I believe that part of the impulse towards *horizontalidad* was related to this—this inability to trust officials; the feeling that all the leaders at the time were corrupt precisely because they were leaders. Regardless of who held whatever formal position, inevitably they were corrupt, had abandoned you, and were totally out of touch with your problems and needs. This reaction seemed specific and defensive, but I think that later it became something else in practice. There's a phrase that I think works here: "bringing virtue out of necessity." Here the necessity was to go out and ask one another what was going on. The virtue—that your neighbor was the only person who was going to answer you. And relationships were re-formed.

In Argentina, we have had a very hierarchical political culture, especially in the years of Peronism, when it was based on a strong leadership figure. In general, even in the more emancipatory groups on the left, political groups were always organized around a strict hierarchy with a strong leader. In the 1970s in Argentina, practically every leftist group had a hierarchy, from those that were armed, to those against arms. All had hierarchy, leaders, and the like. I think one of the changes we see now is that there's much less trust in this kind of setup.

Two things seem to come together in the assemblies: the rejection of all forms of representation, and the search for a way to make decisions ourselves, using direct democracy and a horizontal decision-making process—with equality. These things have come together in such a way that I don't think they can be separated. Maybe *horizontalidad* is the concept of equality, for everyone to be on the same level, in all things.

I think *horizontalidad* has been established as a foundation that all of us share, even if some are happier with it than others. Autonomy? No, there are still people that don't know what it is or how it works, as well as people against it. Even so, they participate in the assembly and accept the criteria of *horizontalidad*.

Horizontalidad is much more than an organizational form. For me, it's a culture. It's not simply that we all have the right to speak and vote. This is only a part of it. The rest of it has to do with what we can all do to claim our rights. If you technically have the right to speak, but every time you open your mouth I insult you, and I'm in a position of moral authority, or I'm a guy who has more... Well, you don't have the same right to speak that I have, even if formally or technically you do. This culture has a particular dynamic, in that as much as you have the same rights as I do theoretically, my way of exercising my right to speak deprives you of yours. This is where we need to change our culture completely. For example, something that is generally a challenge, and really difficult in my neighborhood assembly, is the amount of time it can take to come to a "good" or "right" decision, however that's defined. It often takes more time than it might, and the outcome may be the same, but it's the process of discussion that creates real participation. To come to a decision quickly might seem more expeditious—to just vote and be done—but then you lose the most important part, which is the walk—the process of arriving at a decision.

Martín S., La Toma and Argentina Arde (an occupied building and alternative media and art collective)

What does *horizontalidad* mean? First, that there isn't one right way; there isn't anyone that has the truth and tells us what we have to do. It means seeing each other as equals, or trying to see each other as equals. It also means—and this is something that's a challenge for the assemblies—learning to listen to one another. The assembly is like a game, it's really interesting. Someone comes with an idea and the idea is elaborated upon by someone else, then someone else expands or changes it, and then as you listen, another person improves the idea, or says something totally different. The initial person might say "no" or agree, and this is how we move forward. It's like the game where a group makes up a story together. One person says "the house" and the next says "the house is" and the next "the house is in" and then "the house is in the mountains." If someone is in the assembly not listening, but talking, and trying to move forward with something else… Or if that person just makes statements or speeches, which sometimes happens, things really don't go anywhere.

In La Toma, we have to stay in touch with reality all the time, and pay particular attention to social conflicts that can come up. It's so important that we make sure to listen to one another and resolve problems as they arise, paying attention—all of us—to what's happening around us. If something isn't going well, or a discussion goes badly, we take the time to resolve those things. It isn't abstract. The only way to resolve things is to engage with real problems every day.

Something that I remember from the first assemblies is that we voted on millions of things, and then didn't do any of them. We learned that to vote was really easy. It was like, "yes, let's do this, let's go," but then no one did anything. The issue came from the practice of the assemblies. People got a little tired and frustrated and were like, "why do you come and say these things and then not do anything?" Since then, we've learned that there are more diplomatic ways to say this. What also began to happen was that over time people began to get to know one another and learn from experience who only speaks, and who acts.

The organization of the assemblies includes coming up with agendas and proposals, which are always discussed in the assembly. We discuss all sorts of things, from what day and time there will be a meeting, to what activities we're going to take on or be part of. Everything is proposed in the assembly, then discussed by everyone, and finally an agreement is reached. In the very beginning, soon after we had taken over this space, we had assemblies every day and night. It made sense and worked really well. Later we moved to four per week, then three, then two, and one day there was a discussion where we decided to have the assembly once a week. On Tuesdays. But then on Tuesday only half the folks came, so we couldn't talk about important matters. After discussing this problem, I suggested two weekly assemblies, one on Thursdays, where we would take up the internal organizational questions of La Toma (workshops and all of that), and the other, a more general assembly. This proposal didn't work because another person felt that everyone in La Toma should take part in all decisions—from workshops to legal and other important decisions. There were various stages to this discussion, with all sorts of variations, including the question of what's an interesting assembly and what's a boring one, relating day-to-day questions in La Toma to the larger picture. In the end, we decided that all the areas are important. One example came from the group that organizes the popular kitchen. They brought up how they ended up not only working in the kitchen, but also took responsibility for more general cleaning of the space. After a number of conversations, we decided that the work they were doing wasn't just part of the public kitchen, but part of La Toma, as a whole. We learned together that everything that happens in La Toma is a part of everything else.

Paula and Gonzalo, HIJOS (a collective of the children of those disappeared during the dictatorship)

In HIJOS [For Identity and Justice and Against Forgetting and Silence], we always try to reach consensus. We vote when it seems necessary, but most often, based on the level of agreement we generally have, it doesn't seem necessary. When we're discussing something that's really complicated, we might decide to go around the room and have everyone share their position. Sometimes people get frustrated or angry, but that's usually because we have been discussing the same thing for two hours or more. Clearly, at four in the morning we might decide "okay, let's vote," but that doesn't happen often. There's almost always an agreement.

Lately, we've been discussing our conceptions of *horizontalidad,* and we have found we have a lot of consensus. We see a lot of indiscriminate use and practice of *horizontalidad,* or what dominates today in the majority of the popular camp. To talk about it honestly and democratically, we have to recognize that there aren't equal conditions for all people, and that means that the same possibilities don't exist for everyone, especially related to our ability to communicate. Sometimes a hidden bureaucracy emerges because of this, and of course, this isn't true *horizontalidad.* You have to discuss what *horizontalidad* is and what it means. What is implied when we talk about *horizontalidad* in HIJOS? We talk about there not being leaders and about everyone being equal and able to express themselves equally. There are many spaces, like the MTDs and neighborhood assemblies, that are attempting this.

We aspire to achieve horizontal relationships, but at the same time, we're conscious that true *horizontalidad*—true equality of conditions— does not yet exist. For example we have *compañeros* who have ten years experience in the movements and others that have two months. We all come from different places and experiences, and one of the things we try to do, as much as possible, is bring everyone to the same level. This is not to say that difference doesn't exist. It does, and we still need to acknowledge that. Knowledge is always power and often, in an assembly, we're able to use this power in ways that are good. But it can also be bad—when someone uses their abilities, whether in language or knowledge of history, to manipulate other *compañeros,* for example. We try not to abuse knowledge ourselves, and also try to prevent others from doing it... We work together.

Claudia, lavaca.org (an alternative media collective)

We can't try to understand how the movements are organized by thinking in terms of models of domination or other concepts of power. It isn't a question of massive numbers either. We can't let ourselves enter the mindframe of who has more or who can do more. It's this very logic that needs to be changed; the logic of how the system of power organizes people. We're doing something else.

I believe that if people are left to their own devices and we pay attention, we'll find that people naturally organize horizontally, and the rest is a process of unlearning hierarchy. Children are a good example of this. We can observe how they socialize naturally, how they come to agreements, divide roles, and generally come together as a group. It's not that they immediately elect a leader and other children have to get permission from him to play in the group. This sort of natural coming-together appeared in Argentina when everything else disappeared. Everything in Argentina disappeared. Money disappeared, the institutions disappeared, and trust in leaders and government disappeared. The system had been becoming increasingly decadent, and then it was left naked. And it was a natural response, for people to begin to organize horizontally.

Carina, Argentina Arde (an alternative media and art collective)

I think all of this is a process that requires a lot of time and patience. There are people who go to an assembly and speak for the first time in their life—people that have never spoken in public and usually stay home. I think people are so much more engaged and excited about being involved in things because now they have the space to express themselves. There are moments when you don't speak because you don't have anything to say, and other moments you're dying to speak, and you can't say the things you want. I am talking about myself here. At first, I didn't speak and I waited for someone to tell me what I should do. This happened in almost every group. Later, when all of the idols and leaders began to fall, I saw young women with really clear things to say, who were saying them... Well, I noticed that...yes, yes, I can.

A movement can't depend on one person for a lot of reasons. First, one person can't really take on everything. Or what if this person gets sick and dies? It can't be one person that makes up the movement. A movement like that—really vertical—where one person speaks and waits for everyone else to respond to them is for shit.

For me, this is a sort of personal work, a sort of internal revolution. You start to see it in yourself, based on your experiences, not on theories—from where you are. From that point, you notice that others are also growing, and that we're all changing because there isn't a leader.

Colectivo Situaciones (a group for political and militant reflection)

The first impression that social protagonism gives us is that there is only a base, only those who are on the bottom. One of the discussions taking place today in the social movements, is between those that say we have to construct from the bottom up, and those that say we have to construct from the bottom to the bottom.

We see a problem with the way *horizontalidad* is sometimes perceived as an ideology and discourse, or as an etiquette, which is just another way of negating the multiplicities inherent. The key is the multiplicity. It's also vitally important to recognize the death of individualism, and to move toward the existence of more collective figures. All of this implies an inability to be subordinated to someone else's notion of how things should be. That is to say that the reality of the situation is never subordinated to the ideal—like the concept of a "correct" assembly. We're much more on the side of reality than the ideal. In this sense it's of great interest to us to see movements practicing multiplicity, and that there's a new idea of how we can make *horizontalidad* possible. Of course, it's also important that we understand what the politics of *horizontalidad* are, including the many concepts, as well as a lot of the creativity and research.

The question of leadership is an important one. The politics of *horizontalidad*, in the most moral sense, supposes that when a group of people exercise leadership or tend to be organizers, there's a danger of *caudillismo*—or a danger of verticalism or institutionalization. This is something understood in that context. For example, if there is a person who is very active in a discussion and speaks a lot, but who also generates affection and love, could that person be accused of being an institution that restrains the movement? We think this way of thinking reveals a lack of context.

Sometimes, at first glance, it might seem that there is *horizontalidad* because everyone speaks equally, or because nobody does more than anyone else. But it's necessary to see that often subjugation isn't directed at a person, but can also be the subjugation of an ideal, or a subjugation that prevents action. There's a helplessness and sadness that can exist in forms that, from the outside, appear horizontal.

We don't celebrate the fact that there are assemblies in the abstract. We don't find all assemblies interesting as a general rule. For example, there are those neighborhood assemblies in which people only talk and don't do anything. In others, there isn't enough creative thought—there isn't really an opening for it, there isn't really an active *potencia* [power/potential]. Other groups might be accused of not being horizontal enough. Others are recreating possibilities and hypotheses, and changing people's lives so much that it generates an attraction that's very strong and a *potencia* that's very powerful. We've seen that with *Zapatismo* and in some MTDs. We do not need to pretend we make an experience that functions as the best model.

There's something dangerous about thinking that the purpose of *horizontalidad* is to replace something else. *Horizontalidad* has the capacity to construct other forms of organization, and to ask what the organization's significance is, but it isn't a form of organization in itself. It is not a technique that replaces earlier ones. It is precisely this idea that causes so much confusion. Some think, for example, that *horizontalidad* is the number of minutes each person speaks, or a quantity of techniques that will make all communication work. The real question of *horizontalidad* is: What does it mean to organize ourselves? What will it be today? What does it mean for us? And it is only possible to respond to these things in a concrete situation. It is in this way that all of the literature that has been theorized before now can be turned into an ideology. When you talk about rhizomes, the rhizomes of Delleuze, one might suggest that if each person talks for five minutes, then everything is fine. And if one person talks for an hour and another for five minutes, then there's no rhizomes, there's power. It seems to us that you have to work hard so that every experience, every thought is valued for all of its intensity. We don't think *horizontalidad* should be thought of as a new model, but rather *horizontalidad* implies that there are no models.

It's really difficult to live without knowing, without having... There are no good or bad concepts. We're constantly reexamining ourselves, asking questions, and that's a new thing. We all come from having old structures in our minds and bodies that have so much of the old ideas of established understanding—what has been called Marxism-Leninism, or the forms of democracy in a political party. And it's hard, but powerful to break from these old ideas. It's a process that has started to happen. It is also still very fragile, and can go back and forth.

Horizontalidad is a tool of counter-power when it's a question. *Horizontalidad* is a tool of power when it's an answer. Power is socialized, it's democratized—it is the power of all of us. But as an answer—as an end to the search—is shuts down all questions. *Horizontalidad* is the normalization of the multiplicity, and the *potencia* of the people who are different, not those who follow the conventional. And so we ask how and what, but we don't have the answer. The risk is that *horizontalidad* can silence us, stop our questions, and become an ideology.

Compañera, MTD Allen (an unemployed workers' movement)
The meaning of *horizontalidad* is up for interpretation. If you talk to the left-wing political parties, they schematize the question. They be-

lieve that *horizontalidad* is a straight line, an association of points, in which all are same, in which differences don't exist. If you don't see that *horizontalidad is* a relationship between different people with the same quantity of rights, we won't understand each other. That opposing view implies that you believe that *horizontalidad* presupposes a machine that cuts the chorizo [sausage] into equal parts, and that is not *horizontalidad*. We're different... We're all different. The issue is how each person is thought of and how each sees him or herself inside a community, how each person is integrated, how that produces community, and how that community creates collective thought. That's *horizontalidad*.

Something else that comes up is the difference in how we express ourselves. Some people speak a lot, while others speak less. Some express themselves with words, while others use their bodies. Sometimes *compañeros* say three times more with their bodies than one can express with words. What we learn from all of this is that it's important that the whole community comes together in thought and in practice.

Nicolás, Argentina Indymedia (an independent media collective)

I don't know how you would, or if you could, define the movements. At the most basic level, we have a foundation of principles that we all form together, which are those of *horizontalidad*. In Indymedia, at least from my perspective, we develop our different activities from the things we have in common. We talk about the practices we try to use, whether horizontal or anti-bureaucratic, and how these practices help us to be more flexible. Personally, the theory I like most is anarchism. I also believe that the way of relating in many assemblies—without it being a conscious choice—is an anarchist one. Now I don't know if it is the right definition, perhaps it is something that still doesn't have a name. I'm not sure that

"Solution. Popular assembly. Autogestión."

the same protagonists will end up defining the movements. Maybe it will come with time. One thing that is true, however, is that we are creating a new movement and this movement doesn't have much to do with previous ones. There are some points in common with ideas of socialism, but there is not one particular definition.

Sometimes people talk about what the movements have in common with *Zapatismo*. A lot of people in the movements say things like "We are more Zapatista than socialist." That said, *Zapatismo* doesn't have a definition either, and I'm not sure how they might refer to themselves.

Natalia, La Toma (an occupied building)

In our assemblies and activities, we sometimes observe that what we want to do and what we are doing aren't the same. For example, we recently saw this with the issue of yogurt distribution in the *merendero*, the popular public lunches we organize for children. Yogurt is really expensive, though we were able to get some donated for our lunch program. Many people began to approach those of us who volunteer there to ask for yogurt. It was then up to us to decide who did and who did not get it. We realized that, in making these decisions, we were reproducing a power relationship. Then we asked ourselves, what do we do with this? How do we resolve this? And so we began to have assemblies to discuss these things collectively with the people who worked in the *merendero*— people who aren't necessarily the same as those in La Toma's assembly.

Some of the questions we discussed in this assembly were how to distribute yogurt and food, generally, as well as who we are in relation to others in the community, the assembly, and the *merendero*. We also asked ourselves if our getting the yogurt from donors gave us the power to decide who gets it and who doesn't. Or if we should give it all out in one day, leaving no yogurt for the following day. One of the proposals we came up with, in light of these questions, was that those who eat at the *merendero* should also come with us when we ask people to donate yogurt and other food. We decided that we would all—children and adults—go together to ask for food. This was especially important for us because it reflected that we're not the owners of the food, or in charge of the process of getting food. I guess this is just one example of power relationships that are developing, and how we're learning to think about them. It's all a real process, and one that is created as we go. It takes time, and we're changing both the process and ourselves along the way. It's wonderful that we can see these changes. Now, for instance, we have assemblies every day with everyone involved in the *merendero*, and in each assembly we decide who's going to prepare the food. We see this process as much more collective. Another change we made is that all of us in the *merendero* eat and drink together—those preparing the food, as well as those coming to eat.

We continue moving forward as we break with, and learn from, the various positions that we all have. We're all together, and that's how we learn and move forward.

Neka, MTD Solano (an unemployed workers' movement)

We began learning together. It was a sort of waking up to a collective knowledge, and this had to do with a self-awareness of what was taking place in each of us. First we began asking questions of ourselves and each other, and from there we began to resolve things together. Every day we keep discovering and constructing while we walk. It's like each day there's a horizon that opens before us, and this horizon doesn't have any recipe or program. We begin here, without what's in the past. What we had was our life each day—our difficulties, problems, and crises—and what we had in our hands at the time was what we used to go looking for solutions. The beginning of the practice of *horizontalidad* can be seen as a part of this process. It's the walk, the process of questioning as we walk that enriched our growth. That helped us discover that strength is different when we are side by side, when there is no one telling you what you have to do, and when we're the ones who we decide who we are. I don't believe there's a definition for what we're doing. We know how it's done, but we're not going to come across any definition—similar to *horizontalidad*. More than an answer to a practice, it is an everyday practice.

My personal perspective has to do with the idea of freedom, this idea of discovering that we have collective knowledge that brings us together, gives us strength, starts the process of discovery. This is beyond revolutionary theories, theories that we all know and have heard so often, theories that are often converted into tools of oppression and submission. The practice of *horizontalidad* can give the possibility of breaking with the old and creating something that gives us the security of self-organizing, and the ability do it well, far away from those that try to tell us politics must be done in a particular way.

Constructing freedom is a learning process that can only happen in practice. For me, *horizontalidad*, autonomy, freedom, creativity, and happiness are all concepts that go together, and they're all things that have to both be practiced, and learned in practice. I think back to previous activist experiences I had, and remember a powerful feeling of submission. This includes even my own behavior, which was often really rigid. It was difficult for me to enjoy myself, and enjoyment is something sane that strengthens you. If it's done collectively, it helps even more.

Under capitalism, we were giving up the possibility of enjoying ourselves and being happy. We need to constantly break with this idea. We have life, and the life we have should be lived today. We shouldn't wait to take power, so that we can begin to enjoy ourselves in the future. I believe it is an organic process.

We begin by believing in what's possible—with a positive—and then we push aside all of those things that don't allow us to create this possibility, breaking with all those things that are obstacles. I think that this system is very well equipped to keep people from doing this. It isn't just any system of domination, but one that's made specifically for this—for trying to keep us from all of these possibilities. There are other institutions too, that powerfully keep us from what's possible: the church, schools, universities, the media, and the police. All of them exist so that life can't really be life.

I think that creativity is the key word. The way I understand what's happened in Argentina is that we exhausted all the previous ways of understanding reality, of understanding not just how to get through the day-to-day, but how to change things. When you exhaust all your resources, even ones that you theoretically have, you begin to invent others. It isn't that you resign yourself. To the contrary, what appears is like a new moment. "I explored a lot but didn't get anywhere, but I keep trying." The search for freedom and a better life is a natural process.

Horizontalidad permits us to be in contact with a reality that hasn't been totally interfered with, so we can still see diverse ways of looking at the world. The leftist parties try to destroy our differences. It's a form of power to make us one thing. That power, of course, is false and fake and would have everyone obey a capitalist or Trotskyist boss. But there's also the possibility of beginning to discover what's true in the situation, and from there start suggesting responses that are possible. We begin where we are—still small—but we begin.

Martín K., Asamblea Colegiales (a neighborhood assembly)

I'm going to talk about *horizontalidad* and direct democracy in relation to the neighborhood assemblies. One of the first things we decided as an assembly was that voting just isn't worth it. In an assembly, you can't suggest proposals and then ask, "Who's in favor of proposal one? Who's in favor of three? Raise your hands." The idea of democracy, in this case, is something else. This idea of raising your hand to vote was, in some ways, reproducing the same logic that we were fighting against. What we did not want at any point was this passivity that is implied in delegation. Direct democracy, in the assembly, is consensus that we reach collectively in different ways.

One powerful thing I remember from when we first came together in the assemblies was that everyone was there—housewives, students, and re-tired people, professionals, and *cartoneros* [cardboard collectors]. They were there on the corner, talking, and there was no difference between us. It was crazy and really fun. This is part of what *horizontalidad* is and what

Assembly at *Enero Autonomo*

it allows. I say we are equal, but we did have a hard time finding a way of speaking a common language, and we've had to work this out in different ways. But still...the main principle that allowed us to organize is *horizontalidad,* where each voice was valued equally.

I understand *horizontalidad* in terms of the metaphor of territories, and a way of practicing politics through the construction of territory. It's grounded there, and direct democracy has to do with this. It's like it needs to occupy a space.

Urgent situations come up all the time in the assembly, and it's a real challenge to use direct democracy under conditions where you have to respond quickly. Not having sufficient time to make decisions can complicate the democratic process. It's as if, once again, the enemy is able to force you into a time paradigm that is not yours, and one that doesn't permit you even the minimum conditions to effectuate your process. Direct democracy, in this circumstance, can express a tension with representative democracy, which because of delegation, can seem more expedient.

It is really difficult to sustain all of this in practice—from *horizontalidad* and direct democracy, to autonomy. These are all ideas, ways of being, and reorganizing society that are very much against the established logic we live under. We don't live in a horizontal society. You can be horizontal in the assembly, but maybe in your daily work environment you're subordinate and forced to do things that aren't horizontal at all. This contradiction is really difficult. You can't live in two worlds and say, "Ok, I am changing worlds now." Click. Just like that. It doesn't happen that way.

Daniela and Marta, MTD Almirante Brown (an unemployed workers' movement)

DANIELA: We're in four neighborhoods and each one has its own assembly. The assembly is the highest authority, where decisions are made, and where we deal with all issues, doubts, and proposals.

The assembly is the place where all of the groups can come together. It's so important, because each week every working group and project has their own daily routine, and we don't get to all come together until Tuesday, when we meet and talk about what's been going on. There are other spaces, as well. For example, each neighborhood has a "neighborhood table" where the group coordinators help all *compañeros* bring up their questions, doubts, and proposals to be discussed collectively. We talk about all sorts of things, like plans for the neighborhood. In the Cerrito neighborhood, for example, we talked about the water pump. That's a problem we have right now. *Compañeros* discussed how to get the contributions we need, what kind of pump we should have, and how to handle it so the project will work well. Then the issue goes back to the different groups, and they work on the proposals. If there are any doubts or questions, they're brought up again in the assembly, and that's the way it works.

As I said, we are four neighborhoods, and there's one general table where the neighborhood coordinators and the *compañeros* responsible for the different work and projects meet. There are also general meetings, where *compañeros* bring up proposals from the different neighborhoods. Everyone discusses proposals, and then they go back to the neighborhoods. It goes back and forth constantly. All decisions are made at a group level, collectively, through discussions. All decisions go through all *compañeros*.

MARTA: The neighborhood coordinators participate in the general table, and bring ideas to and from the neighborhood assemblies—but not as bosses or leaders, just as *compañeros*. They are the same as everyone. They don't have a salary, they just agree to act in the role of communicator. In the work groups, there are also coordinators, but we are always clear that the coordinator isn't a boss. They don't just stand there and give orders. In the past in Argentina that's what it was always like. There were always bosses and owners. Today, we're all unemployed, so we try not to have anybody acting as boss.

If there's a problem in a group, like in the community garden, or if something happens between *compañeros*, it has to be resolved within the group. It goes to the "general matters table" on Fridays and is discussed collectively. It isn't that anyone from any group is going to tell the *compañeros* what to do or anything, it's just that it's discussed collectively.

There are ten people in each garden project and no one is valued more than the others. The same is true with the construction groups, who are building spaces for the movements. For example, right now they are building a work shed and a bathroom that we all need. They divide tasks within the group, and it works out—there has to be a work shed and a bathroom. They also have other duties. If someone doesn't have anything to do while assigned to work on the shed, and a *compañero* needs a hand building their house—like putting up walls or something—they help.

Candido, Chilavert (a recuperated workplace)

In Chilavert, we're in a permanent assembly of eight people. Actually we recently brought a new person into the cooperative, so now there are nine of us. To be clearer, there was a person who had a heart operation, so we decided that he would still get his salary and work as much as he can as he waits for retirement, but he no longer has to work in the factory. This is one of the small differences between a recuperated factory and any other type of workplace. We take care of each other, and make decisions together.

We always try to be as horizontal as possible, with everyone participating equally. *Horizontalidad* means getting to the base, getting to the core of what we all have in common, and when you get to the base you say we all work together or we will all go to hell. There's no other option. As part of this getting to the bottom, we all begin to row to the top together and then we float.

Toty, MTD la Matanza (an unemployed workers' movement)

We understand *Horizontalidad* as the idea that it's the same backstitch for all *compañeros*. We all believe in the importance of the assembly, but we also believe in the meetings of the core. All the different meetings are places where we discuss various political questions and proposals, and each *compañero*'s ideas and words have equal weight. This is true for the *compañero* who's been a part of the movement for seven years and for the one who's just joined. Our organization doesn't have official spokespeople. Everyone can speak, everyone says what they want, and when we go to a workshop or some *encuentro,* everyone shares opinions. This is how we come to agreements. That's not to say that something might be said totally against our politics, which sometimes happens, but we figure it out together because we're all committed to resolving things collectively. This has been an issue and it brings out some really interesting antecedents. Many researchers come to study the movement. One time, a young Swiss woman was visiting... I remember the day well since it was raining really hard. We were all there and said to her, "Feel free to talk to whoever you want." We were sharing our history, and a *compañero* who works in our bakery began to share his life experiences. This young woman was really interested in what he was saying, and did a long interview with him. At some point, he began saying things that were pretty contradictory to what some of the older members of the MTD felt. At the end of the interview, she asked him, "So how long have you been with the MTD?" and he answered, "Five days." He explained that he came to the movement five days ago looking for work and is now a part it. After five days he was sharing his opinions, and none of us, at any moment, despite the contradictions, said "No, that isn't what the MTD thinks," because he was sharing his vision and each person has their own. That, to us, is *horizontalidad*.

What we're constantly trying to do has a lot to do with breaking with the ideas and behaviors of non-participation. We work hard to value what each *compañera* says, and to create incentives so that everyone participates. Sometimes there's silence, or some *compañeros* speak more than others. One of the things we do when this happens is go around and have everyone speak, and then we try to respond to all the ideas. It's all about active participation. We also try to define what it means to be a subject in our organization. I believe it's

"We all participate and share opinions"

really important to identify as subjects in society. We all have potential, but capitalism tries to dominate us, and we have to struggle against this domination.

The movement is trying to reject what we call the apparatus—this thing where each *compañero* who is part of the organization is merely a number and has a predetermined function. That's where participation stops. We don't want to repeat these sorts of relationships, so we're looking for creative new ways to relate to one another.

This new way of relating is really important to us. It permits us to have a really diverse movement. There are a lot *compañeros* who don't think like many others—*compañeros* with distinct positions and ideas—but this is not a problem in any way since we love each other. We can have really difficult discussions and disagree, but we all stay part of the organization. We try to love each other. It's difficult. Imagine being in a neighborhood like La Matanza, which is full of really tough men—men who have lived, and still live, a violent, macho life—and we're talking about new, loving relationships. No, it isn't easy—not to talk about or even practice. This is part of our changing culture, and as we change we notice how much we really need to. There's a huge desire to all be together in the movement and to continue creating together. In some ways this is the most important step that we're taking, because we're conscious of what we're doing, and that makes us realize how necessary it is.

The basis of these recent social movements, especially relating to organization—which is deeply connected to democracy, collective decision-making, direct democracy, and *horizontalidad*—is that we are against hierarchy. These social movements are developing because traditional institutions don't offer any answers. There's no answer from the unions, for example, precisely because of their vertical nature. There isn't an answer from political parties either. Not only the parties in power who write policies that have nothing to do with workers, but also those that say they are workers, but are really reproducing the same old hierarchies. The new creation in the social movements is precisely against this form of organization. We're looking for other ways to relate. This is where *horizontalidad* comes into play. The most fundamental principle is that participation has to be developed by the people, and it can't be coercive in any way.

Carlos G. and Julian, Zanon (an occupied factory)

CARLOS: We try to make decisions using consensus. In the assemblies, we try to create a space where each person and position is heard, so that whatever decision we make is ultimately based on all of our opinions, or at least the majority. Here in the plant, we're organized into different sectors based in areas of work. Every day, each sector has a meeting. The factory-wide meetings, where each group shares what they're doing, are on Wednesdays. This is where we make decisions, including ones like paying everyone the same 800 peso salary.

JULIAN: Something we've observed is that each assembly is increasingly participatory. We've seen all the *compañeros* go through a sort of waking up process. It's not just talk—everyone is putting their all into this. In this waking process, new critiques are constantly developing, and in a way that is a part of always moving forward, towards the north. It is from there that we put aside our differences and try to get to this north, the solution to this conflict. This is how we organize ourselves.

There are so many discussions in every assembly that it feels like we're flying. For example one person presents an idea and...Pa! Pim! Pum! We explode talking, and it all goes great. Through everything that happens, we're always united. In the first assemblies, we had to vote about unity, but now we're living it and applying it every day. It's more than a vote.

Before we took over the factory, the only thing we had to do was work, and we didn't worry about the rest. But now with this, with this conflict, we have to move forward, and we know that the company isn't going to solve any of our problems. Of course, we don't want them solving our problems for us. It's like an older *compañero* said: "We shouldn't wait for the very people who tortured us to solve things for us." We understand that now.

Every day we all participate more. We all have the possibility to speak and seek solutions, to be more active and create change together. We can see this in how we make decisions. For example, one person throws out an idea, and then another puts out a different one. People discuss the ideas, and there's a conflict that someone else clears up, but someone else disagrees. Eventually, we'll all come to a conclusion together.

———————

Maba and Orlando, MTD Solano (an unemployed workers' movement)

MABA: The movement is organized under the principles of *horizontalidad*, direct democracy, and autonomy. We're against vertical structures, where there's someone who commands and others who obey. Everything is decided in assemblies with consensus—always trying to reach consensus.

ORLANDO: The seven neighborhoods that are part of the MTD Solano are organized this way—all of them involved and interrelated through the general assemblies. It's not just one general assembly for the whole movement. Each neighborhood has its own assembly, *compañeros*, workshops, and projects, and all are part of that neighborhood collective. No neighborhood can decide for others in the movement. Proposals are brought to the "inter-neighborhood table," as we call it, and that is where we discuss them.

Different *compañeros* come to the general assemblies: spokespeople and delegates from neighborhoods, as well as others who aren't delegates and just want to come. Some neighborhoods don't have delegates anymore, just *compañeros* that go to the neighborhood table and share their assembly's opinion, and then bring what happened back to their neighborhood. No one can bring up personal things, like, no one can talk about something that was voted on in assembly if it's something personal or from that local neighborhood assembly. We see everything standing together as *compañeros*, not like bosses. Sometimes there's confusion, and *compañeros*, who've been delegated a job, feel like they have to be the boss.

MABA: It's like we were saying today, in the *encuentro*. We're all so full of the habits of capitalism, it's hard to shake them all off. Sometimes there's a *compañero* that has just joined the movement and has never felt like a protagonist. Suddenly, they're chosen as a delegate and they misunderstand and think they're the boss. But, as we were saying: autonomy, direct democracy, and *horizontalidad* are built. We don't say, "Today we're all autonomists, we're all horizontalists, and it's a rule that has to be complied with." It's a process.

autogestión

Liliana, Brukman (an occupied factory)

We are all older women here—almost all of us are over forty—and our only source of employment is this factory. What we know how to do is work with the machines that are inside.

Because of this whole experience, I have now begun wonder why the worker always has to keep quiet? The boss doesn't pay you. The boss owes you money, and you're the one that has to leave, to hang your head and go. Well, we made the decision that we weren't going to be quiet anymore. They've done a lot of things to us and I believe that, well, enough already with staying quiet. No? All our lives we kept quiet. In the past, we would have left and looked for another job. I don't think that way anymore. I want to be clear about that. I want all this corruption that's carried out against us workers to stop. We, as workers, have stopped being stupid, and that's it. We're steadfast.

In reality, it wasn't a factory occupation for us. We stayed on December 18, 2001 because we didn't have enough money to get home. Where were we going to go with two pesos when the bus costs four? Together, everyone in the factory thought about our situation, and decided to stay to see if the bosses would decide to give us a little money so we could celebrate the holidays with our families. The bosses had families, too, so they understand the desire to be together on the holidays. This wasn't an occupation at first, but it became one without us intending it. We waited two months for the bosses to come back. We went to the unions, the Ministry of Work, all with the intention of getting the boss to come back and offer us a solution. He never came. So we decided to work. That's how it started, and we were doing a really good job, working well. We even paid the electric bill. The boss had a deal where he could owe money to the electric company without them cutting off his power. They told us that they would not only cut off our electricity, but that in order to keep the power on, we also had to pay the boss' debt of 7,000 pesos. We did it, and we paid the water bill and the gas bill—which is the most important—and that's how we worked. But what we were doing bothered them from the beginning and they came around all the time to harass us. They claimed we were destroying the machines, for example, but that didn't make sense since there was a ton of media people around us and they saw that nothing was broken. Why would we break the machines in the first place? How would we eat? How would we pay for everything? We were working, despite the boss' lies.

So many of the unemployed workers' movements have come to support us. What we've done is pretty big. We're an example of how to fight for a workplace, an inspiration for the unemployed making 150 pesos, which isn't enough for a family. What a worker needs is to work.

We aren't political. We're surrounded by politicians, but that isn't the type of politics that makes sense to the women workers of Brukman. What we want is to work, and we struggle for our work, for our livelihood. Especially women—women think more about their children. I think that women are better fighters than men, and this pushes us to continue fighting for our livelihood.

Candido, Chilavert (a recuperated workplace)

The decision to take the factory was a very difficult step for us to take. Most of us here in the print shop have been working together for forty years. We've always more or less shared in the union struggles, like the ones over wage issues, and generally we've won. We always ended up doing pretty well. So taking over the business, the factory, was really powerful. It was a huge decision that included all the *compañeros*. At first, we didn't know what to do, but when we realized that they were going to come and take the machines, well, then we had to make a decision. The time for thinking had ended and we took over the workplace. That step was reflexive, instinctive. You know that if they take the machines from you, you'll end up on the street. It's a reflex—you don't think about cooperatives, you don't think about anything. Defending your source of work is a reflex.

In Chilavert, you could pick up your foot, and someone from a movement would come out from under it. They were everywhere. It was amazing, the support we got from everyone. People that didn't even know us were there, on the front lines, being clubbed. Everyone fought to be on the front line. It's really emotional [eyes tearing]. Today, it's a little calmer. Now we talk about the day-to-day running of the print shop. But when you struggle for something…it's your obligation to fight for what you want, and that moves you. People you don't even know—who you've never seen before in your life—are fighting for you. [Starts to cry.]

No, look, I can't explain it to you... When they came to evict us for real, they came with eight assault vehicles, eight patrol cars, everything in eights because they knew that there were eight of us. They brought two ambulances and police with dogs. The repression was intense for just eight workers. They started with the assault vehicles, the ambulances, everything with the determination that they were going to remove us. We had already predicted all of this, and had advised the Pompeya neighborhood assembly, which is around the corner, who mobilized, and the IMPA [a recuperated metal shop] assembly, who defended the factory by standing in front of it, linking arms to make a chain... I never expected to see so many people. There were an impressive number of people. There were members of the Parque Centenario and Parque Avellaneda neighborhood assemblies, everyone from *asembleístas,* and people from other recuperated factories.

We were inside during all of this. We were even printing. We were printing the cover for the book *What Are the Popular Assemblies?* That was Thursday, and the book was going to be presented at noon on Saturday in the Palermo Viejo assembly. That assembly had been doing a series of events, the last of which was the presentation of the book, which was written by participants in the neighborhood assemblies.

And that's how it was, from 3:00 in the afternoon until 10:00 at night, skirmishes back and forth. Our lawyer, who was with us, went to the police station to speak with the judge directly. The guy was inflexible and wanted to evict us at any cost. He gave the order to the police commander to remove us. The police chief came separately, and by then there were a few legislators with us. A bunch of them came by, sometimes giving their support. Almost 80 percent of the legislators were involved with the Chilavert issue in some way. And that's how they started talking—the police, legislators and our lawyer—with all the pressure of the movement of recuperated factories and neighborhood assemblies.

We were still inside the factory, following the negotiations going on outside. In the meantime, a man from one neighborhood assembly parked his truck out front, and people from IMPA brought another one, so the door was blocked and the police couldn't push it in. Barricades were made out of wood and tires, and women were putting paper into the tires, threatening to light them. I was inside and the cops were outside making threats. There was some pressure on the police because the media was there, airing it live. There was also the paper that was put under the barricades, like in the tires. There were so many people out front to defend us, not just from assemblies and recuperated factories, but also neighbors who had never been involved before—people who changed after the nineteenth and twentieth. A group came out of the retirement home, which is across the street from the factory, and they made their way up to the front line. Eventually, the commander decided to back off.

The police chief and the judge, who had ordered the decision, reversed it because there were so many people defending us. Meanwhile, inside the factory, we had made a decision that if we were evicted we would set the place on fire. They weren't going to take the machines. The only way they were going to take them was in an urn. That was our pact. But we didn't know how long the people outside would hold up. So we held an assembly outside while the judge's order was still standing, and asked, "How far are you all willing to go?" "Until the end!" they responded.

You have to know two things. We don't take over all workplaces—as some people are asking, "they take over all the businesses?" No, we don't take over any workplaces that are in operation or that pay the workers. We take the businesses that were abandoned by their owners. That's the first point that has to be made clear. Another point is that in all the recuperated workplaces, the workers are owed at least six months' worth of wages. The other thing that should be clear is that these are workers that are in debt, impoverished, and that can't invest anything because they don't even have enough to eat. You sometimes have to depend on a bag of food given to you by the city government to survive. Another thing you have to keep in mind is that many of the workplaces have already been emptied of raw materials, machines, etc. That is unless someone hasn't allowed them to be emptied. So, workers always have to fix the machines, tune them up, or get new ones. We're talking about workers without money, in debt, and factories without raw materials, with machines that aren't in good shape because they haven't been maintained. These workplaces are now producing. So how do we do it?... Don't ask me how, because I don't know. Ha. I know. [Smiles.]

How do we do it? In some ways it's like how a housewife manages the house's economy when there isn't anything. What do you do when three of your kids need shoes? You go out and buy shoes for the one that needs them the most. That's how we're prioritizing things, too. We didn't know about economics—we didn't know anything, but we made our priorities. What do we have to do? Fix the machine's cylinders. We did as little as we could, but to be able to work we had to change a series of the machine's press cylinders. It cost us a lot. You need cash, and you can't just spread that out over the first jobs that you do. We also try not to get to the point, economically, where we don't have a cushion in case a machine breaks down. Those were the first principles. Home economics. For example, when we started, we bought two plates for offset printing, just to get started. Now we're buying packages of fifty plates at a time.

We brought a new printing press into the shop. Our press, not an expropriated one. We repaired the cylinders of the presses. We've got insurance against theft, against fire, and we care for the environment, or at least we contaminate less. We have to acknowledge that the owner was respectful of the environment, but we're a little better because we scrub the ink cans to get all the ink out. We also pay taxes and we put up with the audit that they just did. We don't have any debt with our distributors and generally follow the rules. Our primary commitment is to make sure we're paid and paying our bills. After that, we have our commitments to other recuperated businesses, society, and the neighborhood assemblies that defended us. The police have tried to evict them, and we've defended them just like they did for us. We also have commitments to several popular kitchens and we work as intermediaries for a bread factory. The bread is brought back from the supermarkets and we distribute it among the popular kitchens. We have a new project where we're turning part of the factory's office space into a clinic. From the beginning, we've promised that we're going to use all the space.

Everything is possible with solidarity. When society struggles, we can get through it. We started the struggle, but others followed—the assemblies, and other recuperated workplaces. Besides being in solidarity, you've got to struggle. You can be in solidarity, but if they are going to try and evict us or any other workplace, and if you don't join the struggle—no matter how much solidarity you offer, no matter how many pesos you have—they're going to get rid of you.

Here we struggle for Chilavert. Today we also struggle for the Hotel Bauen. Saturday we're going to struggle for PEN in Venado Tuerto, in San Antonio de Areco. There's another ceramic factory that's going to be taken over soon, and there's the Conforti printing press, where the workers are struggling, and we're supporting them in forming cooperatives. The moment they get ready to evict them, we'll be there.

The unions are screwed down to their easy chairs, no? And if you're screwed to your easy chair, you're going to make sure no one pulls you out, see? Then, solidarity is lost. The same thing happens with all the political parties. They don't want to lose their positions, they don't want to lose anything. People aren't worth anything to them. There are a few exceptions, but the majority doesn't care. They just want to keep their power, their political positions, all that. This struggle isn't like that. This struggle... Here they don't pay me to come here, it's a moral obligation. It's different from an obligation to stay seated in an easy chair, understand? No one pushes me. I come because I want to, because I feel obligated. That's one of the differences.

I'm optimistic about the future because when there's struggle, things are achieved. If you don't struggle, you don't get anywhere. The way we look at it, we're uniting people, assemblies, recuperated factories. There's more energy and more power—more power to defend oneself. There's hope, and you see a change. It's not huge, but if you want to pick up a mountain from here and move it over there, you have to start with a pebble—with something you can carry. And in ten years, the mountain will be over there. We're showing that it can be done. Just as we recuperated these workplaces, there will be a time when YPF [the company that exploits Argentine petroleum] will be owned by the state. But not the old state, instead a state controlled by worker's assemblies and university students. That is to say that this is going to have power. Decisions about energy will be made by the very workers. There won't be some big nobody, not that he's not going to be there, but he won't have control over the workers.

There's a hymn of the recuperated businesses: "We're the present and the future. To resist and occupy. The factory will not be closed. Resist and occupy. With our banners high, we'll lift the country up. We are the present and the future. To resist and occupy."

Flora, Ava Guaraní Community (an indigenous community)

Iyabeche, what does that mean? That you're free, that you're not in slavery. You're free. We were free, *Iyambae Coroico*, that means that we're free.

Life in the jungle before, was natural. Everything was natural, and we lived naturally. We lived a life where nobody came to pressure us, no one told us do this and don't do that. We didn't have any bosses.

I remember when I was a little girl, I'd see my father cutting down trees, but I didn't realize he was being paid. We didn't realize it because my sisters and I were little. We'd go help him arrange the trunks. The Ledesma Corporation would give him a few vouchers he could use to get a food ration. We didn't know about sugar or noodles. Everything we used was from the ground. My father knew how to cultivate the earth, and we had a little plot. Really, we had everything we needed. We grew *selabati* corn, *poroto umanda, tupi, umanda*, which is the one that has the longest veins and the biggest seeds, the *anco*, the *zapallo, guete*, the *batata*, the *mandioca* [Guaraní crops]. We grew everything that the

Guaraní knew how to grow. We lived off that, and when we harvested, we already had a place to store it. It was a two-story building, and we didn't have stairs or anything like that. My father made a ladder out of thick rope, and that's how it was. Back then we didn't have sodas. We drank *chicha*, *cabi*, *siripi*, all things that you make yourself. We drank that. Now we drink soda and we get bloated—it makes us ill. Before, everything was healthy. Everything was nutritious.

I can see the changes. For example, now my daughter says, "I've got to buy yogurt for my baby." And I tell her, "Make her *anchi*." It's corn that you boil with a special process, and it keeps children healthy. Nothing used to make them sick, and now everything does. As babies, we were breast feed on mother's milk, no sticking a bottle in our mouths, nothing artificial. That was our life in the countryside, until we came here.

We all lived as families in a single *oca*, a single patio. Everything was shared with the neighboring families. Food was put in a common pot, cooked, and shared. No one ever had food stored only for themselves. The Guaraní always shares food with visitors. They are always hospitable, very hospitable. And we poor people that now live in the city, lack all kinds of food. If there's *corepoti* [money], we eat, and if there isn't, we don't. We can't raise hens to eat either. No, you can't do that. That's how we used to live, and we divided up the food, the wild fruit. All of our food came from the mountain. And now the *caray* [pejorative for white landowners] call us the *chahuancos*. They call us that as an insult. They say we're lazy, that we don't like to work, but at that time we had everything. We called it the land without owners. Before the *caray* intervened, our fathers could grow things. We had fruit trees. We had what we needed.

Front of the recuperated clinic, FÉNIX,
months after the occupation.

Elvira, Fénix Salud (an occupied clinic)

We decided to check into the clinic [smiles]. I'll explain what that means. It was difficult, because the cooperative is made up of doctors, technicians, administrators, many people—it's a very heterogeneous group. The moment we decided to enter and occupy the clinic was a really difficult one. One doesn't take over workplaces every day. It's a little scary. Some people didn't support the move, and many others agreed, but didn't participate. Many of them were professionals and were protecting their prestige in the medical community. So, well, it was only a few of us that made the decision, and then entered and occupied that morning.

From the moment that we occupied the clinic, people from the movement started approaching us—that is to say, other recuperated workplaces and people from different organizations came to offer support. So we didn't feel alone. It felt, to me, like when you're sitting at home being visited by friends. That's how if felt with all the people that came supporting us. They brought us so much. For example, there's a recuperated printing press, Chilavert, that brought us fliers for free, and there's the bakery cooperative that brought us sweet bread. They were super fond of us. You know how people say "all of a sudden two faces?" It was like that. Suddenly people that you didn't know came and gave you unconditional support, staying with you and keeping you company. Sometimes they'd come and stay here drinking *maté*, chatting and sharing their experiences. It was very emotional, because it was forbidden to come in and show support, but they did it anyway. We took risks struggling for something that we consider our right, and everyone showed support. The process was really powerful.

With all the growth of the social movement... I hadn't thought of this before, but I think, since we came from a time of not doing anything, of not participating, I think people are slowly seeing that we need to participate. Before, we delegated everything to functionaries in the government, and now we realize they aren't going to solve our problems. We realized that there's no leader that's going to come and solve everything. So if there's not participation, you don't get anything—there's no moving forward. While I think that consciousness is still lacking, that not everyone is aware yet, I see a process where people are slowly becoming more conscious.

Now it's our turn to tell the world what's going on. We said to ourselves: those of us who have participated in this process have an obligation to let others know what we've lived and gained through our experiences. It's hard, because you can't really communicate a lived experience with words. I can't tell you what I felt, although I'm going to try to get something across to you.

Elsa, Fénix Salud (an occupied clinic)

In the beginning of January 2003, except a few people, everyone was suspended. Ten days went by, twenty days, six months, and then the clinic went broke. The owners of the clinic were going to shut it down. I spoke with Murua from the National Movement of Recuperated Workplaces and he asked, "What do you think about forming a cooperative?" I replied "Are you crazy?" Then it all started coming together and I was... I don't know, I was talking to people in groups of four, asking them how they felt, until one day we called a general meeting and we all came to an agreement.

How did we come to this decision? Well, I'll tell you, but you know, it was the first time in my life that I ever did anything like that.

Tuesday at 8:00 in the morning we met and decided to peacefully enter the clinic, knowing full-well that we had a lot of work to do, since the day that the clinic closed, all the books and such were left there. We entered through a side door, because this one [pointing to the front door] had locks and all that stuff on it. That's why I say that we did it peacefully, because we didn't break anything at all, we just went in the door, and closed it when we were done. That's what we did every day and night in the beginning of the occupation. Then at night, some of the young people would stay in the clinic to help take care of everything, just in case.

It was really recently that the police brutally evicted us, but we got back in. It started with the police harassing people from the clinic, and then they grabbed a kid from here. When we arrived and saw the number of police surrounding the whole building, as well as assault vehicles, fences, firefighters, and helicopters flying overhead, we were asking, what are they doing? Especially considering the number of people we had, what the hell are they doing? Pretty soon, we saw them bring a police van inside the clinic. We heard welding and saw that they had broken a lot of stuff. See [pointing to equipment], some of the inside doors where we keep the oxygen. They welded down the door, and ripped down parts of the fence around the area where the ambulance comes in.

When other cooperativists, others in the movement, began hearing about what was going on, they all started to come here. This is what solidarity means. First there were ten of us, then twenty, then a little later fifty, then more and more. Someone brought a big truck for us to use, and with that, the 200 people now outside the clinic shut down the street. We blocked Díaz Vélez. We put a big banner in front and all went together, because there were 200 of us, at that point.

I tell you, I never would've imagined that someone would send a helicopter to fly over me all night, or that I would see people with shields, helmets, and clubs wanting to hit us. Before this, I didn't understand anything. The truth is, I was more lost than a child in a maze. As the hours went by, it gave us an overwhelming feeling that we were right. We might be crazy, but still people were coming to help us and support us in this. People from the legislature started approaching us, neighborhood assemblies came out and supported us, and even our neighbors came out to help. It was all so powerful and so strengthening, it was so good, it was all such a beautiful feeling. The only time I got scared was when I saw one of our supporters with blood flowing from his head because of the police hitting him.

After the 30th it was over. We eventually negotiated our way in again with everyone's support. For a month they left a police watchman. Not any more. Now I'm a watchman, and we share the duty within the cooperative. We have no intention of taking over the clinic to do something bad. No, we have taken it over to make it work again, to bring back our source of work. It's as simple as that.

You know, really, all of this is just about our wanting to work again. This isn't about conflicts or wanting to incite a conflict. It is about recuperating our workplaces. It is really just about all of us wanting our jobs.

What we're getting at with all of this—and this is how I explain it especially to people who are used to being managed—is that we're developing as human beings now. How it used to work, like here in the clinic, was that there was always a limit to how far you could go. Each person had their thing, their area, and there was structure. For example, on the nursing floor, or with the treasurer, or that guy over there, everybody had only their role, and even though we had lots of ideas and proposals there was nowhere we could go. This is changing now. We're open to shifting what we do and how we do it. What happens is that workplaces run by bosses and managers have a ceiling, and they don't let you grow beyond it, they don't let you advance, change or create, don't you think? But what we're doing is letting human beings develop, giving people the ability to think and contribute ways of resisting and creating. We believe that, this way, we can produce some of the most marvelous fruits. So that's where we're going.

We're human beings. There's a diversity of opinions in the clinic, but it's like if you have a tree with many branches, it's the entirety of those branches that make up the tree. The cooperative is the tree, and we're each branches with different shapes and edges. We place a lot of importance on each and every one of us, and in all that each individual does.

A sandal making project of the MTD Solano

Group of compañeras, MTD La Matanza (unemployed workers' movement)

COMPAÑERA 1: We are creating a model school. Not in terms of a model of perfection, but in the sense that there's not another one like it. We're in the process of legalizing the school now because we want it to be part of the educational system, but not on the same terms. Our school will have a design, and especially a curriculum that's very different. We're developing the school together within the movement and with neighbors, and without state interference. We're going to make the decisions that we think are right for the school. The goal is to create a true educational community where we can all participate in all of the decisions. It's possible to teach so much, so why not do it? Our starting point is to figure out our needs, the real needs of this community. And then from there, we'll start to find ways to recuperate and repair all that the educational system has done to us, and what it's engendering in the children. It's like a big go around of ideas.

COMPAÑERA 2: The idea is that this new school would be sustained in the short- and middle-term by our micro-enterprises, like our silk-screen printing, sewing, baking, and book publishing. The idea is basically to start to create a different culture. The idea isn't that this new educational community gives to the larger community, but that the parents and community participate in the project, are involved in their children's education, and together remake community. We have a very difficult task, but we also know that it's practice for us. It's an experiment. We don't know how it's going to turn out, but we know that we're going to do it. The only way to see how this experiments ends is to do it. We think this school could have a ripple effect. We believe that in some way we're going to be able to change the education system from what we experienced. I'm twenty-three years old, and primary and

Signs advertising after-school help and the schedule for the neighborhood assembly's meetings

secondary school were terrible for me. For example, in secondary school, they taught me that during the military dictatorship, those 30,000 people who disappeared were disappeared because they were up to no good.

All the things that we're taught are carried inside ourselves, and they're difficult to remove later. We think that it's more difficult to struggle with the enemy inside of ourselves. We want children to learn things that will really help them to defend themselves later in life.

COMPAÑERA 3: Teachers are used as a tool of the government to promote the system, and we want to break with that. Teachers aren't tools, they're the medium children have for learning. Learning and teaching at the same time; the pedagogy here is a back-and-forth. The traditional way that teachers and students relate is where the teacher has the power. So we're starting differently, from the place where power is in all of us, in the group, the collective. This new freedom, this new form of mutual learning and teaching, shows us how children can disentangle themselves from power.

COMPAÑERA 4: The government's education system offers a curriculum that you're told to respect, but that methodology has little to do with what we're talking about in the movement. How do you teach? Do you teach that Columbus discovered America or that the indigenous were discovered by Columbus? It all has to do with the way you teach things. You can teach math by force and coercion, or you can teach it with bread—that is, in a way the children can relate to. Children can understand what it is that you're trying to explain to them, including the most abstract things that they might not see every day. It seems to me that we need different ways of treating and educating children.

Here, you have to deal with violence all the time. We want to take the secret of violence and make it more open—acknowledging that it's a part of daily life, so that we can change that fact. If you don't acknowledge it—like in today's schools, where they say don't use violence, but then don't recognize real life daily experiences—then learning doesn't happen. We don't want our school to have violence either, but start from reality, since it's a reality they live with every day.

Parents are an important part of the educational space. Not that they are necessarily going to be in the classrooms, but they are going to be involved with different things, and one of the first issues they may be talking about is violence.

Fernando, Bauen Hotel/Callao Cooperative (a recuperated hotel)

We're from the Callao Cooperative, former workers of the Bauen Hotel. The hotel went bankrupt in February 2001, but it was kept open by a trustee until December 2001, when the closure was decreed, everything was stopped, and all the employees were thrown out. Over sixty belonged to the company, plus those employees who did work related to the hotel, like security, bar, theater, etc., making more than 150 of us who ended up out of work. They owe us back wages, bonuses, and vacations. A little while ago, about a month ago, we got in touch with the National Movement of Recuperated Workplaces [MNER], who told us it was possible to take over our workplace. So we formed a cooperative, the Callao Cooperative. Friday of this week was when we took the building. Then, after the occupation, we went to talk to the judge that's responsible for the case, and he's given us temporary custodianship of the hotel.

Our principle objective is the reclaiming of our workplace, and then in two months we're going to open the hotel. There's a new law in the city legislature that's sort of temporary—basically only enforced some of the time—that says there can be a vote on an expropriation, and then we can open the hotel for a period of two years, which can be extended for another two years, and again, until we make an offer to buy the building out of bankruptcy. That would make the building ours.

Our idea is to continue offering the services the hotel originally offered. It was a five-star hotel. The hotel is really huge, with six main halls, a theater, a bowling alley that you can dance in, 220 rooms, and a pool. The idea now is to open it soon, with fewer rooms, maybe seventy or eighty to start, and to begin using the halls, restaurant, and theater, and do all sorts of cultural and social events with the community.

Our movement helps former workers from workplaces that have closed or gone bankrupt to see how they can reclaim their jobs. It isn't on a national level. It's not some national organization. It's a movement that helps workers locally, giving us information and advice. There are certain agreements that can be reached with the government, and others in the movement have information about this. For example, the day before yesterday, we had a meeting with the Secretary of Economic Development of Buenos Aires to look at the viability of the hotel, discussing things like how much reopening would cost, looking at the possibility of a subsidy or an easy loan to get it running, etc.

There are now people from every section of the hotel participating in the takeover. The idea is to organize it ourselves, and to not let in any investor who would offer money but then want to participate in the decision-making. All decisions will be made by the workers. We're from every sector of the hotel—from reception, maintenance, maids, bartenders, wait staff. Everyone. The idea is to obtain capital through credit from a state subsidy, but not through investors or anything like that. We want to be independent, and not to ever have to give up managing the hotel for financial reasons. We want to manage it ourselves.

I don't think that anything is ever lost, when you have hope and the motivation to achieve something, either at work or in life itself. Nothing is impossible if you have desire and you know where you want to go.

Jesus, Asamblea Cid Campeador (neighborhood assembly)

Ah! This [gesturing with his arms], this was a bank. Banco de Mayo. This was a bank that practically didn't have an owner. We took over this space seven months ago. It was recuperated for and by the neighbor-hood. At no point did we break the locks. There was no violence in tak-ing the place. Nobody lives here because this belongs to the assembly. It belongs to the neighborhood. We do many things here, but no one uses it for housing.

Here we have lots of activities that are open and free to the whole neighborhood. You've got theater workshops, where you teach theater and perform plays; there are workshops on silk screen printing; the group Arte Arde, which does all kinds of political sculpture; and the group Etcétera, which is another militant art group that does work and work-shops here. There are expositions, tango classes, and all of these things are free. There are also tai-chi classes, Arab dance classes, educational support for the kids that go to school, and a library. There are lots of activities. Later, on the weekends, it becomes a huge popular kitchen and big bags of food are delivered to people who need it. There's the outdoor snack bar, which is now open, and is for the children that go to school. When they leave school, they come here to have snacks. In the evenings, there are a lot of public talks. For example, every Thursday at 8 o'clock, there are different discussions with journalists and writers who come to present books or give lectures. We have a pretty large variety of activities that are useful to the community.

Toto, MTD la Plata (an unemployed workers' movement)

The first priority for the families in the movement is meeting our basic food and nutritional needs. We're still in the very early stages of orga-nizing projects, the most useful of which has been the organization of popular kitchens, which hasn't been easy. As soon as a group begins to organize in a neighborhood, they almost immediately organize a popu-lar kitchen. It's not planned. It happens naturally, because if you had to make a list, the first thing to take care of is food. Popular kitchens, in particular, help do this, and later we add things like baking bread and tending organic vegetable gardens. All of these projects are done collec-tively. It's not like there's a bread oven in someone's kitchen. Everything organized in the neighborhood is for everyone.

There are many other groups and movements that are more ad-vanced in what they produce, how much, etc. For example, some move-ments are able to produce more things than the neighborhood needs, and then they can sell the extra and use the money to meet other needs.

There are also many groups that have a wide variety of projects, including things like raising animals.

As we organized and were able to resolve the immediate question of hunger in the neighborhood, we soon realized that the food we had was very low in vitamins and protein, and not really nutritious. There was no meat, which really wasn't an option to buy because it's too expensive. Today, there's no family that eats chicken once a week. It's unthinkable with the price of chicken here, not even fried, which costs even more. Eating meat once a week is unthinkable. With this in mind we decided to raise animals. It wasn't planned in the beginning, but came out of the necessities we observed. There's a lot of interest in making this happen. One discussion we haven't resolved yet is what we're going to do if there's more than we need, beyond the neighborhoods necessities—how we would distribute it, etc.

Another project we have been talking about is building a more sophisticated bakery. Right now what we have is rustic, with ovens made of mud and wood. We would like to get electric ovens—ones that could be used inside instead of the ones we have now, which only work outdoors. The inside space could also function as a bakery. We're looking for improvements in these projects so

An oven made from a recycled washing machine in the MTD Allen

they can grow, and expand production. We're also thinking about other projects to meet some of our other necessities. Like being able to produce shoes—that would be an important accomplishment.

The way we organize is much like many other of the MTDs. We're all different, all the MTDs, but there's something that lots of us share, which is having neighborhood meetings and making decisions collectively. Each neighborhood has meetings, which are open, and anyone can speak. There are also joint meetings of all the different neighborhoods that are part of the MTD. There are different types of participation in the meetings, which sometimes has to do with what we're discussing, like whether it's an everyday matter or a larger question. We call these larger meetings plenaries. In our meetings, any *compañero* from any neighborhood can participate if they want to. In these meetings, we often work on and develop things that are common to the neighborhoods—projects like health, our collective press, etc. It's a space where we discuss and resolve all sorts of things related to our projects and relationships. It's been this way since the beginning.

Adriana, Clínica Medrano (a recuperated clinic)

We felt like we couldn't do anything at first. Formal regulations wouldn't let us keep working in the clinic. The managers left, closed everything, and all our jobs were eliminated. After a little while, we organized assemblies on Thursdays, and that's how we started. We started to come up with ideas about how to go back to work. We put some money together so we could open the clinic again when the time came.

In September 2001, a new business group came and reopened the clinic. After that, it operated for about a year, but we still didn't have nearly the salary we deserved. Then they stopped paying us altogether. That was in June. Then they issued us an official letter saying we had to take a twenty-one day unpaid vacation. We had problems.

We decided to stay in the clinic—without wages and without the businessmen. It was difficult. You know, it was so, so difficult [crying]... Excuse me. We were in here fifteen days and nights. We had water, but that's all there was. There was no food. The last time the lawyer came, she told us we had to go home because we couldn't go on that way. She said that we'd eventually get paid, but she didn't know when, because the client didn't have the money. It was really too much for us to swallow.

Lots of *compañeros* from the Italian hospital, which is on the next block over, came and brought us things. They'd also come at night to support us. They would bring food and support [crying]. It was a really difficult situation and really painful. It isn't the sort of experience everyone can handle. For me, I feel like I'm more experienced now and can take on much more than before, and I'm ready to continue no matter what, and no matter how long it takes.

At the same time, many *compañeros* left and got odd jobs. We also went out to fundraise. We'd carry a donation box and ask for help for the clinic. We went wherever there was an assembly. The situation was making us more sophisticated. A congressional representative showed up at one point, spoke to us, and looked for government-related solutions on our behalf.

Then, in one of our assemblies, the idea came up to start a health cooperative. Of course, we had no idea what to do first. We started studying, we consulted the congressional representative, and we began to look into what the regulations were for getting started. The first thing we had to do was to get permission from the Municipality on Public Health, and we had access to all these things through this representative. We found that we could do it, and so we continued on this trajectory, got the registry, and complied with the rules. We discovered we could offer outpatient care and have custodianship, and so we opened on November 18, 2002.

Alberto, Clínica Medrano (a recuperated clinic)

We started to work as contract workers in about August or September, 2001. We were contracted even though we knew this new company would have trouble paying us. We knew they would fall behind, but we accepted that because we thought maybe, eventually, the pay would be normalized. But it didn't happen that way. They got further and further behind on paying our salaries, accumulated more and more debt, and around June 2002, the clinic's former owners decided to sell the stock package to another business group. The new group brought us together for a meeting, told us that they would honor the debt, but that they had to close the building eighty days for repairs.

In the eighty days we were suspended from work, we would go to the clinic anyway to see what was really happening, because we had some doubts. We didn't know what was going on, but we saw that they weren't doing repairs of any kind. The new owners had hired some armed guards.

So we began an occupation of the clinic. The owners came and tried to pressure us. On the one hand, they said what we were doing was fine, because we had filed a claim and everything, but that they thought that the method of occupation was wrong, etc., etc. We said we thought they were only there to pressure us, that they didn't have the money to pay us what they owed us, so they couldn't do anything and needed to leave. There was tension, a lot of tension… A lot of nervousness, you could see it, but in the end they decided to leave. When they left, we filed a report claiming control of the establishment, and from there we came up with the idea of reopening the clinic ourselves. The only viable possibility that we saw was forming a work cooperative.

At first, there were thirty-eight of us, but it was all mixed. Some of us had filed the initial claim to get them to pay us the debt and all that, and many others had joined the project later. People who decided to join understood that this was a very serious project, and that we really didn't have any other way out. We all agreed that it was possible. At first, I think half of what we were doing was clinging to anything we could to keep from falling into the abyss—clinging to a root, grabbing at anything so as not fall. Starting there, we developed the idea of reopening the clinic.

We all got involved in this project for the same reason: the lack of work prospects and the need to make a living. But we also decided that we didn't want to offer the same kind of care as before—where your money was what mattered, not your health, which is the type of medicine that's traditionally practiced here and many other countries. Our idea was to be able to make a living, to bring home a salary, without having to rob or exploit anybody.

We want to provide a dignified and professional service—as professional as possible—offering services to people that need healthcare the most. We even have a day where we take care of the unemployed. We have to charge some people because we're not subsidized. We're trying to find funding though, because when we treat the unemployed, we can't afford to send samples to the lab or take x-rays. We don't have a way of dealing with it because we don't have the resources. We're facing a lot of challenges in this project.

We want to provide healthcare to everyone who's marginalized in society. We're connected to all the different groups and movements. Diverse groups of people have reclaimed their workplaces, and each has different structures, affiliations, and relationships. We're politically independent. All our decisions as a cooperative are resolved in the assembly. Everything is dealt with there, even the smallest individual problems, like changes in our schedules. We do this partly so we don't make mistakes.

Compañer@s, MTD Allen and MTD Cipolletti (unemployed workers' movements)

COMPAÑERO, MTD ALLEN: We began our health activism, because we believe that capitalism produces sickness. No. Capitalism produces sick people and sickness, in that order. This is because we live in a society where everyone is permanently desperate, and that makes people sick.

Alienation itself, as well as subordination to power, is a huge part of the healthcare situation. So our health projects start in resistance to capitalism. In the end, we can have a good supply of medicine, we can heal a lot of sick people, but people keep getting sick. We try to encourage caring relationships, including new relationships with professional healthcare workers, not just amongst ourselves. The *compañeros* manage their own healthcare relationships, all from within the movement. *Compañeros* who are doing this don't necessarily know anything about medicine, but understand the dynamics of subordination, particularly the dynamic between doctor or nurse and patient. One of the movement projects then became health management. No, we don't like the word "management" at all, so why we call it "health management" is a good question. There's an elaborate buying and selling relationship in today's healthcare system. You have markets, pharmacies where you get medicine, hospitals, and the professionals, and they're all businesses. We, in contrast, try to manage all of this health business based on our everyday needs and on our desire for a different way to get care.

COMPAÑERA, MTD CIPOLLETTI: Yes, it's really important not to fall into some kind of determinism. If we lose sight of our goals, we could lose the whole embryo of our newborn autonomous construction here. We're aware of this. If that weren't the case, we'd have everything figured out already, and the path ahead would be short and straight. There is nothing that says that what we are doing is "it," or "the way." We have spoken with *compañeros* in the MTD Solano and many others about these ideas, and it's possible that we're messing up in some of these things.

Carlos G., Zanon (an occupied factory)

Everybody comes here. More than anything it's to see the phenomenon that's happening here—the workers' control of the ceramics factory. They come to see things like our working in assemblies—all of us working together—and our equality in pay. I haven't read much Trotsky or Marx, or anything about what socialism or capitalism is, but according to what people have come and told us, what we're doing here is the epitome of socialism.

Everything began much earlier than 2001, when we took over the factory. It started when we took over the leadership of the union. The union here, as in so many places in the country, was bureaucratic, and had the same corrupt leadership for over fourteen years. Anyone identified as opposing the union was put on a list to be fired. At the end of the month, and at the end of the year, every year, there would be a restructuring of the factory, where they would throw out, like, eighty to a hundred people. That was the restructuring. It was out of this experience that a group of *compañeros* was born. We needed to resist the insecurity of being threatened with losing our jobs every year; waiting every year to see if they would get rid of you or not. The movement came from this resistance.

Compañeros began organizing around the need for job stability. First, they had informal meetings outside the plant, with various workers from the factory. These conversations were so successful that when the next internal election came, there were two candidate lists presented. One was the official list, the one we always saw that had all the bureaucrats, and another, which was "the maroon list." The maroon list was the one made up of the *compañeros* that, even today, still make up most of the leadership of the union. We still have a union here, even under worker control. The maroon list made it into the plant and won. Their platform was simple: they promised not to deal with the bosses, that they wouldn't sell out, and that the only thing they would fight for was the rights of all the workers. Those promises are the reason we now toast everything that's come to pass.

Once they won the leadership of the union, they immediately began working on the problems inside the factory. It started to rain complaints—complaints about the lack of safety within the plant, about work accidents, and related hazards. That was the *compañeros'* first focus. Pretty soon the *compañeros* began to notice that our paychecks were late every month, so they started keeping track of all the factory's sales and business.

The *compañeros* also organized events intended to help us build unity—a soccer tournament, for example. Everyone in the plant participated in the tournament. We set up teams by work sector, and we organized delegates based on these teams. So the tournament wasn't only for fun—many discussions about the plant happened there, too. Soccer was a way of combining fun with our lives in the factory, forging more unity and organizing from that unity. And it really worked.

The new union leadership's trial-by-fire was the nine-day strike. In the history of the plant there had never been such a large or long strike. There had been one-day strikes—nationwide strikes and all that, but a strike in the plant? No, never. The company started to fall behind in paying us at the beginning of 2000. So one payday when they didn't pay us, we decided not to take it anymore. We said, "No, we worked and you have to pay us." We knew the products we made were selling, but our salaries weren't being paid.

The company had declared a preventative crisis that was based on the national economic crisis. Crisis declarations allowed companies that couldn't pay salaries, to suspend workers and sometimes even dismiss them. The workers began to rise up against the company, this rising fueled partly because we could see that the products we produced were selling.

Our products weren't just selling—we were producing a huge amount, up to a million square meters of ceramics. There's a gigantic lake here, Lake Marinemuco, and you could cover the entire surface of the lake with all the pieces we produced in a month. Imagine that. An article came out in our regional newspaper, the *Rio Negro*, saying that Zanon was one of the most productive factories in the country, and that it had earned 56-million dollars in 1998, and was projected to earn 56-million in 1999 and 70-million in 2000. The idea that a such a productive factory couldn't come up with two months of salaries, and that it was declared in preventative crisis was totally false and laughable.

I think that once the internal commission won the leadership of the union and the company couldn't fire anyone else, it began to look for other ways to attack us. The way they opted to do it was these crisis prevention measures. These measures made all of us nervous, mostly scared about being fired. One of our *compañeros,* Daniel, was so stressed out because of all of this that he had a heart attack one day while walking into work. *Compañeros* brought him here, to the clinic, to the nurse, but the personnel that were here at the time weren't trained for that type of situation. Our *compañero,* Daniel started to deteriorate rapidly. The conditions in the clinic were so bad that we discovered—right when Daniel was dying and needed it—that the clinic's oxygen tanks were empty. Daniel was dying, and his *compañeros* were trying everything to keep him alive, but the ambulance from Neuquen takes twenty minutes to get here, and while we were waiting for it, the *compañero* had a cardio-respiratory failure and died. This was at the very beginning of the nine-day strike. Daniel's death made everything come together—fighting against the crisis measures and fighting for improvements in health and safety. The plant was totally paralyzed for nine days. Everyone agreed on the strike, and the whole plant was shut down. Nothing was running.

In those times, we weren't scared. We were strong. Daniel's death gave us a lot of strength. For us, Daniel was…as the sign says over there, he was the reason we have such a strong foundation.

It was a very large union, and there was a certain roughness that still had to be filed down for there to be full unity. This was the moment when we really came together and, as we say, clenched our fists and started to hit—we started to strike. And we struck hard. We hit the bosses, we hit the union, and we struck in unity. We demanded an ambulance inside the plant, we demanded nurses on every shift, that they not shut down the cafeteria, and that there be a committee inside the plant that met with the business administrators, because the business was in charge of security. Well, them and the competent health personnel and our *compañeros*.

We won. It was our unity and teamwork that allowed this victory. The mood was really happy at that time. Everyone was euphoric, so content, and the next day we came in and started working. We want to work and we always have. We weren't looking to become owners of anything. Working, we're fine. They exploit us and we know it, but all the same we keep working. We're laborers, so we started working again once things seemed resolved. As time went on, they started trying to suppress us again. This was in around July of 2000. They started to try and set us back. Using salary set backs, for example. And our reaction? There was a two-day strike. They weren't paying us? Bang, an instantaneous strike. That was the conviction we had. If we worked, they had to pay us. If they didn't pay, we struck.

There used to be around a 150 supervisors, which was just insane. You had a supervisor in every sector. In my sector, I had a line supervisor, a production supervisor, a porcelain supervisor, and one final supervisor for the oven. There were four supervisors behind and above me, pressuring me all the time to put out more material. It was that way everywhere. So you lived under pressure of… They were always pressuring you. If you suffered an accident, then they fuck you because you messed up. So we lived with them pressuring us all the time. Go! Go! Go! This is also some of what was changing. We were advancing, and as we continued getting stronger, things changed. All the while, time was passing and April came. April, for us, was the beginning of a great struggle. Almost the beginning of this struggle we're still in today.

There was a huge fight around an assembly for the internal elections of the union before this point. The bosses and the union bureaucracy tried everything possible to prevent us from attending and then from voting. But in the end, we not only participated, but also won with a 95 percent margin. It was huge.

We had to keep fighting for our salaries. One struggle lasted thirty or forty days—we had been paid the previous month but not the current one, and we lived on nothing. It was a hard time. It was then that we started to get the word out about the conflict; making pamphlets and other things so that different organizations could understand and help us. We would ask them, "Look, you really want to help? Good, can you give us at least a thousand pamphlets for us to hand out?" We started to hand pamphlets out all over the place, telling people about what was happening here—that the pretty girl wasn't so pretty. The pretty girl had her faults inside, because this one, the biggest factory of Neuquen, was untouchable. It was an island where nothing ever happened. Here everyone was paid equally, all those sorts of myths, but it was nothing like that. There were a lot of things here that no one knew about.

That's when we first learned to communicate with people so they listened and joined us. Sometimes they'd come and bring us a package of rice, a package of pasta. All the food that arrived would be gathered in different bags and then divided in equal parts and handed out to each of the *compañeros*. We had to live for a month like this, and we made it.

By now we had started negotiations to end the strike, and the bosses were going to pay us for the month that they owed us, but they didn't want to pay us for the month of the strike. It was a back and forth, back and forth, and we weren't going to budge. We were tired of them not listening, so we said: "Enough, we're only going this far, and then we'll shut down the bridge to the town." So we went and blockaded it. We shut it down. That was our first time blocking the bridge. We had an assembly at 5:30 in the morning here with all the *compañeros*, and then went out to shut it down.

We planned to keep the bridge blockaded as long as we had to, night and day, until the conflict was resolved. Then, around 1:30 in the morning, *compañeros* came out like this with a huge smile, like this [grinning], and said the conflict was resolved. The bosses were going to pay us for all of the time we worked and were on strike. We had won again. They paid us what they owed us—330 of us.

Six months went by with us working well, except that we noticed that they were emptying the factory. The company didn't repair anything, went on selling material, and instead of twenty filled trucks leaving the plant each day, there were thirty. The first of October came around and the company said, "No, enough, we can't pay your salaries." Meanwhile they had cleared so much out of the factory. We went on strike, knowing that this time was going to be rough. When they turned off the ovens, it was like a dying man's heart stopping and his being put on life support. It's more or less like that. Turning off the ovens was terrible. We had known that the thirty-four day strike wasn't going to be the end—that the real war would come later. We had to prepare to survive whatever came along.

The day they shut down the ovens, they also took away the transportation, the clinic, and the cafeteria. They took all of it away. They also wanted to suspend us and reduce our salaries. All together like that, a package. Bam! We said no, and we planted ourselves so that nobody would be able to get us out of here. They took away our transportation, so how were we going to get to or from the factory, anyway? It was a way of keeping us from getting there, because if we didn't show up, they would send us a telegram firing us. We said no, we've got to get to the factory, we've got to keep working. We biked to the factory. Some people even walked. However and by whatever means, we had to get there. We were there for eight hours, and that's how we started.

Zanon, the owner, thought he'd beat us with hunger. In the first months we had nothing. We didn't earn anything. The community responded, bringing us more and more food. We went from door to door saying we were Zanon workers, and asked if they could help out the *compañeros*. They knew what we were going through. We went through all of Neuquen and Centernario. We went to the universities and got some things over there as well. We also got help from some of the left-wing party people, folks that could lend us money to get to Buenos Aires to do collections there. Everyone was part of the movement. We fought for each other. We couldn't stay still because we learned that if we all went out and kept busy, we could get things. For three months, we didn't earn anything and the community supported us.

We faced struggles in our own homes, our family lives were being disrupted. Everyone suffered. Many of us—and this happened to me—had credit cards, and were up to here with debt, and we had to pay the credit card companies who were threatening us. The credit card agency would call you everyday saying, "When are you going to pay?" "Hold on, I'm going to pay. Don't cause any problems. I'm going to pay." I was scared of losing everything. They put a lien on everything. With all the sacrifice that you make to get to where you are, it can all be taken away by one person whose only objective is making more money for himself and who doesn't think of anyone else's needs.

The time came when we decided we had to do something else, so we started legal action. We won. It was the first ruling on an offensive lockout, and not only did we win in the first ruling, but we also won in the appeals court of the Superior Court of Justice and in the Supreme Court. Each one looked at the lockout and determined that the workers were right.

The courts also told us we could protect the factory. Who better to protect a factory than the workers that work there? So we started to protect it, creating a sort of workers guard. And they ruled that we were to receive 40 percent of the stock to sell—to cover the wages that were owed us from the first time we were locked out.

When the ruling was announced, we asked an organization to print some fliers for us—very simple ones that said, "We won and by judicial order we can sell the ceramics, which will be sold at the factory door." We shut down the road so that cars would pass slowly and we could hand them

"Zanon is the workers'"
This sign has been destroyed and replaced a number of times after fights defending the factory.

fliers. Bam, bam, bam. We did tons of outreach. Then we started to sell, and on the first day people came from as far as Bariloche. It was great. We used that money to pay our back-wages.

On top of that, in the middle of all this, on November 30th comes a telegram from the boss telling us that our services are no longer required and that's it, nothing more. In response, we had a demonstration at the government house, where we burned a photocopy of the registered letter. Then we started to burn tires, like the *piqueteros*. That was the day when they seriously repressed us. So on top of being fired, the police were repressing us. They chased us through every street of Neuquen. They started the repression around 2:30 and at 4 o'clock, they were still chasing us, ceramic workers, throughout the city. Then the police went on a hunt for all people wearing purple shirts, assuming they were all

Zanon workers, since we all wear matching shirts. A lot of people were wounded or detained. The repression against us was really fierce. I ran fifteen blocks with a drum on my back. You know the type I'm talking about? Afterwards, I was grateful for the drum because it was covered in dents from rubber bullets. My drum literally saved my back. We took refuge in the hospital, and the police started to teargas the hospital to force us out.

When they saw us running, people from the neighborhood opened their doors to us. Small children were leaving school at that hour, but the police kept lobbing tear gas at us. We told the kids to get back inside the school, where it was safer. There was of all kinds of police violence. People came in unmarked cars, and if they saw a ceramics maker, bam! They'd throw him inside and take him away like that. All this made it so, I don't know…we wanted to hide, to take off our shirts that showed we were from Zanon. But we were ceramic makers, right? What other shirt did we have? If they take me away, they take me away. So, several *compañeros* fell. In the end though, Zanon, the boss, came out looking bad and his plan to silence us backfired.

That same afternoon, after the repression—after 4 o'clock, when we had just left the hospital—a march was organized to free the *compañeros* that were arrested. People came out to march with the ceramic workers. Bringing together a march of four- to five-thousand people is impressive. It was crazy. What's more, it was a march to liberate the *compañeros*—to free the ceramic workers. It was such big march, and people were really determined. We were advancing on the police station, and just when we were about to get there, the police freed the *compañeros*. I remember Boquita. Boquita is a *compañero* that always wears a Boca hat. He's a huge fan of Boca, our soccer team. Boquita never gets in any trouble—he's an angel—and when they released him he came running out, and all the *compañeros* opened up their arms like this, and put him up on their shoulders, and he took off his hat to us. And there was Juan's kiss. Juan was one of the leaders arrested. His wife was also part of the march. When Juan was released, a path opened up and his wife went running up and kissed him, a three-minute kiss with cameras all around. All these things gave us a wonderful feeling.

We went back to selling things from the factory and when March came around, we'd sold the last of what remained. We asked ourselves, "What do we do? We're done selling the stock that the legal ruling gave us and now what? Do we shut down the road to demand the subsidy of

150 pesos from the government? Do we go into the factory? We have the raw materials, the machines, and the labor power. Can we make it work? What do we do?" We voted to start working. We had to. Crazy! But we're workers and we can do it, even though we didn't have anyone behind us. Even though we had to start over from scratch. Just as we had to learn how to sell, we had to learn to work without bosses. We had to go in. It was our livelihood, and we knew what to do. On top of that, the electricity, gas, and everything had been cut off. So we turned on the gas ourselves. As for the electricity, we reached an agreement with Lepen, which is the electric company in this province, and they helped us out. They gave us a little boost to be able to start working. And we started working, following our own rules.

Ricardo, Esperanza (an occupied sugar plantation and refinery)

In 1997, the union installed a group of "leaders" that didn't care about the well-being of the workers. The union's policy was to make alliances with the employer, which is anti-worker, and as a result, the workers were silenced. So we called our own meeting and organized a group of workers to fight both the boss and the union bureaucracy. We started organizing ourselves in 1999, with almost everyone participating, because we were tired of taking so much abuse from the boss, and tired of having a union that always sided with the company instead of us.

An important part of this struggle was raising the consciousness of people in the city so that they would join us, and so we didn't end up just making demands and never getting any results. We wanted two things—to make sure that we, the workers, wouldn't end up isolated, and second, the participation of the people of San Pedro. It was important for them to know that this industry was failing, and that everyone's survival depended on it, because the mill was the economic motor that moved the city.

We started handing out fliers so people would know the truth about the situation with the mill. The owners, with all their economic power, tried to quiet everything down. They wanted everything to happen quietly, and tried to isolate us. They told people that all we wanted was raises. They were trying to claim that it didn't have anything to do with saving our livelihood, and the livelihoods of more than 3,000 people in the town.

The struggle had it advances and setbacks. This powerful boss didn't just have national connections, but also connections to the provincial government, and they were trying to create smoke screens so that when the time came, our struggle wouldn't grow. Fortunately, we had a lot of people that were connected to the group, Combative Class Current, at the national level. That's why we tried to make our voices heard beyond the border of Jujuy. The goal was to let everyone know what was happening in Jujuy.

The year 2000 was a lot better because of what we accomplished in the struggle. There were a lot of obstacles, and a lot of marches and counter-marches. In the end, we were able to take over the factory and throw out the bosses. In 1999 and 2000, while the factory was under worker control, we had a small harvest. When we took over the factory, there were thirty days when production was stalled, so we had to restart the task of harvesting. Within twenty-three days, we reached production. I think the owner would have asked, "How could these folks have done that?" We were able to get what was needed, and that's how we got to the 23rd of December—two days before Christmas in 1999, guaranteeing that there be a sugar quota so the factory would run during the time it was usually off, from January to March.

In those twenty three days, we had an excellent mini-harvest, and excellent production. We aren't talking about a huge amount, but it was still excellent. We thought the low production that happened before was due to poor administration, spending beyond budget, and often losing track of where they were selling sugar. It seems to me that the old bosses had a very defined goal. Their idea was to go back to a ghost town where industry disappears, as has happened with other large industries in Argentina.

Ernesto, Chilavert (a recuperated workplace)

We're still working, and this year in particular, we've learned a lot of things. Certainly, the situation in the country has changed, generally. About a year ago, there were expectations of more factory takeovers, but in reality there have been more business closures than factory takeovers. Still, there have been many takeovers. There's not much new. We're still working in the same way. There are now two more *compañeros*—that's the only news. We're still making decisions collectively, and now some of the meetings are thematic, based on having to take care of this or that need. No one gets tired of making decisions. No one!

In the past, we lived off our salaries...if they paid us, right? In the end, they didn't pay us and we had someone to blame. We had limited responsibility—even the person being blamed. Now things are different. Now I feel that if there's a wrong decision, it doesn't only affect me, you know? It affects many *compañeros* that have children. They have a family to sustain, and errors affect the families too. There are certain responsibilities, because there are people that depend on you.

I'm talking about production, but more than that. There are new ways of thinking. You're a person, instead of an object.

Mariana and Vasco, MTD Allen (an unemployed workers' movement)

MARIANA: I'm very new to this project. I wasn't one of the *compañeras* that developed these projects, but I participate now. Hilda was here from the beginning, and whenever we have a little time, we chat about how things started. It's a really inspiring and lovely process.

The way we decide on projects in the movement is that they are first presented in an assembly with all of the *compañeros*. Together, we discuss the project and decide if it's viable. *Compañeras* present things like what resources they have and need, what the project's goals are, and things like that. It doesn't have to be a bakery at all, though most do begin with bakeries. For example, some *compañeras* started a knitting group. They began with a bit of yarn, made a few things, and then with the money from selling things at a fair price, they were able to get more yarn and a little more for food. It's something that they're doing themselves. It's *autogestiónada*. We initiate our own projects with earnings that we stash away to pay for expenses like the flour and other things that needed to make bread. The idea is to not ask for anything from the municipality, so the project begins to grow and is self-managed. The idea is *autogestión*.

VASCO: What we're trying to do is think about how to work with the resources of the region, and at the same time show *compañeros* what it's like to organize in the movement. The movement has to be the thing that revives healthy relations.

Elsa and Neka, MTD Solano (unemployed workers' movement)

NEKA: When we talk about production, we talk about it in a holistic sense. For example, when we talk about producing the clothes we wear or our shoes, it's all related to other things. We're working a lot on a network of food production. We have dairy products, preserves, sweets, a popular butcher's shop, organic gardens, fish nurseries, hens, rabbits, and pigs. The idea is to raise food and crops, and distribute them to the *compañeros* working in the different areas. It's a sort of network of production. Some of the projects are here [gesturing around a recuperated piece of land], and others are in a different recuperated area.

Right now there are seven centers of *autogestión* and production. We have one space for working with children, and another space for security, which we don't separate from other projects in the movement. Security is an important area where *compañeros* do a lot of work. For example, when we go to a demonstration, the security people stay more aware of things than the rest of the *compañeros*. They help protect and defend *compañeros*. We also talk about producing autonomous healthcare and autonomous education. We're talking about a network of production, not productive groups in themselves—but a network of production, one that is communitarian and collective. For example, we have a people's pharmacy where a lot of *compañeros* work. What's produced there benefits everyone who needs it, including those that don't have an income. We also have a lot of people working in libraries and with children's projects. We're trying to become self-sustaining.

ELSA: Every neighborhood has a weekly assembly, and then we have monthly plenaries, where all the assemblies from all the neighborhoods come together. There's an assembly of people working on healthcare, and one on popular education, among others.

NEKA: The situation we're in has to do with the precariousness of how we're living, as well as the lack of resources we have to work with. For example, *compañeras* bake bread in a mud oven. It would be better if we had a space with more machines.

ELSA: I work in the bakery, and we do a little of everything here. We make bread for the children, and some to sell collectively so we can be more self-sufficient. We also get voluntary donations of ten pesos from *compañeros* and neighbors, so that we can not only bake the bread to sell, but also exchange money or bread for things we need, such as medicine and groceries. With each neighborhood making bread and doing this, we can become a little more self-sufficient. So far it isn't working so much with the neighborhood as a whole, but it's pretty much working with the *compañeros*.

NEKA: We have put all of this together with patience, and a lot of love and affection. Without this foundation, it would be impossible. To get together, get to know one another, and know that we struggle together creates a lot of affection. This is really powerful and important. I believe that if there's one thing that sustains us in the movement, it's this relationship of affection. Sometimes we quarrel, but since we love each other, we can move forward.

Graciela, MTD San Telmo (an unemployed workers' movement)

When we began, we were a few unemployed *compañeros* from the neighborhood who started to look around to see what we could do about what we needed. We asked ourselves if we were going to stay home feeling bad about not having work, or if we were going to do something about it. And that's how we started. We got together with other neighbors that had the same needs. At first there were four of us, then there were ten, and then even more. The first thing we did was produce detergent. We bought soap concentrate and bleach, and started to package it. That's how we started to come together. That was the first thing we did, and right after that we started a popular kitchen for the kids. In the beginning, we would each chip in some change and ask our neighbors to give us things. That's how we started the kitchen. Eventually, there were too many kids to sustain it as it was. It was then that we had our first march. The first march was to ask the Social Help Agency for food for our popular kitchen. Soon after that, we went out to fight for the *planes de trabajar* [work subsidies], which had been won by previous movement struggles. What we've produced so far hasn't been enough to subsist on, so we've asked for more subsidies.

We started by talking and seeing what we had in common. We didn't want to belong to any party, and we didn't want anyone bossing us around. We wanted to work without a boss. These were the things we agreed on. We didn't depend on any political party, church, or state organization. Instead, we defined how we wanted to do things, and we wanted to *autogestiónarnos*.

Group of compañeras, MTD Solano (an unemployed workers' movement)

COMPAÑERA 1: We came from a variety of struggles—from different places of resistance: those for life, for the earth, for work, for health—and we all got together in Solano, working together on these various things.

Unemployment started to hit us really hard, and it started to take on a structure that was progressive for us in a way. We started getting together within the framework of a church. This was in 1997, that we came

together to talk about the increasing phenomenon of unemployment.
We saw that it was here to stay—not
just some momentary problem. So we
started talking about it and one of the
possibilities that emerged was getting
something from the state. We needed
a few resources to help us resolve
our urgent needs—hunger, the lack
of healthcare, and education. Those
were the topics of the first assemblies,

**Duck in front of MTD
Solano's fish farm**

then the first marches, and the first road blockades, and that's how we
started.

We started getting some money from the state with these protests,
but in the assemblies we discussed fighting for more than the tiny amount
of subsidies they threw at us. Together we decided that we had to fight
for something much larger, and that's where the whole idea of fighting
for dignity emerged. Fighting for freedom. Fighting with *horizontalidad*.
Horizontalidad, because we believe that we all can participate—we can
all explain what is happening to us. All of us together can search for new
paths. And those were the first steps.

COMPAÑERA 2: We started as... We found each other, met each other,
and started to love each other as neighbors. We discovered that we were
a lot happier when we were together confronting the crisis, and a new
potential developed, a new subjectivity, no? There was a personal transformation, something communitarian. We all came from different experiences, but we all met together, and together we could walk. That was
the point of departure—knowing each other, seeing that what we were
experiencing was happening to all of us, and that the solution would be
found together.

We'd been burned by prior experiences in hierarchical, more vertical organizations. We were coming from a very stressful position. Also,
in this area—as in many areas surrounding Buenos Aires—the PJ apparatus, that's the Peronist party, is very strong. Very strong, and there's a
lot of political clientelism. We didn't want to reproduce that in any way.
We were totally fed up with that way of organizing. There was always
someone who wanted to make decisions for us, and to drive things, and
we would always end up in the same situation or worse. So we said,

okay, let's invent a new way of doing things, with new social relationships rooted in *horizontalidad* and direct democracy. A new walk where we create our own subjectivity, our own way of understanding and transforming reality—and these became sort of pillars for helping guide our horizon. Now we feel confident in the concepts of autonomy, *horizontalidad*, and daily struggle, because we don't just announce things like we're autonomous or horizontalist. No! It's a permanent struggle, and something we confront all the time in practice; breaking from old systems all the time.

I believe that we have grown a lot quality-wise—in consolidating ourselves in this experience. We have also grown in quantity, but that is relative, no? We are always going up and down in numbers. There are always new *compañeros* coming around, but as an experience as a whole, we see that we've advanced a lot. Many of the things we're doing today—like the productive projects—would have been impossible in the beginning. We also see this difference in the plenaries, comparing them to what they were before, and seeing how much we have consolidated and grown.

Challenges to Autogestión

Compañero, Clínica Medrano (a recuperated clinic)

We're facing a serious problem. We can have exchange agreements with Chilavert, the recuperated printing press, because it is not a big place—they're just a few people. But if it was a factory with more than a hundred people, how would we do that? It's one thing to exchange the printing of flyers and brochures for the medical treatment of a dozen people, but what would we do if it were 300 or more people? That wouldn't be a fair trade. They'd have to print a lot more to balance it out, right?

Another challenge we see is with regard to all of the recuperated workplaces coming together. We see the path to the unification of the recuperated workplaces as something simple. What we see are different sectors, like the sector of Murua and the sector of Caro, each from different movements. There are many workplaces that are themselves leading, but what we see as the real problem is that some people support the recuperated workplaces out of political interest, instead of the workers' interests. So we're trying to put together a group of recuperated workplaces that's independent from any political party or organization. I don't mean political independence in that people won't have political ideas, but that they won't be affiliated with any institution. We want the recuperated workplaces to be autonomous, without anyone coming and saying what to do, and with the workers themselves deciding the path to follow, constructing it themselves.

It's really difficult, yes. This weekend, for example, we went to a gathering of employed and unemployed workers, and unfortunately it was a huge mess because of the political organizations that were there. What was most important to them was fighting amongst themselves over who would lead the organization, rather than thinking about the needs of the workers. Still, the gathering was good because the recuperated workplaces that were there were able to plan the independent gathering. Right now, it's planned for July 19th, and we have another meeting soon to think about how we can get the most workplaces possible.

Pablo, Asamblea Colegiales, (a neighborhood assembly)

Let me walk, let me ask, and let me learn the answers as I walk. I know what I don't want. What I don't know so well, is what I do want. Don't give me placards of the left or the right. All of that's old. That's what's being said right now, but what's also being said is that we can't stand the ambiguity, this vacuum. So in response to the vacuum, some people are retaking discursive categories of the left. In this case, old forms of organization taken from the left, [making a biblical reference] simply because it was a desert, and the "they all must go" generated a desert through which many were not able to walk. It's really difficult to walk in the desert. Many want to go back, many fall along the way, many want shortcuts to get there the fastest way possible. They want to see the horizon quickly, and many can't handle the way it is. I think this is what happened with a lot of the people in the movements of the nineteenth and twentieth.

It's important to remember the context of the nineteenth and twentieth. This was a movement of destitution and crisis—one that brought a lot of uncertainty, hunger, thirst, and suffering. Some people just said, "I can't take it," and ended up before the left political parties who brought them some water. And this was a real relief. But it was also farce—not a farce on their part as much as a farce in drinking old water. No? It's not like they did it for some bad reason, but that in the movements things are difficult.

Flora, Ava Guaraní community (an indigenous community)

The Ledesma Corporation and the government evicted us from our homes. We didn't even have time to take our animals. They just took us to another place called Lote las Paulinas, where we lived for two years until they brought us here. We're not at all familiar with things here. Ledesma Corporation and the government of Jujuy put us in this little house. We don't know if we have to pay taxes to live here, just as we didn't know if we had to pay for water and light. We're not used to living like this, and many of our elderly have died because of this change. Five of them died and were carried away in just one day. They took them away.

We aren't used to the chlorinated water. We didn't know how to do the laundry here, we didn't know how to use detergent. Everything got bleached and we didn't know about bleach. We use *Pacara* [from a tree] and put things out to dry in the sun, but here in the city you have to have money to even do laundry. We miss the water. Our water there was underground, and it was sweet and drinkable. When they brought us here, we went out looking for water because we weren't used to the water here. The water here made all of us sick to our stomachs.

When all the grown-up Guaraníes were working, clearing the jungle, Ledesema Corporation took the little twelve- and thirteen-year-old boys and put them to work early in the morning, while they were still sleepy. They made them plow with a mule, and sow seeds in the part that was cleared. Imagine with all the heat here! They put the little girls in a school with a white teacher, near where we were living. We weren't allowed to speak Guaraní—they taught us Spanish, instead—but we hid and spoke it anyway. They wouldn't let us grow our crops, though we tried to find time to plant and grow them anyway. They made the Guaraníes clear all the jungle. I miss everything about the jungle [crying]. Even just to eat—now I have to have money to go buy things at the supermarket—before my father would just bring home food, and we had enough to eat.

You give your life. We ended up giving up our lives and everything, just so that this gigantic industry gets even bigger.

Compañeras, MTD Allen (unemployed workers' movement)

COMPAÑERA 1: Right now we're still recovering from a decrease in the number of *compañeros* participating in the movement. I believe this has a lot to do with the electoral campaign. The elections have sucked in a lot of *compañeros*. They went to the municipality to work for the campaign. What happens is that the party hacks come to the neighborhoods and they buy them. They offer a bunch of money and some—including some that were really valued and respected—end up going along. Veronica is an example of this. She was deeply involved—even speaking in front of thousands of people on behalf of the movement—and then went to work on a political campaign. Imagine what that was like, and then imagine when she walked back in one day. You could've heard a pin drop. Imagine going and working in a political party with everything that was happening in the movement. But this is the way a number of *compañeros* went. We lost their contributions to the movement, and many of the productive projects suffered—all because of the drainage of *compañeros* during the elections.

COMPAÑERA 2: There were a number of *compañeros* who left, went outside the movement, and now want to come back. But, like everything, this is a decision that we make together in the assembly. It's a really difficult decision, because in many cases, *compañeros* leave because they aren't really clear on what the movement is about—about what autonomy, *autogestión*, and real social change are. I sometimes think that they decided to leave, because none of this was really clear to them.

Compañeras, MTD Solano (an unemployed workers' movement)
COMPAÑERA 1: Right now, there are about 500–600 people involved in weekly movement activity in our neighborhood. At first there were around 300, but we kept growing until we were a bit over a thousand. Then, when the electoral political campaigns began, there was a decrease because the political party apparatuses put up a lot of money to buy people into their campaigns.

During the last electoral campaign in the neighborhood, they tried to buy *compañeros*—especially those that were the most involved in the movement—and they offered them a lot of money. A sister said that someone who works for the government told her that political parties offer more money if a party broker can get someone who's involved in the movements, rather than someone who's not—and even more if they are a leader. It's more cost effective to them to get a *compañera* because she is fighting. They offer a lot—from money to all sorts of material objects. It's really hard. They might even offer a salary of as much as 1500 dollars. They also offer all sorts of dirty work for money—along with immunity for doing the dirty work.

If people who have left the movement want to come back later... Ah...this is a big question, and there are many positions on what we should do. I believe that we were hit really hard in the last elections because they were able to buy really valiant *compañeros*. This was a disaster for the movement because *compañeros* were being transformed into enemies of the movement, and they begin to operate that way. That generates a lot of anger in the movement. We discuss this a lot in the assemblies. There are some people with very closed positions, who believe that those *compañeros* who left have caused so many problems—have really worked to destroy the movement—that they should never be able to come back. On the other hand, there are *compañeros* who left and were less genuinely involved with the political parties and government, and that's more of a grey area. Really, it's for the movement assembly to decide.

COMPAÑERA 2: It's like the *compañera* is saying: the party broker, the political hack, comes and takes not just one *compañera*, but ten or fifteen. They come and offer a lot of money or a salary, and take ten *compañeras* from each part of the neighborhood. This causes us so much pain. It hurts a lot, even now, because some of these were really valiant *compañeras* who fought with us and whom we loved, and the party hacks came in and bought them.

COMPAÑERA 1: We really talk about this a lot and there are different positions, because we don't want to become a movement that exerts pressure on people like the state does. If a *compañero* wants to come back to the movement and feels bad about everything, who are we to say no? That would put us in the position of playing with someone's hunger. We believe people can change, and that we are becoming different people. So what do we do if someone wants to come back and feels changed again? This is a really big debate.

autonomy

Martín K., Asamblea Colegials (a neighborhood assembly)

I have this idea, which I'm not saying will always be true, but it's a sort of impression I have… It's one thing to say we're horizontal, or that we're autonomous, blah, blah, blah. And it's another thing to be able to do it. I believe we're at a point where we are somewhat clear in our understanding of this, though not entirely. It's much more difficult to carry it out effectively; to embody it, don't you think? It's like… I don't know, I can't think of an example, but it's like we came out of a culture at the other extreme—a culture of verticality, a culture of representation, a culture of delegating, a culture of impotence, and we want to do everything differently. But we find ourselves falling back into the same practices. It seems to be a problem that springs from our inner lives. This is a recurring theme. It's as if there's an enduring memory of verticality, of representation, of delegation, that plays out almost unconsciously. No matter how much we say we're autonomous, we suddenly and unexpectedly find ourselves in the same position of waiting for someone else to act, waiting for someone else to speak, or waiting to accept and be accepted by another.

Compañeros from MTD Allen and MTD Ciplletti (unemployed workers' movements)

COMPAÑERO 1: Autonomy presupposes a radical rupture of consciousness, of values, and of capitalist subjectivities that gives rise to twisted social relations. Otherwise, it's merely a facade, a mask. It's those things that were said last night about the movement in Allen. The movement in Allen is surging forth, and from it all the freshness and naturalness of the movement. From the moment that it's born with all that fresh spontaneity, it bursts forth, rupturing the social controls that political parties and *punteros* [party brokers] exercise over the unemployed. The first rupture is the casual dismissal of the *punteros*, the setting aside of political parties, and seeking one's own path. Imagine that. And this is done without a previously elaborated theory about this practice. It surges as a spontaneous expression of social practice that seeks to carve out a different path, like some sort of quest. Don't you think?

COMPAÑERO 4: But in addition to seeking, there's also a rupture away from everything, a firm rupture away from things that have already been tried—all those things that have been experimented with in one way or another over the years. It seems the prevailing thought is: "enough of this," including past revolutionary experiences. We have to break with the past and start charting a new course. Autonomy is a new path under construction, an unfinished roadway, and every day there's something to be learned, something that each *compañero* can learn from other *compañeros* and from various projects. It's something that's constantly under construction and reconstitution. It isn't something that's static. Not at all.

COMPAÑERO 2: This surge of autonomous movements isn't an opportunistic phase of a particular sector that's attempting to channel its pursuit of some future revolution through a social cause. No. As I said before, past experiences are directly and strongly thought about and processed. These interrogations are not synthesized, but rather are, for the most part, expressed in the context of subordination. Nobody wants to change from one form of subordination to another. Since nobody wants this, it's questioned, and continually rethought.

COMPAÑERO 1: I believe that autonomous consciousness stands precisely at the vertex of the contradiction, and this explains its radical stance against capitalism and against all of modernity. Autonomous thinking doesn't only question past revolutions. It doesn't only question the past practices of revolutionaries in their struggle against capitalism. Instead, we're at a point in time when the contradictions of capitalism presuppose either the dissolution of humanity or the creation of a whole new civilization. This requires undoing what's been done throughout the entire course of human history, because the problem of power cannot be attributed exclusively to capitalism. Capitalism takes power to its maximum form of expression, to the most exacerbated perfection inherent in power. But power doesn't reside exclusively in capitalism. Its historical roots lie in the totality of modernist thought and in the way humanity carved out its historical trajectory. That is to say, the issue doesn't simply entail bringing about a change in the system. It isn't simply a matter of interrogating capitalism. It involves questioning our own practices as products of our entire human history. To me, it seems the profundity of autonomy is beyond our comprehension. It's impossible to appreciate the vastly rich qualities of autonomous thought in their complete context when autonomy, in practice, manifests itself as the larvae of power and subordination.

COMPAÑERO 3: And in general, those who formulate that critique of subordination are those who assume there can be no thought that isn't subordination somehow.

COMPAÑERO 1: In the end, they remain subordinated and they remain prisoners. No form of liberation can ever allow you to advance from the ruptures without subsequently converting its very own theories into some form of commodity—into a mechanism for reproducing a new state of subordination. In other words, theory is imagined from a different perspective—from those ruptures that are creating new practices. As the saying goes, "enough of thinking only with our heads." The issue is no longer simply a theoretical problem concerned with the way theory up to now has been considered merely an intellectual exercise. No. Thoughts and ideas are not solely the product of cerebral cogitation. Thought must also engage the physical body. Thought emanates from transformative practice. Thought emanates from a practice that creates a radical rupture against that which has been established. We establish the theoretical framework from this place. It's never the other way around. It's like merging theory with practice. In fact, it's from practice that theories are constructed. Practice is what shows, reflects, and determines what we're going to do at a particular time. For example, we've said that in the particular case of Allen, some *compañeras* have taught us lessons about our bodies' autonomy. What assumptions do they have about autonomy? In Allen, there's a sewing workshop called "discover." They named it "discover" because they realized through the MTD, the value of *compañerismo*, the value of solidarity. Through the MTD, they discovered experiences that enable you to express yourself beyond words.

COMPAÑERO 4: They started buying fabric and making clothes for other *compañeros* with the MTD brand. They are attaching the MTD label. It's spectacular.

COMPAÑERO 1: You can imagine the inner struggle they probably go through when deciding on a price for their work, because something like that is priceless. The value or price of this work is determined by the *compañeros'* need to dress themselves. If they've sewn clothing for someone, and that individual doesn't have any money to pay for it, then they don't have to pay. Especially if that person has no means to pay. Notice how they are beginning to tear apart the established criteria for the sale of goods and for exchange based on money.

COMPAÑERO 3: This is autonomy, because it involves an autonomous mode of production and of value that isn't subordinated to the logic of accumulation by the individual. Notice all the categories I just mentioned. The notion of the "individual" no longer operates. What I believe is beginning to operate, is the notion of singularity. On the other hand, there's still a historical memory that this should be combated by means of subordination. It seems to me that what we're going through doesn't involve subordination, but something different. This is what makes it such a radical process. This isn't about re-articulating forces of the same design.

COMPAÑERO 4: I remember when we began talking about autonomy, when we came up with forms of autonomous thought. We had specifically decided to discuss autonomy. The *compañeros* were clear in their understanding about our desire and intention to be autonomous, and we are autonomous. However, I raised the issue of whether we are, in fact, autonomous, or whether autonomy is the road we're traveling. To be truly autonomous is to come close to not depending on a specific plan. I believe that now is a moment of ruptures, where plans are falling apart, and that little by little we will find ourselves without them.

Claudia, lavaca.org and Neka, MTD Solano (an alternative media collective and an unemployed workers' movement)

NEKA: I don't believe there was ever a time when we said, "Yes, we're autonomists. This is our identity." At one point, we were pressed to produce a much more concrete definition of ourselves. I believe this was the moment when we said we wouldn't allow ourselves to become any "ist" or "ism." What we're doing is constructing an experience-based practice, and it is precisely this experience-practice that speaks for itself. Since this is an open movement, and one that's territorially-based, with ours located in the neighborhood, we're constantly discussing what *horizontalidad* and autonomy are and what they mean for us here. It's an open and ongoing discussion.

We started using the language of autonomy for a number of reasons. There were certain expectations—a sort of need to see us in a similar way to those other groups that had come about, and now are organizations—that's something we felt would kill the experience that was being created. On the other hand, there was also a need to position ourselves within some theoretical framework. This can help generate a sense of security and cohesion, and within the populist camp at that time, there were people who sought such spaces.

There are some things that one must never surrender. We're constantly discussing what autonomy and *horizontalidad* look like in practice from the point of view of the collective, and how can we recreate that without having to give up being autonomous, creative, and horizontal in our relationships. Sometimes looking toward the horizon as we walk helps us find our direction. There's a difference between declaring, "I am an *autonomista*," versus, "I want to create or construct *autonomy*." To say, "I am an autonomous autonomist" sounds dogmatic, as though something is finished and closed, like a program. And, I don't know, for me that isn't a good fit. It's like some kind of title. I don't believe the most powerful articulations have to do with defining autonomy, but with practicing autonomy in the day-to-day. I believe that's the important thing. When movements that are engaged in constructing a concept of *autonomy* begin to say that we must hegemonize, that we must unify, that we must build a single national movement, they are, in effect, approaching co-optation, and this triggers forceful resistance, similar to that of the gathering of *Enero Autonomo*. We will continue to resist efforts to promote forms of governance that maintain the status quo, such as populism and all that.

How will we resist in practice—in concrete terms? What is diversity? What is radicalism? What is freedom? What will become of creativity? I believe that if we don't reflect on these things, we'll fall into ritualized dogma. For example, if we don't think about the meaning of *piquetes* in the present context, and consider how to recreate and reinvent those methods of struggle, then in effect, we would be abandoning autonomy. We would be repeating outmoded schemes that are of no use in the present. This isn't to say that direct action loses all meaning, but that it, and other similar methods once considered radical, have become commodities.

CLAUDIA: One of the problems we're facing as a movement is how to articulate what we are as a movement. Any previous attempt was frustrating because, in one way or another, articulation would amount to reification of a particular social order or ideology.

NEKA: I believe that the purpose of communicating what we are as a movement is not about building a unified movement or hegemony, but a step toward creating diversity.

This is where articulating what we are as a movement becomes interesting. You have a voice. It seems to me that you, lavaca—as a communications collective for counter-reporting—have made a tremendous contribution to this diversity. I believe some of our work is carried out horizontally across different movements, and along the way it generates a web of many meanings. This is much more powerful than building a single or universal movement. It seems to me, this carries much more potency, much more force. I believe you are also constructing this type of autonomy.

Zanon workers' weekly town radio program

CLAUDIA: Yes. The thing is that we must figure out how to promote respect for differences. No movement is the same as any other. No experience is the same as any other. No situation is the same as any other. And that doesn't mean these things can't be expressed accordingly. It might seem like the only way to articulate something is to require complete and disciplined adherence to a limited set of ideas. It's this that amounts to a kind of conspiracy when one is called upon to provide information. It's as if every world is a separate and independent world unto itself—each having its own specific needs and unique logical constructs. From this point of view, we can agree to respect each situation and experience for what it is, without assigning it greater or lesser value than any other situation or experience. Each situation has its unique features, and everyone contributes something different. The thing is, all this amounts to "information" or an intellectual exercise, for lack of a better word. Later, when it's time to put these ideas into practice, nothing comes of it because reading alone doesn't make the revolution. Clearly, the idea has to be paired with action. Otherwise, everything would amount to mere rationalizing.

NEKA: It's precisely those rigid, closed, and structured definitions that limit us—they limit our ability to be free. As we discussed previously in the workshop, once you taste freedom, you will forever fight to remain free. When the criteria that served as a basis for organizing begins to operate like dogma or law, I believe that's when movements naturally begin to seek ways to combat the status quo. When something is emptied of its contents, and it becomes a hollow convention that lacks any consideration for our humanity, lacks respect, and lacks *compañerismo*, then the *compañeros* are naturally inclined to reject it. At this time we must revisit, rediscuss, and rethink our options and actions because we're missing our mark. What about the essence of things? What is freedom all about? What is our humanity all about? I believe it will be part of our lifelong struggle to deal with the fact that criteria and agreements that were useful to us at a certain time will have no useful purpose at some other time—when different circumstances have emptied them of their meaning. It's like our conversations on the tactic of road blockades, the *piquetes*. At one time, they were a more useful tool in radical struggle.

CLAUDIA: In some cases it may also serve a new purpose in the future.

NEKA: Today, in some cases, the *piquete* is still used, even as an appropriated commodity. It serves no purpose when used this way. At best, this serves only to permanently reproduce and reconstruct it in its original form.

CLAUDIA: I believe the change we're undergoing is of utmost importance. Sometimes I think—and I'm not exaggerating—that this is a historic moment of vitally important changes. Changes that are altering the culture of politics on a scale proportional to the level of violence that characterizes this era. There wouldn't be a need for so much violence if there weren't so much resistance. This reflects the fact that we are experiencing a powerful cultural change. Indeed, the cultural change at hand is so powerful that it provides a basis for hypothesizing the rise of a permanent legal war, a war that could break out at any moment. It's a cultural change so powerful that it has literally triggered the rise of a police state, which, though it may not be fully deployed at all times, nevertheless remains active through surveillance, intelligence gathering, and the profiling of citizens. One can observe a rupture so profound in the hierarchical system that it simultaneously cleaves into, and tears apart, the current culture of power.

Emilio, Tierra del Sur (a neighborhood assembly, occupied building, and community center)

We don't need anyone to impose a new "Communist Manifesto" on us and throw us into that camp like a bunch of fools. After I abandoned that form of a communist idea, I said to myself, "What is it that we want? What is our project?" The good thing is we have no program. We are creating tools of freedom. First is the obvious: to meet our basic necessities. But the process of finding solutions to meet our basic needs leads us to develop tools that make us free. For me, that's the meaning of autonomy. If you start to think about what constitutes autonomy, and you then start to discuss the notions of *autogestión*, self-sufficiency, web-like articulations, noncommercial exchange of goods, horizontal organizing, and direct democracy, you eventually end up asking yourself, "If we achieve all these things, will we then be autonomous?" Autonomous from what? No. If one day we achieve true autonomy, we won't be autonomists or autonomous, but will, in fact, be free.

When the day comes that autonomy as a construct is on the verge of disappearing, it will cease to exist all together. This is because on the day when it's possible for us to be autonomous, there will be nothing from which to declare ourselves autonomous. There's no reason to believe that we can actually be autonomous within a given geographic space or at any given time. The notion of a noncapitalist community lacks believability. That was a "hippie" experience that clearly won't work. As long as capitalism exists, we'll continue to dwell within it. Through autonomy, we can create zones that aren't governed by the logic of capitalism. This isn't the same as claiming that the capitalist system isn't the dominant social order. For now, capitalism is everywhere and it will be the prevailing order until it ceases to exist altogether.

And yes, we will reach that state. If I didn't believe it was possible to end capitalism, I wouldn't be attempting it. That the idea of autonomy can exist within the capitalism system often becomes a stumbling block. The idea that we can be non-capitalistic within a capitalist system is a fallacy, because capitalism intersects our lives all the time. What we can do, however, is build and create different things without following the logic of the capitalist system. We can attempt to create the revolution in our day-to-day living. The day when all these things succeed, when we truly succeed in all these things, we will have arrived. We will be free, rather than autonomous. Autonomy is a bubble that exists within the larger system. Autonomy is not, in and of itself, a system of governance. Autonomy is a tool for gaining our freedom.

Toty, MTD la Matanza (unemployed workers' movement)

It isn't that a group of individuals charts the course for larger societal concerns. On the contrary, it's the larger social unit that influences the particular path that will be taken up by particular groups. For example, in our case, the position we took with respect to government assistance services was very controversial. We were conscious that the Argentinean people, having lived through the strong welfare state of the 1940s and 1950s that gave rise to what we have termed "Peronism," wouldn't dismiss a return to that original state of affairs. So we were patient. We presented a controversial position, and explained it coherently. Now what we're seeing is that autonomy is a process each individual has to go through. Nevertheless, beyond the fact it's a quest, it's like the culture of Peronism is beginning to rupture among those movements that are addressing the most severe forms of deprivation. Maybe there will be a return to the past, to the way things were before. It depends on how autonomous organizations exercise their capacity to develop the inherent potential that's at the core of this social movement. This is the fundamental issue the social movements have yet to discover their own potential and activate it. I'm speaking out of ignorance. I know nothing about sociology [laughs].

Gabriel, Ava Guaraní Community (an indigenous community)

We think about the things that might become a reality for all our sisters and brothers who think in independent terms—decent housing, a hospital, schools—all created by us, independent of everything else. We would say independence means working and producing on our own, on the same land. We know how to be independent. I was raised on the land, and my father often said, "To work as a company employee is to be a slave," because one day the company will say, "you and you are fired," and you're out of a job. If you have your own land you're independent, you're independent of everything. We have confidence in ourselves when we say that if we have land, we'll work. Because if you work, you will have, but if you don't work, you won't have.

We hold assemblies where we all come together and talk about things. We talk about how we think things are going, as well as various other issues. We seek and act on the consensus of the Guaraní people.

We all participate. That is, it isn't just the indigenous leaders who attend, but instead we seek the consensus of all the constituents. As long as the people stand, we wouldn't think of giving in, because it's through our unity that we gain strength to move ahead.

What I think about autonomy is that it is important to have solidarity between various organizations and communities, in general, so that we can achieve our goal of being autonomous and independent, and arrive at a happy ending. This is what I long for as a constituent of this community: to go before the government with dignity and for them to come before us with dignity.

Maba and Orlando, MTD Solano (an unemployed workers' movement)

ORLANDO: The process of autonomy... Over there at the Ministry of Labor, we were told in the past what projects we had to complete. They imposed projects on you that you were required to finish. We'd say, fine, we'll attend a workshop on tailoring and dressmaking, but in the end it turns out a bakery is opened. We had no autonomy to explore our own interests and do what we wanted to do. We couldn't do and create what we desired until we fought for, and won, our autonomy. We have an alternative economy that we were able to create through this autonomy. Every *compañero* who belongs to this movement we're building, who receives a work subsidy from the state, makes a voluntary contribution to the movement—in solidarity with the movement—but they're not obligated to do so. Through these contributions, for example, we were able to buy some tools to open the shops, rent the mini-buses to continue attending demonstrations, pave new roads in the neighborhood, etc. We aren't a movement about making demands, but about creating things. We're creating projects that don't necessarily produce material goods to sell, but instead build knowledge, and professional and vocational skills. *Compañeros* learn a trade. *Compañeros* in the health field get good training so they don't take the easy way out by simply giving a pill, and presto! You have to discuss people's ailments with them as well as give preventative care. Not just preventative in terms of "I have a cold, a fever, etc." Rather, I'm talking about preventative care in all aspects of life, including the illness of capitalism. When you're sick, you go to the doctor, you get a prescription, and you take the medicine. And that medicine gives you an ulcer. There might be something else you can do that doesn't affect you that way—remedies that are more natural. Let's find those alternative remedies. These are things we discuss.

MABA: It's not as if we expect that the movement itself will solve our problems—it's the workshops and skill-sharing that are part of the movement that help us resolve things with other *compañeros'* help. When there's a problem, you can't expect someone else to solve it for you, but instead you have to think of ways to solve it together. It's a difficult process. In Solano, there are many elements adopted from Brazil's MST, and from the Zapatistas who are using similar forms of construction and creation, this is not a new invention [laughs].

ORLANDO: When we said, "they all must go!" just like the assembly members had, it was an act of rejection—we no longer wanted any bosses ordering us around. Perhaps this led to an awareness of personal autonomy. Some people eventually recovered some of the money that had been lost by the banks. Others continued to build something else—concrete things like gardens and child care programs, and with other *compañeros,* they kept thinking critically and self-critically. In fact, some assembly member *compañero*s have said, "Imagine how wrong I was when I said we ought to kill you if you blocked the road. Now, I sit before you to explore what we might do together." These are some of the things that have changed—our relationships with one another. It was also them, the *asamblistas,* who approached us for a relationship. We didn't initiate their participation, nor did we give them any sort of line to follow. We don't give any line to anyone. I believe the point is that they have discovered things on their own. They build something autonomous on their own, and then come together with others, who we've seen have a basic level of autonomy... Well, this is a beginning place, and from here we can discuss many things and begin to take steps toward something new.

Oscar, MTD Allen (an unemployed workers' movement)

Above all, this is our struggle. The struggle isn't mainly on the outside. We know who we have to struggle against on the outside, and in this respect, we're organized. We know what we have to do and how we have to do it. But everyone's interior struggle is really difficult. Each of us is struggling. Don't think we were born ready. It was a wonderful thing to state our preference for autonomy, to state that that's what we want, and to be able to define for ourselves what that means. We create autonomy daily as we struggle with our own values. All of us do, because we were all raised in a particular era, one with a different set of values, one with competitiveness and egoism. You have to get ahead, no matter who you step on as you rise to the top. This is how we've been molded—in the workplaces and everywhere else. To suddenly begin to change those values requires a struggle against yourself. This is why the most difficult struggle is here [touching chest]. Within. This is why some of the most heated and powerful discussions take place at the assemblies, because we're struggling against our own selves. It's about our own egos, and our own personal situation, but we're learning. We're making progress.

Toto, MTD la Plata (an unemployed workers' movement)

For me, what autonomy means is rejecting a whole slew of things, and nobody telling you what you have to do. It's a matter of rejecting a whole set of impositions. In the assemblies and newspapers there are lengthy and important discussions about autonomy that really intrigue me. I once asked a person from the Basque country in Spain why there was all this talk of autonomy, especially since, out here, autonomy was unheard of and had never been discussed the way it is now. I once read this publication from Spain that laid out the issues of autonomy. In the final analysis, what is referred to as autonomy differs, even within the same country. Autonomy doesn't mean the same thing for a Basque and a Catalan, or for the members of ETA [Basque Movement for Nation and Liberty], as it does for anarchists. It seems to me like it's somewhat fashionable here. Come to think of it, if one were to walk into any neighborhood and walk up to anybody and ask, "Are you people autonomists?" of course the majority would respond, "I don't know." On the other hand, if you were to ask, "How do you relate to the other movements, or to the government?" then I can assure you the response would be, "We will not allow others to impose foreign interests on or make decisions for us." The same thing would happen if you asked a *compañero* in the movement, "Are you a horizontal or vertical group?" But if anyone were to ask them, "How do you people make decisions?" any one of the *compañero*s would mention the process where some of us get together and hold weekly meetings, make decisions together, everyone participating, and so on. That's why I say that the issue of attaching a label to certain ideas comes from the outside. We talk more in terms of how we do things as opposed to what to call the things we do. Because what might happen otherwise is we'd constantly refer to ourselves as "horizontal," and then end up forgetting what that means and act in some other way. To me, it seems much more important to remain attached to certain ways of doing things than to start attaching labels that ultimately contradict what we do in practice.

But, you know... I'm not sure, I am still thinking about all of this.

Neka and Sergio, MTD Solano and lavaca.org (an unemployed workers' movement and alternative media collective)

NEKA: One of the most marvelous things is not thinking solely about the future and not turning your life over to those who'll guarantee the future for you. We're about reclaiming life. It's as if we started living again and believing that, above all, our life and everything else that we transform belong to us. That's the most marvelous thing.

SERGIO: What you do in life is learned from your own lived experience. From analyzing your experiences, and then using that analysis, you're able to resolve things better along the way. It seems to me that we arrive as some level of maturity—of clarity—where we think about everything that has happened and how it happened, what worked, what didn't work, and we continue taking things in and building on everything. It's wonderful to be unattached to what was previously written and declared, and to base your life on what you're living, on what is happening right then, and on how you're interpreting and integrating all of it.

"True democracy is in the streets: Election 2003"

Ezequiel, Asamblea Cid Campeador (a neighborhood assembly)

From the very beginning, the assembly took a very clear stance against having any links with the state and government. For example, my assembly's meeting place is located very close to one of those City of Buenos Aires Government Administration and Participation Centers. In theory, these centers are intended to decentralize government action and to encourage local civic participation. We've always flat out rejected having anything to do with that center—to the point of absurdity. For example, even though the center allows anyone to walk in and make free photocopies, we'd rather pay for photocopies than enter that place for free copies. In this respect, our intention was always to remain on the margins of the state, but not out of the belief that we were creating an autonomous space. Rather, it seems to me, that—at least initially—we were manifesting our rejection of representative government, our rejection of politicians, in general. I believe our de-linking from the state came from that.

As an assembly we have always been somewhat schizophrenic with respect to the state. On one hand, we've been vehemently opposed to having any ties with the government, but there've been cases when we have accepted state support. For example, the city government started giving us bags of food a few months back. We accepted them and used them to start a popular kitchen. These things soon result in a *de facto* link to the state, though we don't accept it as such. We don't want to view this as a tie to the state. In assembly jargon, we refer to this as something we snatch away from the state, as opposed to something we ask them for or something they give to us. At the very least then, our distance from the state is kept alive in our conversations.

Our participation in discussions over the city's Law of Communes is in a different realm altogether. This law would divide the city into smaller communes, with a mandate for local representation and a participatory budgeting process and so on. These issues are being discussed and the assembly is participating in the dialogue, albeit with constant distrust and fear of having any contact with the world of government, representatives, and the like.

I think that the state, the political regime, in general, is gradually losing something it needs like it were the air it breathes—and that's our trust in them. I mean, the entire political system is based on us believing that it's real and it works. If that commonly held belief falters—which is what's happening—I believe that people in Argentina, like in other places, will begin to vote less and less. And that's partly because they won't believe in their elected representatives' honesty. The failure of that trust precipitates problems because, when it fails, all the populist energy starts to leak from the institutional framework and reappears in other places—in direct actions, demonstrations, or in autonomous groups. It's at this point that the professional politicians, the leadership, and the theorists who work because they believe in the system, take note and realize they have to redesign institutions to recapture those who are slipping away. I think certain types of initiatives, such as participatory budget processes and communes, have something to do with this. These are attempts to make us feel a little more enthusiastic about government and representative politics. That's not an altogether bad thing since, in an effort to achieve those goals, they have to cede things we might be able to use to our advantage. In general, these things seem like a trap that works against us more than anything else. At times, things work out well though, as in the case of the unemployment subsidies. There are ways of using the government to strengthen the movement, but there are also times this leads to deactivation. This is really ambiguous terrain that intelligence can occasionally help you navigate.

Elections

Paula, feminist and GLTTB collectives

I haven't voted in years. In Argentina, elections are mandatory, but I don't give a shit. Make sure to translate it that way in the book. I don't give a holy shit about the elections and the obligation to vote. I have not voted in a very long time. I have absolutely no faith in parliamentary representation. I don't believe in anything that's ever elected in this way. It's a total political farce. It's an enormous problem that Argentina has had military governments, because one of the supposedly progressive discourses insists that we take advantage our ability to vote, since there were periods in history when we couldn't. This is absolutely ridiculous and false, because our vote today doesn't have the same weight that it had when voting wasn't permitted.

Porque no sólo rechazamos lo que nos imponen, también queremos desarrollar nuevas formas de organizarnos para discutir cómo seguir en el camino de conseguir el

Que se vayan todos

para hacer posible una sociedad justa.

EL 27 DE ABRIL
DECIDIMOS ELEGIR NUESTRO FUTURO

GRAN ASAMBLEA POPULAR
EN PLAZA DE MAYO

"Because we not only reject what they impose on us, we also want to develop new forms of organization to discuss how to follow the path that will achieve the slogan "They all must go" to make a just society possible. On the 27th of April we decide to elect our future. Huge popular assembly in the Plaza de Mayo."

When voting wasn't allowed, the vote would have resulted in the election of a parliament that people might more or less agree with. I've never believed in bourgeois institutions, but it isn't the same to have a fascist in government as having a democratic guy. Nowadays, the vote means nothing. Voting legitimizes perverse functions of the political and economic system. In other words, when someone goes out to vote, the only thing he/she accomplishes is the legitimization of this perversion.

That's no longer a middle ground, because capitalist society is very complex. Things aren't necessarily clear, but in this case, it seems to me that the decadence of Argentina's political system stems from the fact that you, when you vote, are only legitimizing a political system that is absolutely perverse. This is why I oppose elections. For me they have no meaning whatsoever, and I know that many people who voted think exactly as I do.

Daniela, Marta, and Ariel, MTD Almirante Brown (unemployed workers' movement)

DANIELA: In my opinion, the guy didn't want to admit defeat. He alleged fraud and stepped down, because he knew he would likely lose. Admittedly, Kirchner is no one's idea of the best solution, but he is the lesser of two evils. For us, he's terrible, just terrible. Moreover, Menem was a new threat in all of this. The struggle would continue, but at a greater cost, because this guy would be very threatening to us. If there were more road blockades, there would be more of a military presence in the streets and that would be rough on us. It would destroy more organizations. This guy and his people would infiltrate the neighborhoods and destroy the organizations.

They're there now and they will always be there, continually oppressing us. But what we're building is out here, day in and day out. I think that for us, the change in presidency is so false that we see no difference among Duhalde, Kirchner, or Menem. Although the latter, Menem, is somewhat rougher. Regardless of who's in that seat, the situation will stay the same and our struggle will have to continue. And I think that's the reason, along with the fact that our communities are tired of the politicians acting as puppets, that there's a feeling in this society that no one is believable. That's why not many people want to work hard. An example of this can be seen in a workshop that was organized around the issue of the elections. A ballot was circulated for each individual to specify who they planned to vote for, or what they planned to do. I read a couple of these and most of them said, "I don't want any politician, I vote for work. I demand something different." Those are our causes. We talked about our real issues outside the discussion of the voting process.

That widespread discussion on the elections was of the utmost importance to many outside the movement, but we didn't even touch it.

Like many others in various movements, we express things through the ballot box. We express our desires, our hopes, and dreams, because ours is a vote of protest. I personally didn't vote because I have no faith in that. I know that it won't bring about any change, because change isn't at the polls. Change happens because of the things we do. That other thing [voting] is something they're trying to sell you. It's what the system wants to sell you: Vote, there's the solution. Not for me. All it does is sink you a little deeper.

ARIEL: Today at the assembly, we discussed water issues relating to the orchard, which is important to us because it supplies the dining hall. Now, with the run-off just a few days away… I don't know.

DANIELA: Out here, they tried to co-opt the comrades by appealing to domestic issues. They have penetrated so completely that you just know someone on top is going to screw you over, and you're going to have to fight it daily from the bottom. The penetration is so pervasive that you worry about whether you'll have produce to cook with tomorrow, or whether there will be any water, or whether we'll be able to finish the shed, whether the library will remain open, or whether the healthcare system will have medicine.

ARIEL: All of the autonomous organizations were planning to meet in Claypole, because they have dining halls there…this was within a week of the election. These are not *piqueteros*, rather they are dining halls operated independently from the municipal government—autonomous dining halls. There are other groups, like the indigenous Mapuche group, that are closer to us here in the Almirante Brown neighborhood. We talked about getting together, getting to know each other, and examining all sorts of issues without even discussing the elections. I went to a meeting yesterday, and we never talked about who we were going to vote for. On the contrary, we discussed what the Cerrito neighborhood would bring to the meeting. Lights, ricotta, bread, and lettuce samples from our garden. The Mapuche were planning to make and bring honey to sell. Since we also consume honey, sweets, and marmalade, we even talked about purchasing their honey if the price is right. And they can buy our bread. As we discussed these things, we never considered, nor did we stop to think about, who might win the election. Regardless of who wins, we know we have to struggle to meet our basic needs.

Emilio, Tierra del Sur (neighborhood assembly, occupied building, and community center)

Lately there has been tremendous fear about what might come after the elections. The elections aren't a good time for the movements—for movement time. As the Zapatistas say, "This isn't our time." Violence and state repression aren't good times for us either, but we still have to respond. If we don't, we cease to exist. I am very fearful about what might come out of the elections, about the type of government that might emerge, and about what might happen to the social movements. I predict difficult times after April 27th, regardless of who wins.

One issue involves what actions the state will take. In all probability, it will adopt new measures against social movements. Since the electoral era isn't our era, we'll continue to pursue building in our neighborhoods—building locally, while thinking globally. At this moment, we exist in a state of resistance. This is a time to build. The revolts of the nineteenth and twentieth of December have passed. The upheaval and agitation phase is over. We've achieved all that could be achieved through revolt, in terms of sudden impact. Now we are advancing step by step. At times, we need to stop and affirm the progress we've made, and wait. And, in time, continue advancing. This is a time of resistance.

I personally believe that right now the need to expand our work in the neighborhoods is more important than the road blockades, than the marches, than direct action—obviously with an anti-capitalist notion of creation. It seems to me that in these times of resistance, it's more important to expand our gardens, expand our reclaimed factories, expand our vocations, and expand all these construction processes. We need to remain realistic about what it is that we are doing and why... Until we have another nineteenth and twentieth.

Political parties are the most pacifying commodities. It's much more comfortable to vote, and to remain within the system of representative politics. It's easier, for example to eat at McDonald's when you can afford it, to drink Coca-Cola, and to blame the President, than to participate in the day-to-day creative initiatives of the assembly, the *piquetero*s, the occupied centers and factories, indigenous communities, and other self-organized initiatives throughout Argentina. It's much more comfortable to complain and vote, and to vote and complain.

For some people, this business of the revolution can be very annoying on a personal level. Going to the assembly and taking on a whole bunch of responsibilities can be very unpleasant because, when one starts getting involved, one becomes aware of huge contradictions at a personal and social level, including within one's own family. One begins to see how one's been deceived and then becomes aware of many other painful things. This causes great personal pain. Therefore, it's much more comfortable to avoid participation and just complain instead. In this day and age, it's hard to ignore the real crisis. Until the nineteenth and twentieth, more or less, one could try to ignore it. After the nineteenth and twentieth, it was impossible to ignore that Argentina was in deep trouble, and that we were in very bad shape.

At this point, a person who won't evade the truth finds it very uncomfortable to change things and will vote for one of the leftist parties, or will nullify their vote. They believe in the system. It's much easier to believe in the system by voting for a leftist party, than to attack it.

Vasco, MTD Allen (an unemployed workers' movement)

Out here, we don't vote or anything. This worries the government. Now, they're trying to pacify us with regard to the elections by trying to get us to vote for a low level administrator, and they're asking people to register to vote. I've never voted, because we always elect the same people. In this relationship, you have no autonomy and you stay dependent. It's important that people not vote, because voting only perpetuates dependence.

Myra, Asamblea Colegiales (a neighborhood assembly)

What we did in the neighborhood assembly with respect to the elections was create a carnival against that farce—which it is. It's turned out to be quite ridiculous because nothing ever changes. I don't know if anybody invested their hopes there. Since we respect differing opinions, there are people who go out to vote for someone, there are others who vote in protest, and still others who will not vote for anyone. This isn't the same as submitting a blank ballot. To vote and register a blank ballot would favor certain groups. The protest votes aren't counted. There are those who won't show up to vote. I still don't know if I'll go vote or if I'll vote a protest ballot.

Martín B., Intergalactica (an anti-capitalist collective)

What we're doing in these next elections is reminiscent of the 501 Movement, a movement that emerged in July of 1999. The actions associated with the 501 Movement took place during the elections of the October

24, 1999, when De la Rua won the race. In Argentina, voting is mandatory, however, there's an exemption clause that says if you happen to be
more than 500 kilometers away from your polling place for work or a
health-related reason, then you can go to a local commissioner and say
that you can't vote. A group of us traveled more than 500 kilometers.
There aren't any provisions that allow this sort of thing for politically
motivated reasons, but that's exactly what we did.

Sometimes I say the 501 was one of the precursors of the current
movement because it was organized horizontally, in an assembly format.
When all is said and done, this turned out to be a movement that kept
many of us politically active. What we were saying was very simple: this
isn't a democracy nowadays, our vote has no meaning, we don't want to
vote, we don't want to be extorted in this manner, we're outta here.

It turned out that 400 people—which is a lot—ended up 500 kilometers away. It was huge. The idea behind 501 was "Politics Beyond
Voting." The assemblies were the means for organizing. And this was
wonderful. As far as I'm concerned, this led to many other things. In
retrospect, the best thing about the 501 Movement was the peculiar relationship with the media it started. We didn't appear in any publication at
all, with the exception of two communiqués. But there was a commotion
among the media. They pursued us for interviews. It was a compelling
mystery.

Compañer@s, MTD Solano (an unemployed workers' movement)

COMPAÑERA 1: We don't participate in the elections. It's not as if there's
a rule in the movement prohibiting participation in the electoral process,
but the vast majority of us haven't voted. For quite some time now, we've
abstained from voting. I'm not sure you can really judge whether this
is good or bad—it's just different. As far as we're concerned, in terms
of state, nothing's ever changed, nothing's ever improved, and we suffer the same conditions of misery and poverty. We see a lot of political
campaigning going on out there, tons of propaganda, but we don't see
any change in our neighborhood, so we continue organizing in the neighborhood and reclaiming power from the state. We don't believe in the
discourse that claims things will change or improve through elections.

COMPAÑERO 1: In many ways, it really isn't about Kirchner or Duhalde.
We know they're not the root of the problem, nor are they our fundamental challenge. As far as we're concerned, this is just a moment in time

in the prolonged struggle that's unfolding now throughout Latin America and around the world. We've chosen, at least within the movement, not to become auxiliary to, or supporters of, the government—not this government or the ones that may follow. We understand the limitations in this and know there are others who are doing it.

True, there are movements that are way more involved in the street-action and road-blockade aspects of the struggle, and it might seem like there's a withdrawal, right? But in Argentina—well, Argentina is very special—today you might find a whole nation destroying an entire institution, and tomorrow 80 percent of the population goes out to vote. That's how Argentina is. It's very unstable.

As for Kircher, we don't underestimate him at all. I think he studied the effect of the nineteenth and twentieth, and his speeches and writings reflect the desire to create a politics of reinstitutionalization, an attempt to regain credibility. It suits us better to have a government that at least isn't trying to openly annihilate or kill us when we mobilize. We're not saying things aren't tainted as they are, but if Menem had won we might not be here now.

Pablo, Asamblea Colegiales (a neighborhood assembly)

The system had completely lost its legitimacy, and the main challenge it confronted was the need to reconstruct this legitimacy. There were two ways to reconstruct authority and order: repression or rebuilding consensus and legitimacy. They tried both options. Well, they tried repression, and that didn't work. Soon it'll be the one year anniversary of the famed *Puente Avellaneda* of the *piquetero* movement, when the state killed two *compañeros* who were participating in a road blockade. After that happened, they tried to conduct an election to rebuild their legitimacy—the legitimacy of state power, the legitimacy of the political system.

On the 19th and 20th of December, everything exploded. The president was physically removed from office. One week later, another president was removed by consensus and popular struggle. After that, there was no authority. That's why elections were held. A part of the neighborhood assembly movement thought it would be important to do something to ensure that the wound wouldn't heal. The fissure that existed didn't allow the system to heal its own wounds. It was important to prevent the elections from helping the state gain any legitimacy, and a lot of people got involved in election-related activism to help fight the state. One campaign asked people not to vote, or to vote a blank ballot, or to nullify their vote, so the state couldn't renew its legitimacy. Despite the effort, it didn't happen. We didn't achieve a counter-campaign. In the end, the regime successfully set the stage for elections. Part of the reason we failed is that more than a year had gone by with neither the assembly movements nor the socialist movements helping people imagine a different path. After a good number of the people had rejected institutions, they returned to an institutional system once again—this time with less confidence. Nevertheless, they returned.

Most people were alienated from the electoral process and rejected the campaign. One significant factor that set this election apart from any other before it, was that for the first time the campaigns weren't held in public spaces. All the campaigns were on television or in closed stadiums. Usually, in the final months of earlier elections, street corners like this one drew people from all the political parties, and the candidates walked through the street campaigning. This time nobody was out here. They didn't come out onto the street for fear they would be rejected. The people were absolutely disinterested, which was reflected by many people saying they weren't going to vote, or that they didn't know who to vote for, or even know who was running.

Disinterest can manifest itself in two different ways. Either you don't vote, or you do. If there's a movie that doesn't interest me, I don't go see it. Or I can go and vote a blank ballot, or I can go and tell everyone to get lost, or I can write something else. But if I go and vote for a candidate, I effectively transfer my power to someone else, even if I do it with extremely low interest and extremely low confidence. In effect, this situation involves widespread extortion. It seemed that at any given time, the neo-liberal far right might win the government seat. As a matter of fact, Menem won 25 percent of the votes. There was very low voter turnout, but he still won the first part of the election. At one point, there was a real threat that it might be Menem and the other version of the ultra-right, Lopez Murphy. I think this marked a big change in people's attitudes in the final ten days or so. Many people decided that, even though they didn't believe in anything, they wouldn't allow these characters to appropriate the governmental apparatus. I think that caused many people to go out and vote for the non-Menemista candidate with the greatest odds of winning, which was Kirchner.

This was an anti-vote. If there had been a second round, 70 percent would've been anti-Menem votes, but not pro-Kirchner votes. Kirchner won 22 percent, and out of the 22 percent there may have been 10 to 12 percent who knew him and wanted him, and another 6 or 7 percent of the vote came from the party's apparatus. In other words, these might've been people who didn't even know who he was or trust him, but who follow the party apparatus managed by President Duhalde and voted for the candidate he [Duhalde] supported. Also, another 2 or 3 percent were people from other left-of-center parties, or people who weren't planning to vote, or people who reject elections, but when faced with the threat of a Menem victory decided to vote while holding their noses, so that the other guy wouldn't win.

creation

Gabriel, Ava Guaraní Community (an indigenous community)

A small group of us brothers and sisters got together and said, "What are we going to do? We're all unemployed, but we have that land over there." I've seen the cemetery when everything was in place and completely well kept—before 1972—not like it is now with the crosses all burnt. The cemetery reflects generations of living and dying on the land. We have land, we have rivers, we have canals, we have everything. I was raised on the land, as were many of our brothers and sisters, and we know how to work the land, how to raise cattle. My father and mother, who both worked the land, raised me. I was raised with abundance and great respect, because I was raised working, without bothering or asking anything of anyone.

Having such a large piece of land that we shared and was ours became a part of our mindset. "Ours," but not in the sense of ownership. So why should we be suffering from hunger? Why should we be running behind politicians begging for handouts, when we have land and we have our arms raised ready to work that land? So we thought to recuperate our land. We took it back and now continue to struggle to keep it. It's crucial to have something to throw in the pot every day. For that, we have to work and we need land. But we have land. So this is what we have in our hearts and minds: that if we don't have our land at our disposal, we can't discuss projects, let alone culture. If you ask my children today to say "water" in our dialect, they don't know. So I would tell those "leaders," who claim to be Indigenous leaders, who speak of culture this and culture that, that words come and go, but there isn't anything positive, nothing positive at all.

Without land, there will never be anything positive; never in a thousand years or in 10,000 years. We should make this clear. I want the government to understand this. Without land we're nothing.

**Bridge made to re-enter
la Loma after the Guaraní
community were evicted
from their land and their bridge
destroyed**

Martín S., La Toma and Argentina Arde (an occupied building and an alternative media and art collective)

We're in La Toma [The Taken], which is what those of us who have occupied this building decided to call it. Everyone involved in this project, including people from the assemblies, social organizations, and unemployed groups made the decision. The building is huge. It had been abandoned for eight years, and was under some sort of federal fiscal ownership. Nothing had been done with it, so when we decided to take over a building, this one made sense.

I am not really theoretical, but it seems like words are institutions in a way, and there's a power in naming something. This feels like something we need to break from, because if you say, "you're this or that," then *ciao*. From the very beginning, when we entered this space, we decided to call it La Toma. The whole process, including deciding on the name, has been really beautiful. There's a short story by Julio Cortazar, who is a very famous Argentine author, that's called "The Taken House," but in his story the situation is reversed. In the story, there were people whose house was taken over by fear, had been forgotten, and stayed empty. Here it's the opposite. We've reversed the story and opened up a space, recuperated it, and it's beautiful.

Taking over the building began as an initiative of the various neighborhood assemblies. There's a history of building occupations by neighborhood assemblies. Necessity was one of the main motivating factors for our occupation. We wanted to have a physical space where we could develop things beyond what could be done in the plaza, which is where the assembly had first been organized. The idea was to bring people together in a physical space, and in a place of general political agreement, in order to maintain all of this. So we began to talk with individuals and organizations in the southern zone of Lomas, where we are, to see what they thought. It began with the assemblies of East and West Lomas, and then Fiorito and Lavallo, and soon there were fifteen other organizations. Here in Lomas de Zamora there's "The Network of Organizations in Struggle," which tons of organizations actively participate in, including neighborhood assemblies, unemployed groups, cultural and social groups, and even a few political parties. We all get together to organize projects and coordinate street actions.

That's where we decided to look into what space we might take over. We also had a lot of conversations about what it would take to maintain such a space. Once we found this space and came to a consensus, we picked a day, and all entered the building. From there we began to "give it life," as we say.

We began to organize a whole bunch of activities, the most important being a popular kitchen, which now feeds over 120 people every day. We also opened the space for educational and artistic workshops on topics like health and popular education, as well as for theater and social events. Most recently, we've started to edit a small alternative paper.

One of the other groups I collaborate with is Argentina Arde, an alternative media and art collective. Our approach to our work is to place ourselves in situations and then reflect from the inside out. We always try and do this from the point of view of counter-information, being conscious of the situation in the country and what the media's saying. Argentina Arde works with La Toma, including on La Toma's paper. One of the intentions of the newspaper was to communicate more with the community that walks past the door every day, looking inside, but rarely asking what we're doing. The paper helps us communicate more generally as well, and to break with different prejudices. I feel like there are two different forms of communication: one is the paper of a political party, where they tell you what to do, and the other is the paper of counter-information, where the idea is to generate discussion, which is the kind we're attempting to create.

For us, one of the most important things is the way that we communicate to, and amongst, ourselves. We try new ways of communicating, like what we're trying to do with the paper. The idea is to create a permanent conversation, always from the inside out, and from the outside in. What happens on the outside of La Toma or in Lomas, our neighborhood and community, has to be something that's ours. For example, if we really want to change things…if there's a problem in the neighborhood, we have to make it our problem. We can't see things only from inside this space, as if only we understand things, and we can't only talk amongst ourselves. There has to be a constant dialogue, a constant back and forth. It's with these dialogues that we are able to write articles. They're not written from the inside, but from our relationships; from conversations with and among neighbors about the popular kitchen and food, or how things are evolving. We try to always involve different voices.

Daniela and Marta, MTD Almirante Brown (an unemployed workers'
movement)

DANIELA: Here, in Brown, we have a number of productive projects, like
the bakery that we're sitting in now. Here, there's a group of *compañeros*
that work four hours a day, just like in the others projects, making bread
and other things that are then sold to *compañeros* at a really reasonable
price. Our bread is healthier than the store kind because we don't use
preservatives. We also go around and sell it to the neighbors, which is a
way of expanding the movement, and showing the neighbors what we're
doing—what the MTD is about. We see our productive projects as a way
out of dependency on government subsidies. We know that we can't fit
everybody—all 140 people from the neighborhood—in the bakery, but
this is one of many projects, and a way to bring in some income. One of
the other projects is the organic garden, which is a community garden
that provides vegetables for the popular kitchen. When there are some
vegetables left over, *compañeros* bring them home.

As I mentioned before, we're organizing lots of projects, it's not at
all just about the government subsidy. The things we do in the neighborhood, like having the dining hall, are really important to us—they're
things we're proud of. All the *compañeros* come to eat in the dining hall
at noon, and then they bring leftover food home to eat with their families. In the afternoon, there's the *copa de leche* [cup of milk], where milk
and snacks are given to all the children in the neighborhood.

In the MTD, things are different. We feel different. You could work
for the municipality and get an employment subsidy in exchange, but it
isn't the same in the movement. We all struggle together, not just for material things, but for the relationships between *compañeros*, for togetherness, and more than anything, for the creation of other values.

It seems to me that what we are creating is our own future; a future
based on what we want and desire, not in what they impose on us. So
what we want for our future—the future for our children who are to
come—is an understanding of these values and these new relationships.
But not just an understanding, we also want the creation of this other
way of living.

It's not about waiting for all of Argentina to acquire this level of
organization, but about doing it now. Our being organized like this fills
our lives, our families, and our neighborhood. We hope to have a good
future, a dignified future. The intense thing is that we aspire to social

change and it's happening every day. It's not easy, and it'll take time, but we're on the path.

MARTA: I believe that when we talk about social change, we're referring to everything as a whole. Maybe revolution, the whole system changing, beginning with work...which is exactly what we do because we believe work is what gives us our dignity and is one of the basic pillars of society, along with healthcare, education, housing, people, children's education beyond school, and family education. These are all things that make up society and things we want to change and recreate. Little by little, and day by day, we are building this new society.

Gisela and Nicolás, Elipsis-Video and Argentina Indymedia (an independent documentary collective and an independent media collective)

GISELA: One of the basic principles that all the social movements seemed to agree on from the beginning, was that we don't want to work with, or be a part of, political parties. We began to organize on a human level, one rooted in solidarity and in helping one another. We based our organizing on the concepts of sharing ideas and opening minds. We opened ourselves to see what was happening to our next-door neighbor, who we didn't notice before. We began trying to figure out how to solve our different problems. For example, we helped neighborhood families that couldn't support themselves.

In the neighborhood, there are a ton of kids under fifteen years old who are *carteneros,* and collect cardboard until as late as four in the morning. In the neighborhood assembly, the majority of us are trying to help them. One of the things some people have done is organizing hot meals for the *carteneros* for when they finish work. We all come together then—*asemblistas* and *carteneros*—and share a meal. These kids probably haven't eaten dinner for a few days, and after work they take a long train journey to their houses out in the provinces. It's a really big collaboration that has been organized. I think, more than anything, the fundamental principal of organization for all of the social movements is solidarity and *compañerismo*. It's about beginning to look one another in the eye, and about helping ourselves and each other through this social crisis—a crisis that has come close to breaking the country and destroying some of our fundamental principles...like solidarity. People have opened their arms to each other in an effort to rebuild all of this, to rebuild what the government tried to break—the middle class, and the working class, those that get up to work and try to earn a salary that will be enough. But it's never enough, especially these days. All of the social movements are trying to re-imagine and rebuild everything.

NICOLÁS: I've noticed a difference in society since the rebellion. Before, there was a great sense of fatalism. Argentines would set things aside and delegate a lot. People had the mentality of "well, corruption will always be there, and so what's the use of mobilizing if things are not going to change?" Or the police, for example, who everyone knows are much more dangerous than delinquents. It's this same police force that perpetrates the delinquency, instead of combating it. But, the perspective was, a sort of, "oh, well, that's how it is," a real fatalistic view that Argentina was in a shitty place, and that things would not change. I think that the nineteenth and twentieth had a lot to do with this sense of fatalism changing. It was something so massive, with all different social sectors participating, and the result was a real shift in thinking. After the rebellion, the way we saw things changed. People were saying things like, "It depends on what we each do and what we do together." It was like one day we said, "Enough! We can't take any more." This was something that was felt everywhere.

Couple at a road blockade

Art also played an important role, nourishing the resistance. Theater, for example, always incorporated something political—some plays address the recuperated factories. Or the performances in the plazas, where the acts always have political content. The generalized hate and rejection of politicians was so widespread that you could see it everywhere. One of the main points that we all agree on is that we don't want what existed before. Now when you watch the *murgas*—which are the popular dances—when people sing, they always sing against the politicians and everything that has happened. It's ever-present. You go to a film screening and there are always movies about the *piqueteros*, and bands sing about them.

There has been a fundamental change. It seems like people are more accepting of differing opinions now...well, as long as they're not too strident. We're also in a country where so many people are poor. This is something that is even noticeable on the street. There are so many people who were left without work and are out on the street. When people come across them, they generally feel that it shouldn't be like this. That's different than before. Well-dressed people notice the intense poverty, and see that even their lives have changed so much. A year ago they were working, and now life has a different rhythm.

Sometimes when people feel a bit fortunate in their position, they're willing to help others. That's how we all began. For example, instead of throwing our old newspapers wherever, we began to gather them together to give to the *carteneros*, or use two trash cans—one for paper and the other for trash—understanding that this is important now, and being conscientious. How do I explain this? Sometimes it is difficult to do things—one resists them initially, but these are the things we now feel and do in Argentina.

Another example is the popular meals organized in the plazas. The church even began to get a conscience, and changed their position to one that was a bit closer to the people, instead of the state. They began to be critical, and sometimes even helped the unemployed try to get state subsidies. I think that part of what happened to the middle class was a big *mea culpa* when they realized that all their lives had been an illusion, that the dollar and the peso were not one-to-one, that that was never going to happen, and that because they had been swallowing the dreams of the past, they were now falling. It's like a person falling from the eleventh floor, and on each floor they say, "From now on all will be fine, from now on all will be good." One day, when they're splayed out on the bottom floor, they change and say, "I knew this would happen."

Eluney, Etcétera (a militant art collective)

It would be so much more interesting if I could tell you about our projects and show you the concrete work at the same time. I should say that I've just recently become a part of the collective and there are still tons of things that I'm learning.

An action we did recently was in support of the MTD San Telmo when they occupied the house next to the Modern Art Museum. That action was called "To EAT!" It was intended as a sort of analogy. We wanted to show how we believe artistic nourishment is like food—it is a part of the necessary sustenance for life. Suggesting these things as analogies, we think, is really important. We often work with groups to help them decide on their own projects or actions. In this case, they proposed doing a popular kitchen—only doing it with objects, symbolic representations of the popular kitchen. They designed the project and put it together, including the selection of all the objects, and together, we displayed and sold it, giving the money to the MTD San Telmo. The idea had two functions, one was to get the general public to see things from the movement's point of view—what their work is—and the other point was to raise some money for the movement, which they really need.

There was another action we did on March 24th. Etcétera is a collective that has always been deeply involved with different groups and movements, like HIJOS—who are the children of the disappeared and have for a long time been organizing escraches [direct and public actions]. The theme was the anniversary of the 1976 coup [which lead to the most brutal dictatorship in Argentina's history], which is a very important date for everyone in the collective. These are people whose parents disappeared, which is an extremely powerful experience. Every year on March 24th there's an action. Last year we built a huge pot that had a slingshot in the center of it, which was the symbol of the piqueteros and caceroleros [those that went out banging pots and pans], who were uniting for the first time. We assembled an army, armed with forks and knives, and attacked the supermarkets and McDonald's shouting "To Eat!" There was a really ludicrous element with lots of playfulness.

In 2003, the action I participated in was oriented towards the April 27th elections. It was a huge parody of the election, and we presented a goose as a candidate. In all of the demonstrations, we all gathered around our candidate. We had a whole security team and a mock pro-paganda team. We were ridiculing the same political parties with an ex-aggerated dogmatism. We presented a goose—truly, the animal—in the elections, and a security team talking importantly amongst themselves surrounded it. All of the team surrounded the candidate, chanting and singing the political songs that the traditional parties have been singing for a thousand years. But we changed the songs so the lyrics were about the goose. "To the Pink House we're going to take it, with the goose, with the goose, with goose, yeah, yeah, yeah!" And of course, "We feel it, we feel it, the goose is president!" Or "Clear the way, the goose is coming!" We also used slogans that are always used in these spaces, only transforming them.

Carlos G. and Julian, Zanon (an occupied factory)

CARLOS: We're struggling against a variety of things. Actually, we're pretty much fighting an entire system. What we're doing might seem utopian, since you can't always prove that the factory is completely prof-itable, especially when so many other people are trying to show that the factory is headed for failure. So, we built up the factory through our own initiatives, like paying three or more times the value of the boxes in the beginning. The idea was that then we would have them and would be able to package our products no matter what. As for land, we weren't able to acquire it at first, and it was only through an agreement with the indigenous Mapuche community that we were able to begin to get access to land. Many obstacles were put in our path.

JULIAN: Yes, we always try to have relationships with everyone, whether they're working people or unemployed, working under a boss or not. We don't see our experience as "the" experience, or think that because we're recuperating a factory, that's the only thing that people can do to keep from losing their jobs. We're trying to show everyone that they can de-fend themselves a little from the pressure, and that... How can I say this in just a few words, that they should realize that we're all being used. We want to demonstrate that, together, we can keep this country going—not in the way that Menem says, "I am going to move the country forward," like he's the great maker of the reality we're living. A single person can't move a country forward. The ones who can really move things forward are the workers, employed or unemployed. We fight for everyone. As we say "it's all of us who need to keep this country going."

Ezequiel, Asamblea Cid Campeador (a neighborhood assembly)

For me, there is no dichotomy between creation and reaction. For me, each is a moment of the same, since you can only create if you are reacting against that which has already been created but doesn't work for you. Sometimes the primary impulse of politics is purely reactive.

Front of the Cid Campeador neighborhood assembly, located in an occupied bank

At other times that isn't the case, and you are forced to ask yourself what you'd want it to be. I believe that now we're seeing the most creative moment, which is also the most difficult.

I also believe that these two previous years leaned more toward the reactive side, toward the long and painful process of ceasing to be what we were. It isn't easy, and it requires an entire self-examination and rupture with one's previous self, and with what one is. Maybe you cling to beliefs that don't necessarily work, or aren't always very realistic in order to break with the past—beliefs that, at the same time, you have to cling to tooth and nail, because you're still in the process of breaking with the past. It's a complicated moment, but I believe that the more creative part is still to come.

Colectivo Situaciones (a group for militant political reflection)

At a certain time, we began to see what we think represents the lack of a foundation for change in the libertarian autonomist left. We started to get disillusioned with the leftist discourses of activists, intellectuals, artists, and theorists. So we began to ask ourselves if we should devote ourselves to the investigation of what ought to be the foundation for emancipatory thought and practice. Since then, we've continued to ask ourselves the same questions, and things like *Zapatismo* appeared. Many people in the theoretical fields began asking radical questions, influencing us greatly. We studied their ideas a great deal, and got to know many of them. We exchange ideas with these people a lot. In Argentina as well, new, extraordinarily radical practices put everything into question. The people who engage in these practices have asked some new questions. Around all of this, a few key ideas were appearing, and we decided to develop them and see where they would lead.

One of the main things we discovered was that neither theory, nor practice are givens. Their power doesn't automatically appear, but rather only appears in a particular concrete situation. This is pretty obvious, or at least it ought to be. But normally, the development of thought and practice in a situation isn't easy or obvious. We decided to throw ourselves fully into this sort of work. We didn't then, and don't now, believe that situations can be created. Existing situations have to be taken on. They are to be entered into and assumed, not so much created through an individual act of will.

We decided to abandon all those forms of political organization, discourse, and forms of thinking that presuppose that the space for action is global. We don't think it is. We don't think it has a pre-determined scale, whether national, provincial, or local. We see the global as the sum of the locals. And we think that both the local and the global refer to an unsituated space, one that's too homogenous.

Then we decided to investigate the intense experiences and ideas that emerge within situations. For example, we were inspired when the group HIJOS [a collective of the children of those disappeared during the dictatorship] began the practice of "*escrache*," which consists of going to the homes of people who were directly involved in the genocide from the last military dictatorship. These people were ruled culpable at trial, but were given pardons rather than punishments. HIJOS uses the *escrache* as a way to produce politics in a different way, one that is based in the community and society—based in concepts of society. They created a new method for the application of justice, one not related to the the state's national representative justice. We discovered that in HIJOS, this neighborhood level of organization—a level of organization that requires working with the neighbors for several months prior—produces great connections which give new meaning to every element of that community. It resignifies its destiny, it resignifies the idea of justice, and it is in no way subordinated to the state, to representative justice, to the dictates of a judge. On the contrary, it gives rise to what Gilles Deleuze called "creation as resistance, resistance as creation." I believe that we could say the same about every one of the other experiences that we're investigating. We believe that our very own collective is an experience that consists of resisting and creating, creating through resisting on the terrain of thought, linked with practice.

Maba and Orlando, MTD Solano (an unemployed workers' movement)

MABA: We aren't interested in the capitalist system. We want to generate something different. We don't want the factories to open and reincorporate us so that we can go back to being exploited. We want something else. The principles we organize around are work, dignity, and social change. With respect to work, dignified labor doesn't mean returning to a factory to work sixteen hours, and being exploited. Instead, we want to create specific types of projects—projects with no boss, in which the worker herself, the

Making bread in the movement bakery of the MTD Solano

compañeras themselves, decide what to do with production. This is how we feel about work.

We believe that both dignity and social change need to be constructed collectively. We aren't making demands of government. We believe we're the ones who have to construct it, and the government needs to leave us alone and let it happen.

ORLANDO: Dignity. We're recuperating our dignity through organizing ourselves and fighting capitalism. We don't want to reproduce the old system, but rather to arm a new society in which there are no oppressors or oppressed; a society in which there are no exploiters or exploited. It concerns us that we're supposedly in a democratic country, because if democracy means starving to death, if democracy means that every time you go out to protest, they beat the shit out of you, or that every day kids die in the Solano hospital because they don't have gauze—and this is the sort of democracy that I believe we have today—then we are living in a more dictatorial country than before.

Martín K., Asamblea Colegiales (a neighborhood assembly)

So many of the feelings in the assemblies are similar to the feelings you have when your child is born. I remember that when my daughter was born, I only slept four hours a night and I was fine. Here, something was being born, and we were also individually being born in many ways. All of our lives have changed. I believe that we all have been affected in some way. And this is also a memory of that power, because something political that has such an effect is an incredible weapon. It's important to note that it was spontaneous. All of this helped us to create a wonderful atmosphere, a joyful atmosphere, a militant atmosphere characterized by happiness. The assembly has made me happier.

I believe that the greatest obstacle we have in Argentina today is our inability to reject certain ways of living that have to do with individualism and egoism. I see these as a mercantile mode of existence, and since this appears in all collectives, it also plays a role in shaping them. For example, there's a lot of protagonism in the assemblies, an excessive amount really, meaning that what's most important sometimes is saying what I want to say, and listening to what is most interesting for me to listen to, instead of being open to changing my opinions.

In these new political relationships we're envisioning, we need to create spaces where we can trust that no one is showing off or not paying attention to the other. Maybe it's better to say that we need a level of openness with one another in the movement, and an openness that creates space. This trust is key to shaping the territory we're creating.

To create this cooperation, we have to renounce certain "advantages" of the market. We need to be prepared, from the very beginning, to recognize that there's a value system which is neither unitary or homogenous, and that doesn't have to do with the capitalization of any type of profit. There are multiple values and distinct modes for sharing those values in a collective situation—there's no norm. This is sometimes uncomfortable because we live in a world in which there are many colors, many pleasures and textures, and that's how you have a world that is more, more alive, no? The world of the market is a world of shopping, of a colder light stimulated by things.

I believe we can invent other value systems. In the past year-and-a-half, we've learned that, although it's okay to want to construct new values, we need to acknowledge that doing so necessitates confronting what's ingrained in us and what is constantly reproducing itself within us. It's like a virus, like *The Matrix*. As a society, we need to create an anti-virus, a relational anti-virus. It's as though hate and violence were a memory, viruses infecting our memory, and we need to transform this sadness into joy.

Neka and Alberto, MTD Solano (an unemployed workers' movement)

NEKA: We want to take power [everyone laughs].

ALBERTO: Our experience in the movement is only seven or eight years old. It's not a very long experience. We believe that many societies, peoples, and countries have attempted to transform things, but these transformations have not been realized. It fails to happen, either because of power and decreeing things, or by making laws. We believe that transformation occurs when one begins to have other values, and starts relating differently to people. We don't see our role as merely making claims or struggling for survival. In an emergency situation, one of poverty, misery, and really the deterioration of us as humans, of our values, survival is something the struggle has to take into account. Understanding all of this, we see that we also need a transformation that isn't solely about economics, but one which also includes our consciousnesses. It's about being better in our work and health, but also creating another way of living. This is an experience that we construct on the basis of the collective and collectives, in which individualism no longer figures among our values, and similarly with the egoism, which is a part of this perverse society. Our relationship to the environment, the relationships among *compañeros* and *compañeras* and their children, these all need to be worked on; these relationships are integral. It isn't just about saying, well, "How are we going to survive in a situation of such massive misery?" Instead, how are we going to reconstruct those values that I believe are present in many communities throughout the world?

Our principal struggle is centered around this: the generation of new subjectivities, new relationships, ones that have to do with the new transformations. We don't think this will come about because of a revolutionary president or a revolutionary group. Historically, we've seen in Russia and China, for example, that they fought for values and ideals, but ended up continuing under the same oppression. Freedom remained absent from their lives.

Our struggle began in the south, and then moved to the north of Argentina, and then later in Buenos Aires. Before that, there were not many experiences outside of traditional institutions, like the church or political parties. Suddenly, with a small nucleus, we began this new experience, and it began to be reproduced, without our even knowing, until a ton of experiences began and spread all over the country. These aren't the most numerous experiences, or the ones that are in the press, but there are so many people looking for the same things, without much experience from other practices either, because there just isn't much experience in developing this sort of politics out there today.

NEKA: So, our perspective is grounded in the need for a new construction, no? A new society. Though the goal was to achieve a common good, I believe many things happened that were based on ordering and obeying. I think that many things fell apart precisely because of the shortcomings of this sort of relationship. This is true because the most important thing is effect, or rather, not something superficial or spectacular. Something that is born from human need—the need to recognize others, to feel like I am recognized, and to recover our self-esteem—to recover our dignity.

I think this is the sentiment that we're talking about. We're not going to entrust our individual dignity to someone else who might do things well, but instead we're going to reconstruct our dignity from within ourselves, utilizing our capacity for self-definition, self-determination, and self-valorization. We're not referring to affect provided by the television or propaganda, but another type of affect, with people at the core. One of the things that capitalism robs us of, is precisely this possibility. It converts us into objects, it thing-ifies us. I think all systems of domination convert us into objects. So, to recover our dignity is to recover this capacity to feel like people. For me, that's to feel like a woman with possibilities, able to choose how I want to live, and feel what my role is in relationship to others. It's not for someone else to explain to me, no. And neither is it up to a vanguard to explain it to me. It isn't for anyone to explain to me, but rather for me to feel it and want to do it.

It's very difficult because we live in a very macho society. I believe that machismo is also a product of the domination of capital, and to break with this is also a part of...that is to say, we don't speak of machismo only with reference to the difference between men and women. We speak of machismo as a culture that we, as women, also contribute to. For example, when we speak of our roles as women in the movement, as women fighting, as women in creation, we need to reflect upon how much we might also produce a macho culture of domination, and we need self-criticism. It's like a ladder: the man oppresses the woman, the woman oppresses her children, the teachers oppress their students, etc. It's like the reproduction of a chain of oppression and domination, and I believe that we're implicated in this at the most fundamental level. We're the ones who need to reflect upon this.

ALBERTO: Above all, we're living in a moment of ruptures. On the international scale, this is a moment of very profound changes and transitions whose final result we can't predict. I feel like we know what we don't want. What we want...well, that's what's unknown, but we're going to start building it by trial and error, much like the Zapatistas say, "Walking we ask questions, and move forward with our reflections." No, we don't have a finished manual, but we do know the attempts that have been made on the part of modernity, right? This whole long period we see as exhausted, rather than a period of invention and realization. Our goals are shaped by a disintegrating environment where human life has become endangered. We want to find a way to live collectively, in a community, seeing and relating to others without losing our freedom. We're not interested in a regime that says, well, we are going have better income distribution, but no freedom. So we're searching.

NEKA: There are lots of diverse experiences now. Here in Solano, we don't organize as a closed community, instead, we try to stay open to the possibility of finding different experiences, since people are struggling for different things in different places. For example, there are indigenous groups struggling everywhere, not just in Argentina but also in Chile, in Bolivia, and in Mexico with the Zapatistas. There are many of us, and we're everywhere. The problem arises when we consider ourselves unique and exemplary communities. I believe that by breaking with these hierarchical models, we can encounter another potent reality. The fundamental thing is to be able to weave networks out of all of these experiences. We don't believe that some experiences are more powerful than others, or that they can illuminate all other experiences. Just the opposite. We each come from different places, acting, struggling, and learning to bring ourselves out of our situations. We really don't feel alone. What makes us feel different in some moments is repression, which is sometimes strong, and other times, more subtle. It doesn't cease to exist, but is sometimes more subtle. We're struggling alongside other *compañeros*, and I believe we're powerful.

Christian, Attac Autónomo (an anti-capitalist collective)

I believe we're undergoing a big change. No one can deny that we're facing a historic process. It's like the nineteenth and twentieth—I doubt I'll study it, but my children will, and when I tell them "your father was there," that'll be a proud moment for me. This is true, not only from the point of view of history as it's told in the formal educational system, which tends to be manipulative and make a mess of the situation, but history as told by our *compañeros,* who understand the reality of what was and is going on.

The revolutionary process that we're living is simultaneously slow and fast. Life wasn't like this ten years ago. Before, I couldn't even mention these things because we were living under the dictatorship. So it's slow, but also very rapid at the same time, because we're all starving for something new. We're saying, enough is enough. We don't really know what we want, but we do know what we don't want, and we set out from here on the path to its construction. We begin to look at the alternatives and the different methodologies of struggle in order to move ahead. We live in the day-to-day, but we also live from today to the future. It's a slow revolutionary process. It's like Subcomandante Marcos says, "We take the slower path in order to construct something true, something that is representative of the people and collective." It's as though we're longing for something, whether that's political, revolutionary, cultural, or strategic.

If I weren't here, if you weren't here, if other *compañeros* weren't here, there wouldn't have been the same national and international repercussions that there were. What I'm trying to say is that we're each like a bit of sand, and together we make things happen. Alternatives are being created that the government wouldn't have offered, and people become the initiators. It's an important moment when someone says, "Fuck, my struggle really matters!" These are the small satisfactions that you achieve through all the daily struggles. We're struggling from the minute we get up to the minute we go to bed. We live struggling all of the time... I mean, all of the time. Whether it's in our workplace, struggling with the same idiosyncrasies as other *compañeros,* which we have to do sometimes in order to keep our jobs. But we're able to connect everything, and bit by bit, we move forward, creating a new political construction, a new alternative in the face of all of this system's demagoguery.

Compañer@s of MTD Allen and MTD Chipoletti (unemployed workers'
movement)

COMPAÑERO 1: In the movement, we don't need others speaking for or
about us. I mean, there are the media and the politics of spectacle, but we
don't need that. What's important is that society speaks for itself. We're
social actors and can speak for ourselves. This is the biggest effect we can
have on how all of this can radiate outward. The key is not falling into
politics, while you stay in the political.

COMPAÑERA 2: From there, it's about moving away from the emptiness
that comes from feeling that you're only a thing, and as a thing you're
constantly observed, labeled, and marked by a society that oppresses
you every day. Through participating in the movements, you start feeling
useful, like you have a place. You know that your work is for the benefit
of a collective. It's a feeling of importance, like you have a purpose, and
you reclaim all the things the system has taken away from you. You feel
alive.

Paloma, Asamblea Palermo Viejo (a neighborhood assembly)

Here [gesturing around], where we're organizing and some people are
living, was a market that was abandoned for twenty years. A family
has been living here. I think the father was a shoemaker, and they still
live here. Nothing else was happening. I don't know the origins of the
relationship between the neighborhood assembly and this family. After
the rebellion of the nineteenth and twentieth of December, neighbors
gathered together in the neighborhood plaza and we began the assembly.
I just joined last December, so I'm not one of the oldest participants and
may not have the history exactly right. I work in a number of our projects, like the popular kitchen, where we offer warm meals to the neighbors and *carteneros*. Did you know that some of them travel all the way
from the provinces into the city to collect cardboard?

Natalia, La Toma and Asamblea Lomas Este (an occupied building and a
neighborhood assembly)

This is a new place—a place of creation, a place where different bonds
are made, bonds which are creating completely new relationships. Making new bonds sometimes involves thinking about people in new ways;
seeing each other as equals, whether some of us are more or less marginalized, or have been torn apart by the system. And not seeing these differ-

ences as problems, but just as differences. This is a new place, one that's distinct from institutionalized places. It is a place where we can create new ways of being social, and new senses of sociability. To make this sort of place it's essential that we are all a part of it: the kids that hustled at the train station next to La Toma, the *carteneros*, those that are living in the street, the neighbors. Everybody.

I believe some of what we're feeling and experiencing has to do with what happened on the nineteenth and twentieth. The history we're living shows us that there comes a time when people must realize that the mentality of only saving yourself, or of getting rich, or getting a career and not looking at those around you, are old ideas that don't work. This old frame of mind leads to selfish individualism and really doesn't make sense. I don't know…it feels like so many of us now share this new way of thinking about how we organize together from below, and help one another as we go along. We represent a break from individualistic thinking. I don't know exactly how to break with all of this com-

"We are waiting for you"
Sign for Pompeya's popular
kitchen and snack program

pletely, if it's going to work in the short run, or what's going to happen. Maybe it's too utopian. I really don't know, but this is how I feel.

Alberto, Clínica Medrano (a recuperated clinic)

We aspire to build a big movement of recovered factories so we can confront this cruel system and take care of everyone's needs. We want to collect the political tools that will help us to create new paths away from the system. This is the core of what we're doing, and isn't easy.

Emilio, Tierra del Sur (a neighborhood assembly, occupied building, and
community center)

Reaction is also construction. For me, reaction is a fruit that rots really
fast. Nevertheless, it does have life. Reaction, struggle, the scream...these
are all social constructions.

Today, one of the most wonderful things about the idea of revolution is the revolution that takes place inside of us. What sense does it
make to try to take power if we're not changing ourselves? If we're the
same, if we don't change the authoritarianism and capitalism that's in
and all around us, then what are we doing? Capitalism isn't only in the
International Monetary Fund (IMF), the World Bank, or Monsanto. It's
also inside of us. If this weren't true, it would be easy to just blow up the
IMF and Monsanto, and then there'd be no more capitalism. But in fact,
the Twin Towers were blown up, and capitalism is still intact. Capitalism
doesn't have a physical place. And this is the challenge: to rip it out of
ourselves in order to build a non-capitalist society. The main issue isn't
that we have capitalism inside, but what we're going to do about it. In
other words, the question is how are we going to be effective with what
we're reclaiming, and with our attitudes? And then what does this look
like in our daily life as activists? How do we change our values and how
we relate to other people—our social relationships? How do we change
ourselves and our communities? This is as important as getting rid of the
IMF... More important even.

Bartering Networks

Gisela and Nicolás, Elipsis-Video and Argentina Indymedia (an independent
documentary group and independent media collective)

NICOLÁS: Bartering networks sprang up very quickly all over the place.
People just said, "OK, you're able to do this and I can do this, so what
do we do now?" And we began.

The idea was mostly great, but not entirely. There were times when
people used the network just to get things for themselves, but it really did
help a great deal. In every neighborhood, people were able to eat because
of this relationship, and we were all involved. Also, there were different
relationships in the barter network between the rich and the poor; those
that had a lot of nice things to exchange, and well, those that did not. We
made tickets to represent the exchange values, and each person would
have a quantity of these tickets. For example, with my photography, I
was able to go around and take photos of people, and I was paid in

tickets, and with those tickets I got a kind of credit. Now, these tickets barely exist at all. Very few places use them. Now, they exist in a sort of sentimental way, but before there were millions of them.

GISELA: What happened is that people started to counterfeit the tickets. Since it was just a piece of paper, it was really easy to counterfeit. So barter networks that used tickets fell apart. I don't know who did it, but it seems it was people who could print millions of tickets at a time—people with power... The barter network that used tickets was distinct from the one that exchanged object for object, the difference was the ticket and idea of credit.

NICOLÁS: At one point, those tickets helped pay for train trips to Mar del Plata.

GISELA: And the taxes, right?

NICOLÁS: No, I don't think so, but in some of the provinces and towns, so many people were using this type of money that the government started accepting it.

GISELA: The municipalities. In the beginning it was in the province, in Avellenada. They even allowed people to pay electric and gas bills with the tickets, because people had more of these than money. It's a bartering commission. [Reading from the ticket in her hand] "The Global Network of Bartering Exchange, this ticket is valid only for those that are a part of The Global Network of Bartering."

NICOLÁS: The condition for participation in the barter network was that you exchange something. Someone couldn't enter into the space where merchandise and services where exchanged if they didn't have something to exchange. It didn't have to be an object, it could be a skill or craft or trade, really anything.

GISELA: Each person decided the value individually. There was a sort of base, but it didn't have anything to do with the value of money. Not too long after it began—really from one day to the next, when everything with the dollar began to change—the bartering networks changed too. I mean, before, a packet of sugar cost about seven credits, and then one month later it cost fifty. It started to become impossible. It began to cost money to buy food to bring to the bartering clubs. Then the clubs fell apart so much that people started to bring clothing and objects from their homes to exchange for food and nothing else. It became only about food, and there was no more fun in it. Many people were able to eat because of their relationship to the barter networks.

NICOLÁS: Before, you used to buy raw products and then use them to make other products you could sell. For example, you'd buy flour, sugar, and various things to make raviolis or cakes. You'd sell some products, and with that credit, you could buy more than just the products to make the cakes again, to bring more to the next barter, or you could also buy fruit and really everything that you'd eat. It worked for a long time. In reality, it worked too well. It got to quite a sophisticated level, and there were exchanges that didn't get taxed or anything, so it began to seriously worry the Ministry of the Economy. No one knows what happened with the government—what their position was, or if they were trying to break it up. Some speculate that, at some point, the government started to...

GISELA: To counterfeit.

NICOLÁS: ...to make thousands and thousands of those tickets. What happened was, you'd go to a block where people got together in each neighborhood, where there was a bartering network, and for two dollars, you could buy fifty credits. So then, it wasn't worth anything to bring those products, because with two dollars, you already had fifty credits and that made the prices...

GISELA: It was because of money that people boycotted the barter networks. Food products got so expensive that people couldn't invest in goods to barter with. You couldn't get the things you needed anymore. It broke the balance of the barter economy.

NICOLÁS: Remember when the barter network started in 1999? It was soon after that we were invited to participate.

GISELA: Yes.

NICOLÁS: I teach French classes, and they invited me to come and teach. They explained a little bit about what it was about.

GISELA: It grew a lot after the nineteenth and twentieth of December. Before that, the bartering networks meant going to a fair to exchange something frivolous. After the nineteenth and twentieth, it turned into something for the basic survival of a family.

NICOLÁS: This was true for everyone. People also created barter networks in the rich neighborhoods. If you went to those barters, you would notice pretty quickly that they were exchanging totally different things than us.

GISELA: Now, in the poorest, most humble places and the provinces, the networks have started to work a bit again. But just a bit, because all that happened with the counterfeiting was disillusioning for people. I'm from the province, and when we used to go back to see my family, there were three or four bartering networks, all day every day. It had turned into a supermarket, more or less. Women organized most of the barter networks.

New Language

Emilio, Tierra del Sur (a neighborhood assembly, occupied building, and community center)

The traditional left had an whole way of speaking, a language, and today we're constructing something different, something completely different. I mean, it's old. It's something of the past; from a different historical moment, a situation that expired. And for me, it's not worth the energy to try and continue those practices. So, today we're constructing something different. And in constructing this something different, there also comes a whole new language and different forms of expression. *Horizontalidad*, direct democracy, sharing, and affecting one another's movements, articulation, organizing in networks, are terms not often heard from the traditional left. They're the words of the new social movement, of the new anticapitalist struggles. There are many words from the past that could define today's situation, but since they're old words now used to define new things, they create confusion. And when words don't communicate clearly, it's better to just leave them out.

I don't believe that we need this new language. I think that people, in their need to express something new in practice, already develop a new language. Obviously, we're not inventing a whole different language, but there are many old words that are being rediscovered. This has a lot to do with the people that are involved in activism today who weren't before. Many words were demonized for them. Many people here lived a large part of their lives thinking the devil was communist. The words communism, socialism, revolution, and imperialism are still very loaded. But to the extent that this internal and collective change is happening, many of the old left's words are being recovered and given new meaning. The word "revolution" is a very beautiful word that is timeless and enduring. *Horizontalidad* and *autogestión* evoke something related to our practice, something that arose from this practice, a practice that arose from necessity. For me, *autogestión* evokes a bunch of sensations, smells, and sounds that don't have to do with the intellectual, but rather the practice.

I'm a little scared about what words we're going to use when the system begins to take our words, because capitalism is also a grand appropriator of language in its great mania of co-optation. That is to say, what capitalism can't destroy, it incorporates and modifies, and tries to make work for itself.

Celeste, Clave Roja (an anti-capitalist student group)

Of course there's a new language. Everything that has to do with self-organization, *autogestión*, even the word "democracy." These are all words that weren't said before. And the words that were said have a completely different meaning today. For example, for many people before the rebellion of 2001, the word "democracy" meant going to vote. Democracy meant that the military dictatorship wasn't there anymore. Having had the military there, the conquest of democracy, especially for people in an older generation than me, is something really deeply felt. Most people felt it was really important to have the possibility of voting, even if the candidate is someone you know will lie or steal, but it was still something really important. This changed recently—in December 2001. It seems to me that a lot of people, including me, have discovered another meaning to democracy, which is the democracy of the people. This democracy doesn't have anything to do with politicians in congress, ministers, or the president. It has a new and different meaning, both

"I vote, you vote, he votes, we vote, you all vote, they betray us. We are organizing an active rejection of these elections because we want to deepen the road towards a more open and direct democracy."

for the people that participate in neighborhood assemblies and those who don't.

Just thinking of democracy as something active is already a change. Even if nothing results from it, and tomorrow the president comes into office and nothing happens in Argentina for eighty years, something has already changed forever. When something doesn't seem right, people who thought that democracy happened with a vote will go into the street, bang pots and pans, organize, go to the neighborhood assembly. It is like there are now two meanings for democracy, and for me, this is really profound.

Carina, Argentine World Social Forum mobilizing committee

I believe that new languages have been created within each of the militant groups. For example, we've started incorporating all the antiglobalization language that's part of an international movement, and some of the *piquetero* language, too. The discussions around power, counter-power, and anti-power are part of our language now, as well as the concept of *autogestión*. Yes, there's a new language being created, but it's still lacking because there isn't a real practice yet. There's a process, but we're not sure where it's going. But through that process, yes, we end up generating a new language, a practical language. The language of the assemblies was a practical language. Seeing a bunch of people in a plaza who put a bunch of their time into generating discussions, and really discussing in a way that I personally prefer, which is discussing and not arguing... This is part of the new language.

Daniela, MTD Almirante Brown (an unemployed workers' movement)

We call each other *compañeros*. There are political parties that say *compañeros* as well, but we have chosen to say *compañero* to each other despite that. We say *compañeros* because we share everything, you know? We share in the struggle, we share hunger, misery, a plate of food. Whenever someone comes to an assembly for the first time, especially in very low-income neighborhoods like Cerrito, they come with lots of needs. Once they are here, they immediately find that there is someone in a march who's brought a piece of bread or a *maté*, and says, "Come, sit down at my side and we'll drink this together. We're going to share everything." This is also true in our popular kitchen, where we try to recover the values of how our grandparents lived—or at least this is how I remember their generation living. Before, you could invite a neighbor over to eat: "Come, sit down, and eat some of this barbeque with me." For workers, I remember that on the job, we always barbequed and sat down to eat together. We're trying to get all that back. We'd like to all be seated and eating in our homes, with enough food there, but this is what is left now...going to a popular kitchen.

It's about trying to recover the values that this system took away from us (which is just another form of repressing us). The system tries to separate and isolate us, and makes us worry only about ourselves while others can die. If someone beside us doesn't have any bread, it doesn't matter, I have mine. That's what that system imposes on us, and we deal with this in so many little ways day to day. It's really hard, because people come with those values forced in their heads, whether from TV or from everything else that surrounds us in this system. It leaves us isolated. In the movement, we try to get rid of all of those values, and replace them with *compañerismo,* to call each other more than *compañeros,* and not just call each other that because we're in the same struggle. We're all the same, and as *compañeros* we try to make things easier for everyone, day by day. Not only in regards to food and work, but also with things that maybe we're not capable of seeing on a grand scale—things you feel that, day by day, make you become *compañeros.*

One example that I always think about when I think of solidarity and *compañerismo* has to do with a vice—cigarettes. Sometimes I can't afford to pay for my vices, and I'm down for not having money, for not being able to feed my kids, and my mother over there is not so good because she is out of work. I am just down. And then standing next to me, I have a friend, a *compañero,* who has a cig, and he offers me some of it, and we smoke it together. This is something that this shitty system tries to make invisible. It tries to make us forget that our *compañeros* will share. They teach us to buy our Phillip Morris and smoke by ourselves, and everyone else can go to hell. This is a small story and detail, but something that happens every day. The same is true with *maté.* It's something that happens every day, a small detail that happens all the time in the workplace, in the assembly, everywhere. But it's really not small.

Paula, feminist and LGTTB collectives

New social practices, in general, when they're new, need new forms of articulation. For example, I have an experience that relates to language and the practices that come along with queer movements. In the LGTTB movements, we speak using the feminine. The Spanish language has articles that are not neutral like in English. In Spanish, you've got, "*él*" and you've got "*la,*" right? In English, you don't. The language is neutral. Generically speaking, I mean. Here it isn't. Therefore, in the LGTTB movement, we would never say to each other, "*nosotros*" [the masculine form of "we"], we always say "*nosotras*" [the feminine form of "we"]. This is because we understand that language signifies lots of things, it isn't just a way for people to communicate with each other. It's infused with social relations, gender and otherwise. It seems to me that people who participate in assemblies, recuperated factories, and the MTDs also realize that language is a social experience. That it's not a convention. It's a social experience. And if the social experience changes, a different language is needed. I believe that the fact that new words appear in a movement...excuse me, in a certain historical moment, in a certain place, and that cannot be translated to other languages—that this has to do with what's happening there and not happening in other places. So there aren't certain words in English, because those same things are not happening in English-speaking countries. What's happening in Argentina is happening in Argentina, right? And in Argentina it happens that lots of groups suddenly are living new experiences that aren't immediately translatable into the language produced by previous experiences.

power

Group of compañeras, MTD la Matanza (an unemployed workers' movement)

COMPAÑERA 1: No, thank you. State power? No thanks. [Everyone laughs]

COMPAÑERA 2: I believe we're creating popular power in this space. Anyone can come here and participate in decisions about how things are going to be. It's an open space. For example, in an MTD assembly, a neighbor who comes—who doesn't know us yet, but wants to—is not only able to express opinions, but participate in making decisions. It's not a problem if the person isn't a member of the MTD. We believe that this is how popular power is created. When you take control of your education, work, and relationships like us, that's creating power—not state power, but popular power.

COMPAÑERA 1: Power is within us.

COMPAÑERA 3: Sometimes we talk about how our experiences teach us not to waste energy worrying about this power, but instead to try and create a new power. The idea is that if one sort of power doesn't work, another kind must be created. Why would you think of taking this power that isn't worth anything if you can hope for something better?

COMPAÑERA 4: The other day, a *compañera* at the *Enero Autónomo* gathering asked me if our school project meant there are going to be a lot of schools all over, if we're going to create them all over. Similar questions have been asked before as well. I said that the idea is—like Silvia said today—that the experience will multiply. For example, if one plans something for the country, or even for the province of Buenos Aires, it is unrealizable. First we stay in our own community, working on the basics among ourselves, and then later others can come and learn and choose to reproduce our experience. We have been able to share information and experience with many people who ask us about autonomy and how it can be created, and then from there they can share these experiences with others.

COMPAÑERA 2: There isn't anything secret, really. It's an important tenet of the group that everything is open and transparent. For example, there's no such thing as a closed-door assembly.

COMPAÑERA 1: Something very interesting happens with this question of power. One example took place a little while ago: when we first entered this space, there was a discussion about the key. The discussion was who would keep the key, because in many ways that person would have the power of opening and closing the space. Also, there was a question about what would happen if things were missing. There was anxiety among us, because we all feel like we're part of the projects here, including the machines. There was a very long discussion about the key, where to put it, who would hold it, etc. It's a very long, ongoing discussion.

COMPAÑERA 3: We've noticed that when you start to participate in the discussions and workshops, you open up to new ways of thinking, and this helps you grow. This process feels like some sort of historical experiment of seeking new ways of being and thinking.

Paula, feminist and GLTTB collectives

I have an idea of power, but it is a critical one. The concept of power, at least in the leftist tradition, has always meant that to transform society it's necessary to take power. That means to take political power, to take over the means of production, which is the classic vision. I had to laugh because after December 20th, when there were still many *cacerolazos*, which my friends and I always participate in, there was one that was particularly violent, with a lot of police repression. To escape this, we ran and jumped the fence to the Pink House [government building] and went inside. I was on television. They

The MTD rabbit on the wall of the movement's building in Allen

said that I was encroaching on the Pink House, that I was taking over the Pink House. I had to laugh. It's especially funny because at the time, my friend said, "We can go in there, but we're not taking power." To us, power didn't exist any more. The concept of taking power is archaic. What does it mean to take power? Power over what?

The social movements are thinking of a different kind of power that's distinct from the power of dominance, the power of transforming daily relations. We need to build different social relations in the present, and then later think about a future society. That's what the left doesn't understand. The left has a structural view, not very Marxist, not very dialectic, no? It has retained the least dialectal concepts within Marxism. For me, I must define power in terms of building an alternative power. What does building an emancipating, liberating power mean to me today? It means building, as much as possible, distinct social relations in the present. Of course, there are things that can be eliminated only if capitalism ends. Exploitation is exploitation, and can't be eliminated until the means of production are socialized. But machismo, violence, all the things that transform daily life, these must be changed because without such changes, how can we build a new society? It's contradictory. It's theoretically impossible to construct a new society if we don't first imagine new social configurations. I believe that the idea of power isn't homogeneous now, it isn't the same everywhere. The MTD isn't the same as the recuperated factories or the neighborhood assemblies, but a large part of the spirit of these groups is the same.

I learned many of these political ideas with my friends in the GLTTB movement. I met with many groups of people who were terribly persecuted in their daily lives because of their sexual orientations and their sexual identities. To be lesbian in Argentina isn't easy. It's more difficult than being gay, which isn't accepted. And transvestites? Don't ask. In these groups, there's such a profound respect for other people, and such a real need to change social relations today, because their suffering is yesterday and today. I learned that it's necessary to change the present in order to think of future change. It's not that I'm not thinking about future change, but for me, it isn't possible to construct an image of a different society without simultaneously reconstructing society. For me, that's a Marxist dialectic. I still consider myself a Marxist, and of course, a revolutionary.

Alberto, Clínica Medrano (a recuperated clinic)

I personally don't believe in taking power—that is, not until an alternative power is in place. You can organize from below, but until the system that oppresses, exploits, and doesn't permit you to get ahead is overthrown, no other power can be installed. It's very difficult to think about building any form of parallel society or parallel market. It seems like it's either one society or another.

I believe that all organizations, not only recuperated workplaces, but workers, the unemployed, everyone, must struggle to organize and create a power—not a parallel alternative, but something to replace the previous or present power, the reigning power. This is the power of the huge corporations, the politicians, priests, and business people. Power where workers and other people are marginalized, and then are forced to watch the same marginalization on television. We don't participate at all in the distribution of money by the large corporations and political parties, and that's the way it is. The only way out is to organize with everyone; all who struggle and suffer from these policies of starvation that leave us marginalized from everything. And yes, to organize in order to build something else, something different—in order to establish it, not just make a parallel form—it's a process that won't happen from one day to the next or even one year to the next, but our starting point is organizing differently.

Neka, MTD Solano, Claudia and Sergio, lavaca.org (an unemployed workers' movement and an alternative media collective)

NEKA: The issue isn't just the physical confrontation with the system. Every day, we're forced to confront a system that's completely repressive. The system tries to impose on us how and when we struggle. The question for us is how to think outside of this framework. How to manage our own time and space. It's easier for them to overthrow us when we buy into concepts of power, based on looking for the most powerful—based in something like weapons or the need to arm the people. We're going to build according to our own tempo, our own conditions, and our own reality, and not let them invade it. I think this idea of power as capability and potential—not a control—is a very radical change from previous struggles.

SERGIO: The difference is thinking about power as a noun: to arrive at power, to obtain power—as if it was a thing, when power is a verb.

CLAUDIA: There's a tension between active and passive power. It isn't that one is more important than another. If you apply this concept to the construction of a movement, it's much more difficult not to talk about confrontation. If we're talking about capitalist power, who has more possibility to make a change today, capitalist structures or the resistance? I have no doubt it's the resistance.

NEKA: These new relations that produce new subjectivities are never exhausted, because you never get to a point where you can say, yes, this is subjectivity. That's where we see a change. It's in permanent flux, permanent rethinking.

SERGIO: An idea that I find really interesting is that there's no left, or no autonomy, but there are leftist acts, autonomous acts, good or bad acts. The idea is to give a permanent characteristic to something. It's useful to think of the concrete act in order to label it in the moment, rather than what we believe supposedly characterizes a person, which changes from one situation to the next. I have a leftist friend who could commit fascist acts and realize it. Or a Christian could take over a factory, and at that moment, we could call that act leftist. I think we should change the adjectives we use.

NEKA: One of the many good things that has come from our coordinating together in the movement is that now we are going to coordinate in the neighborhoods without needing someone to manage everything—someone to keep everyone on course, or evaluate every experience. To me, this feels like real autonomy. I'm not saying our past experience was wrong or for shit. I believe that all of our experiences have been worthwhile. The question is how to continue.

Hundreds of neighborhood assemblies making decisions.

Paloma, Asamblea Palermo Viejo (a neighborhood assembly)

Here in the assembly, I believe that concepts of power lie beneath all of our discussions. It isn't that we are always talking about it, but it's always there.

In my opinion, what's important is the construction of another power. What is important is the process of trying to build another power, not one where you submit to someone else, but a power to do things, the power of joining together. A little like the Zapatista movement, who say that we are a world where all worlds fit, and one where we accept that the other doesn't necessarily think like you do.

More than anything, creating a different power means neither being submissive to another person or forcing your ideas upon them, but being inclusive.

Many people say this isn't possible or that it's utopian, and in order to have power one must destroy the previous power. I both agree and disagree with this idea. What is clear though is that if we don't destroy this power that exists now, it will destroy us first. Today we have a clear example of what happens if you don't want to destroy power. Now that Lula is in power in Brazil, he's changing—it is as if power has something that corrupts and changes people.

If you want to build another power, then all the people need to talk about it. I'm not at all interested in tearing down what exists now just to go to the Pink House. No, no, no, because my idea—and that of many people—is about sharing in the true construction of another power.

Fabian, Alavio Group (an independent media collective)

It seems to me that power manifests itself clearly. I don't agree with those who say power is so diffuse that you can't do anything except retreat into your house and build something else. I think that underestimates our ability to self-organize and change the system. Of course, I believe that in your home, you should be absolutely consistent and live your ideals. I believe consistency is a value that's difficult to find and even more difficult to practice. If you believe something, you have to be consistent about it with your children, your neighbors, your *compañeros*, and the world around you. One can talk a revolutionary talk, but keeping different values in your house, no. Really one is a consequence of the other.

There's no lack of leaders in the movement who could assume power, but to the extent that a leader assumes power, he is violating his own principles. So the diffusion of ideas seems to me a more interesting possibility than the preservation of institutions. It's the purest practical application of anarchist ideas. I believe in organization and don't discredit organization, but it seems to me that, at times, it's necessary to have actions fulfilling the dynamic. This permits one to say ok, we're becoming more democratic, more horizontal, we have more autonomy from the state. This is much more important than having someone directing a movement and saying, "we are such and such a thing." When that happens, something crystallizes, and unfortunately that's happening today. I believe it's been occurring for some time. Those who most frequently say "We're X thing," accomplish less. That's logical. When one assumes a hierarchy, it violates all the principles. It's time to forget the idea that your *compañeros* are going to pat you on the back for struggling and keeping the tradition. When you think of these values, of these organizational principles, what predominates is the dynamic—not leaders. Leaders are always temporary, transcending individuals and their organizations that are not institutionalized.

Although I believe in revolutionary organization, I also believe that we lack the tools to destroy power right now.

Nicolás, Argentina Indymedia (an independent media collective)

Power is not discussed so much, though lately it has been talked about a lot. Now power is talked about as an enemy—power, like that of the state.

Power is seen as more of a daily practice now. For example, in my neighborhood there's a very bureaucratic health center that, until recently, has been the place that gives out milk. The problem was that the milk never arrived, or no one knew how much milk was coming, or if it was going to be bad when they got it. The assemblies—I'm talking about my neighborhood assembly—saw that the health center wasn't functioning, or that it only worked for it's own employees, who didn't even do anything. That took away people's motivation to go to the health center. So they began to peacefully take it over, pressuring the doctors and managers to do their jobs. They spoke of power, meaning the power of the neighborhood—not government, but everyday power.

Toto, MTD la Plata (an unemployed workers' movement)

In movements like ours, we don't talk so much about the word "power" right now. We do, however, talk about the implications of a certain kind of power. We also talk about organizing, taking control of our own work, about having control over the decisions that affect us, and the fact that this must be expanded to reach as many people as possible. This is surely a kind of power, but it isn't the kind that's usually talked about, because the problem is something else. We reject the idea that taking power is a path. Instead, there's a confidence in a collective of people that didn't know each other before, who now do, and have developed many relationships that have nothing to do with taking or not taking power. This isn't to say that the relationships have nothing to do with power, but it's a different kind of power. We talk about performance—what we do—not in terms of theoretical power, although we're aware that in each mobilization, in each confrontation, power is and must be present.

This idea of power is nothing new for anarchism, but it's one of the characteristics of the new movements. For these movements this is something new—this idea that change can occur, but not through taking power. It seems to me that for the type of actions and creation we're a part of, it's key that we continue to focus on the practice, on what we are doing and how—which is so much more than slogans and phrases.

Ezequiel, Asamblea Cid Campeador (a neighborhood assembly)

The neighborhood assembly movement as well as other movements that arose around the same time, like the *piqueteros,* are thinking of power in another way. I think that one of the cultural changes that generated all this boiling-over during the last two years is that, while I would not say we absolutely changed the way we think about power, we've begun to question and hold serious doubts about what previously had been certainties. One of the things that's gone now is the certainty that social change occurs by putting one or another person in government.

I believe that the movements have created doubts about a certain concept of power, and these doubts allow us to think in different ways. Before the rebellion, a few circles discussed the idea of the state and read things by people like John Holloway and Antonio Negri, but they were very small groups, mainly people who are now part of the neighborhood assembly movement. For example, the name John Holloway began to circulate, which is strange when you think about it—to talk about an Irishman in the middle of a Buenos Aires assembly. But that's what happened, and I believe that's the moment to think about and relate. Above all because I believe that there was a very strong, but somewhat unsophisticated attachment to some of the old concepts of power. Whether you were for or against it, the idea was to take state power. There was a reaction of the extreme opposite, that is, to forget about the state and build territorial power.

I think the idea to not take state power is right, but in some ways it's a little ingenuous, or at least it's an incomplete analysis. The state exists, it's there, and it won't leave even if you ignore it. It'll come to look for you however much you wish that it didn't exist. I believe that the assemblies and the movements are beginning to notice that something important is being forgotten. A year-and-a-half ago, we began to think of a strategy for constructing an alternative autonomous power, forgetting the state, but now we see it isn't so simple. You have to seek a way to build autonomy while remaining cognizant of the state's existence. There is no alternative. That's a problem that directly affects us, and one that has to be kept in mind. I believe that no one has the remotest idea of how to do this, at least not that I know of.

I see in the movement that there's a reaction with a certain naïveté. We are forgetting the state while we construct a territorial autonomous power. Now people are trying to not think the way they used to, but are trying to look at these unsophisticated ideas of power with certain skepticism. It seems to me there is a very strong rejection to the idea that we are going to live on the margin of the state, on the margin of its theories and laws, and that we can live in this way, based only on our willingness and good heartedness. Change in cultural subjectivity and in the hearts of each one of us is fundamental, but for me it isn't enough. We also have to invent new types of rules and institutions. This is another way of saying we need explicit political agreements with clear rules, which are distinctly ours, and that don't depend only on goodwill. I'm working on this now—how to invent institutions that defend and preserve what we're doing, within the framework of network construction—building autonomous spaces, constructing horizontal places—because power changes in the very small things we're doing, and power is connected to all these things, these very small spaces. One of the ideas is to preserve the good we're creating and, at the same time, to not be so vulnerable to the outside. I sometimes see an enormous vulnerability to many external pressures, and I realize that even the most insignificant and weak of them could destroy us. I'm confident that it's possible to construct rules, institutions, and procedures—whatever you want to call them—in order to protect this, our construction.

Maybe in time, that rejection, which is perfectly sane and healthy, will finally bring about another way of thinking about things, but for now there is a very negative reception to these ideas and perhaps an inability to see that when there are no clear rules, what happens is that ambiguous rules develop. I believe that an unacknowledged leader is worse than an acknowledged one. If we take the example of the job "president of the world," isn't it worse to have a world president who is informal, than one who at least everyone knows is president?

Clearly. Because if you can't vote, you can't control your leaders. Unelected leaders don't answer to anybody. And in the absence of clear rules, what always happens is informal leaders sprout up and the functioning of things revolves around this informal leadership. This leader might be the most sensitive, but when leadership begins to go to their head (which is very common), it destroys the movement. Perhaps it's better to imagine that when a natural leader sprouts up, they carry out some sort of specific function. And then we must think about the institution, mechanism, or procedure we can put in place to relate to this person and the function they are carrying out. A mechanism that, of course, we decide together.

Toty, MTD la Matanza (an unemployed workers' movement)

Whatever state, in whatever system, there is the opportunity for associations to come together and generate power that would dominate large portions of society. The state continues in distinct forms. For example, in Argentina there is a formal state, which is parliament—that is the government—but there is another informal state, which is the mafia. The mafia dominates the economic sectors through drug trafficking and such things that are absolutely illegal, but still done by those who have real power. They become a new institution, like the corrupt police, the political apparatus, or the *punteros* [party brokers]. They all become a new form of state and generate new policy.

For there to be autonomy, there must be a rupture with the state. It isn't easy, and our being relatively isolated makes the path less easy, but it is possible. We've continued as a movement for all of these years, and never accepted the *planes de trabajo* [state unemployment subsidies]. Of course, you must discard the possibility that you'll have a leadership position and that it'll be the sort of movement where one is recognized and looked up to as a leader with power, being well-known for this power. You must reject the seduction of a system that allows a dominant class to decide your values and principles, and instead, you must build other principles, other values, and a different ethic into the construction. Maybe we don't know how to do this systematically, but we do know it's possible.

First we have to have strength in our rejection of the way things are, to be able to say "enough!" and then have the strength to resist what they may offer us as forms of cooptation, from coercion to seduction.

We're constructing a new power, one that is expressed by creation and the possibility of creating. It seems to me that some of what they can't get rid of is our creative power, especially as it relates to our work and production. These aren't ideas in their terms, but things that are within us—things they can't expropriate in any way. If we are cognizant of this potential, it's very difficult to take it away from us.

We say that in many ways, we're on a voyage. Autonomy of the individual is something we're proud to have experienced. No one can take it from us. Many of us are older now and might not be able to keep up the way we used to, but the young people have begun and they have their whole lives to travel this path. They'll have the option to enter the system, but if they do, they'll do so consciously. Or they'll choose another path. We have no doubt that this alternative path is possible and powerful.

"Horizontalidad, autonomy, direct democracy and struggle."

You don't always advance in a straight line—sometimes you have to step back and pause, in order to demonstrate strength. The Zapatistas recently illustrated this, when *Pagina 12* reported that the autonomous communities are losing ground. The Zapatista subcommander explained that they were not retreating, and that strength was increasing in the autonomous communities. The fact that people don't see this from the outside doesn't mean it isn't happening. With these visions of walking, stepping back, and strength, it seems to me that we use another kind of logic.

We aren't many and we aren't tough, but we have another logic—another way of thinking and constructing thought—and we believe this is the power we have. There's no way to beat us—first, because of this practice of *horizontalidad*. To co-opt a leader, they'd have to co-opt all of us. We all contribute opinions, and work to formulate a common strategy, so we don't depend on the movement—the movement depends on us. To me, that's profoundly revolutionary. The second reason they can't beat us is our life experience. While you can't change everything you do, we still think *autogestión* is a viable path to a different, happier life for our children and the community. We continue to move forward by turning our thoughts into action, and continuing to embrace new challenges.

We have so many ways that we do and see this, from reinventing work, education, and culture so it benefits all of us, to returning to the land. We're always thinking of more ways to create even more community.

It's very powerful when social movements arise as a counterpoint to the strategy of the world's great statesmen. I think this is the threat of today's social movements—movements like the *piqueteros*, Zapatistas, and the Landless Movement in Brazil [*Sem Terra*]. We don't present short-term danger to the government. It's more like fifteen or twenty years, not five years. But the importance isn't the length of time till then, but that everyone is thinking about this relationship.

Paula and Gonzalo, HIJOS (a collective of the children of those disappeared during the dictatorship)

GONZALO: The idea of taking power is a very interesting topic of discussion. When we, HIJOS, talk about taking power, we're speaking of the destruction of the ruling power, the bourgeois power, and the implementation of the power we're creating through struggle. That is the power of the people—a new power, a revolutionary power, people's power.

PAULA: There's an interesting discussion on power taking place now, one that's different from previous conversations and conceptualizations. This is happening, not only in HIJOS, but in the entire movement, particularly in different groups of the unemployed workers' movements. Some of the questions we're asking, for example, are: "Power for what? What kind of power?" These new concepts of power are being discussed everywhere, and it interests me a great deal. What power are we creating? Are we really inverting the pyramid? Might we end up creating a new dominant class? Perhaps we'll come to the same conclusion, but first we must ask ourselves what power is, and what we want to do with it. From there we can create more possibilities within ourselves. For me, the greatest problem isn't taking control of what currently exists; it's creating elements of the future in the present, based on what we desire. The key is to keep asking ourselves, "Why? How? With whom?" If we are going to build a revolution, we can't continue with established formula. It is fundamental that we continuously ask ourselves what it is we want in order to really create power.

Martín K., Asamblea Colegiales (a neighborhood assembly)

What we call power, I believe, is the control of societal production. In feudal-ecclesiastical societies, power passed through the church. In a mercantile society, power is economic. That is one perspective on the concept of power. Now we're living in a time when power is changing forms, and the power that operates as external and coercive begins to bond internally. I'll use the oppression felt in Argentina now to explain this. The feeling is similar to that felt during the dictatorship, without the same repressive apparatus and the disappearances. There's a means of domination that produces oppression and pain similar to that which we experienced thirty years ago, when state repression was massacring people. Now it's happening in another way.

I want to share an anecdote to give a small idea of how to think of power today, how power functions. The other day I was on the subway, and I saw a guy with a tattoo of a series of bars on his back, and it caught my attention—it was like a trademark, a barcode, like identification as a consumer object. I thought about how we live in a consumerist world, and in a sense, that is power—the power the system has to create values based on prestige and individual accumulation. Maybe we're entering this phase of bio-power, where life is organized, regulated, and produced in market terms. In some ways, power today is the feeling that life is about shopping, or about talking about how much money you need to live, always something in relation to the market.

Now in the movements it's different. I believe what we have is another type of power, with the individual at the center—self-empowerment. It's a process of generating relationships outside of material worth. We can look around the world and see people creating along similar lines—in Chiapas, Mexico, or in Brazil's Landless Movement. We might not be able to say that they have of the exact same sense value and ways of placing value on things, but like us, they are working on it together.

I get this feeling through our events in the assembly. We organized a neighborhood street carnival against the upcoming elections, and decided we wouldn't charge for food or drinks. As an assembly, we donated everything to the neighborhood. If people wanted to pay for things they did, but we wanted to be able to give everything for free. What's incredible is that people paid and the assembly got back what we put in, without losing money—the same as if the community was paying for things. We don't do anything as individuals, but as a neighborhood without leaders. Everyone does what they can, participating as they're able. We don't have anyone in any position of authority, looking down on others, and no one feels coerced, like they're part of a manipulative political party. It's a climate of trust.

Think about a way of assigning value based on real worth, not what is accumulated, not on the monetary equivalent. For example, the value of what is produced has to do with the community—it comes from the community—so if the community is better or more contented, that contentment is where the real value exists. An individual is happier in a place where they feel good, in a place where everyone is involved, and this is another kind of power. I like this better than a counter-power. Anti-power or counter-power presupposes the same scenario, no? It's the same with autonomy. The individual is operating under another kind of logic. There's autonomy of diverse heterogeneities and that's power. But it's not a power that's going to fight a battle in the market-power agenda. This is difficult because while there are flashes of what we're doing, they come and go with such a fluid velocity that we can't grab onto them and say, "Here, this is it." On the other hand, I believe that when you grab onto something and say, "this is it," you delegate something, you become passive. And we are creating a more passionate, less passive life.

I believe there's something in what we're doing in the movements that brings about other values. It has to do with love, politics, identity, and with a type of identity that is not individual, but is instead, a singular collective.

Pablo, Asamblea Colegiales (a neighborhood assembly)

In the most elemental sense of the verb, power is being able to do something—particularly in the sense of institutions or instruments of power, so called legitimate instruments of power, such as the state. I don't think that many of us who participated in the movement to reject the state and all its forms, have experimented sufficiently with constructing alternative institutions of power. At the time it was better to say: it isn't important what happens in the state, if Menem wins, whoever wins… That doesn't interest me because I am participating here in this assembly, and we're organizing another form of credible power in the here and now.

Ernesto, Chilavert (a recuperated workplace)

Power is extremely complicated, especially because we're talking about how it comes into play in a specific place. We're now in a society where each person feels the effects of power. There are those who order and those who obey. A minority owns everything and in the end, they have the real power, and we, the poors, work so that this small minority can eat and live. My position reflects the idea that power must be snatched from those who have it. For me, there's only one power, and it must be taken. I tend to look at it from my own ideology: We're in a constant class war. If we don't displace the minority who have power, they'll kill us or at least attack us. They find different ways to attack us—from buying us, to trying to placate us. It's all still an attack, as they try and eliminate us as subversive agents of change. It's the same to shoot you as to buy you. The result is the same in that your subversive function disappears. From this

In front of the government building, where the Madres of the Plaza de Mayo have walked in protest every Thursday since the beginning of the dictatorship. "Thank you Madres, Neither god nor country, self-organization."

point of view, for me, one must create power to displace power, or build a path to power to displace those who have it now.

Carina, Argentine World Social Forum mobilizing committee

We're born into situations where power is delegated. We live and someone else decides things for us: what we eat, how we dress, and what language we speak. We incorporate many things into our lives through socialization. Now there's a vision that's different from the traditional Marxist vision of seizing the power of the bourgeoisie. Even though there's a different vision being discussed, I haven't seen much come of it yet. It's difficult for us to break with all the paradigms we were raised and socialized with. We're accustomed to following a leader and a slogan—they're supposed to give us the reason to live. Power is complex, and I don't have the answer. There are many different ways to think about it. What I notice is a fear in radical power, "Power is bad and so I stay here criticizing those who have power." I don't like that way of thinking.

Emilio, Tierra del Sur (a neighborhood assembly, occupied building, and community center)

I believe that it's clear in the Argentine social movements, that taking control of the state and then forming another government, is not the objective. The Pink House was empty and very accessible during many of the *cacerolazos* and none of us were interested, including the groups of the left. Not even when we were being suppressed or killed, or whatever they did. It didn't occur to anyone. It isn't interesting. It isn't fascinating. It doesn't make sense. It is old. We are building the new in the neighborhoods. I don't know what the things we're creating now will look like in twenty years. We're clear in what we don't want. But the multiplicity of what we want... The quantity of positive things we're constructing is too vast, and doesn't convey all the possibilities we are creating for the future. Given globalization, given our state, given so many things, it's absurd to take state power in Argentina. It's ridiculous to take over a state that's billions of dollars in debt. No, no thank you, I'll pass. Besides, we're creating things that are so different and point us in another direction.

"Zanon is for the people"

We can't see the light at the end of the tunnel, but we know there's a light. We're creating other values. We know that what we're doing goes against vertical and authoritarian logic, the logic of delegation. What we're building is not their opposite. That's interesting to consider—we are not creating the opposite, but are creating something else. We aren't building the opposite to the capitalist system, that's been tried and doesn't work. The opposite doesn't work. We are building something different. What? I don't know. It doesn't have a name and I hope it never has one.

When I feel lost and ask myself "What am I doing?" I look at how I began doing this. First we had to resolve our needs, and resolve them with different tools than what we had. It's almost an unwritten law in the social movements. There are hungry people, people dying, environmental destruction, many things that are really evil, and these are concrete things that must be addressed and resolved. And no, I am not referring to one person resolving it for the others, but rather I'm referring to resolving it ourselves—collectively, as a community, resolving our own problems. And obviously to resolve them with the practices that have helped us resolve many things—direct democracy, *horizontalidad*, *autogestión*, practices that appear exactly to resolve the problems. Then, while we're resolving our day-to-day needs, we try for more. We try for freedom, to be happy, to live fully, for the fulfillment of each person. The capitalist system today doesn't allow us to live life fully as we'd wish, so while we're resolving our basic needs with our new tools, we've also been creating tools to regain our freedom.

repression

Two mothers whose sons were killed by the police in Jujuy, the north of Argentina. The sons and mothers are in the Unemployed Workers' movement.

MOTHER OF JUSTINIANO IBARRA: My name is Principia Ibarra. I'm the mother of Justiniano, who was murdered on the road, after a road blockade.

He left home to participate in the road blockade. They were fighting for wages, because salaries had been lowered again and they couldn't survive if wages were lowered any more. That's what they were thinking, that's what they wanted.

So a group of *compañeros* went to be heard by the government people, and then their bodies showed up in Jujuy, in Yuto. Justiniano left on a Monday, and he still wasn't home on Tuesday. We waited and waited, and on Wednesday at 2:00 in the afternoon, the news on the Jujuy TV station said there had been a traffic accident involving a van. Then my brother-in-law came running in and asked if we knew what had happened. He said our son had been killed in a highway accident in Jujuy. I told him, "That can't be true, it can't be." I couldn't believe it, because he was a young man who didn't go out without telling us where he was going and why... He already had a family and everything... We ran to the *piquete*, where they were blockading the road, and I asked if the TV news was true, if there had been this accident.

They said that around 3:30 or 4:00 in the afternoon, the boys drove the van filled with firewood and tires to Cornejo. None of them stayed with the firewood—they left to go back and support the blockade. Just as the van was leaving, a police truck filled with arrested protesters cut the van off, and there was a crash.

My brother-in-law said it would've been better if they'd walked. He claimed that the driver who brought them said everything happened in Yuto, but they went to Salta and left at 4:30. I thought, "My God how could it be that they were so far?" I had all these thoughts while I ran to get documents, clothes, and everything, and we went to the Yuto police station. Just as we got there my friend, Gómez's mother, arrived. She already knew they were dead. I was the only one who didn't know anything.

When I got there, the police began to tell me their version of what happened. They said that there had been an accident. An official took my statement. He asked me how my son was dressed, and I told him he was wearing cowboy pants, brown boots. I told him the colors of his clothes, everything. The official told me that my son was one of the victims and asked if his name was Justiniano, and if I could go and identify my son's body.

We then went to the clinic in Ledesma, and into the morgue so we could identify the bodies. I went in and the first thing I saw was a covered body on a table. I went up close, turned his face, and saw he wasn't my son. It was Gómez. I took hold of his hands and began to notice he was missing fingernails—this one wasn't there and this one was...the middle fingers were missing the nails. I covered him up again. I went to the other table and saw my son. I began to look at him carefully. I opened the bag—he was in a black bag—and I began to look. I looked at his mouth, his eyes, his nose, his head. I touched him all over because the Yuto police official told me that he was a bag of broken bones; that both of their bodies were in tatters. He said that the van had rolled over three times, that on impact the bodies were thrown on the road, and they were all shredded—the bodies were torn to shreds. He said the firemen put them in bags and brought everything, all that belonged to them. If this is true, how did he lose fingernails in a traffic accident?

He told me they had a witness to all of this. First, he told me that it was a garbage truck that came just when the van turned over three times. Later he told me it was a water truck and that the driver had seen the whole accident. So already there was something he was lying about. The guy was going overboard with me. I knew he'd been lying from the beginning, because when I went to Ledesma to identify my son, I looked carefully at everything. His leg had been burned—small burns. I saw his mouth, his ears. I cleaned his face and looked at his entire body. I had uncovered him and I understood that it wasn't really like they said. It wasn't a traffic accident, and I said, "This is a murder. This has nothing to do with a traffic accident." Later, a police diagnostician came and said that blood had collected in his mouth, ears, and nose, but I said, "No, he has suffered blows, and that's what all the blood was from."

And this was much worse because it was murder, not a traffic accident. Because of how he looked, and everything the official had said: that the witness was in a garbage truck, then it was a water truck, that it was before the accident, then during the accident, and the driver said something else. So I didn't trust him. I knew that he was lying. Worse, when I identified my son's body, when I examined his body, I understood that the police had murdered both of them, had tortured them. They'd suffered torture.

MOTHER OF ALEJANDRO GÓMEZ: I am the mother of Alejandro Matías Gómez, who died from the repression of General Enrique Mosconi, on Route 34.

On Monday, the people who'd been arrested on the *piquete* were brought in a truck to Salta. My husband called me and told me to come. The police refused to let me go get them (including my son) out of there that morning. I went with my sister and my older son, and the police told us that there'd been a traffic accident. But when I saw how their bodies were, the condition they were in, I understood immediately it had not been a traffic accident. They had been murdered. The official asked me if I recognized my son. He told me to identify him and take him home with me. As a mother, I wanted to bring my son home, but I left him in the morgue eleven days, because I wanted them to do an autopsy. They refused. They sent me to Dr. Cheer, to Dr. Aramayo, and to the judge, but no one would listen. I even went to the prosecutor there, but he wouldn't help me.

Mother fighting for justice for her murdered son.

Assistant Governor Guayar had already made an announcement about the van and the truck bringing the arrested protestors to Salta. The truck arrived, but not the van. The truth was that those in the van weren't being arrested and being taken to Salta… They were kidnapped, tortured, and murdered. My son died on the 10th. If, as the police say, there was no delay in his release, and they freed all of them after midnight, as they say, how did the accident happen at 11:30? I also heard that they didn't die at the time they say, but that they died at 7:45 in the evening, and then they brought their dead bodies to throw out in Yuto. I know this from the marks they had—one pupil more dilated than the other, his mouth open pleading for help, the mark of the bag on his neck, the marks of the handcuffs on his wrists. I know this because my father was with the police, and for six years I worked with lawyers in San Nicolás. I'm good at making these assessments. All I ask is justice, and for everything to be cleared up according to justice.

This proof I'm presenting now is a recording from day eight of the *piquete*. It's the last time I heard my son's voice. He is asking Commander Hidalgo to not punish them, to not repress them. Let's see if President Kirchner, when he hears this recording, will give us the courtesy of an audience so that we can explain to him in person, as mothers, what happened. Hopefully, the same thing that happened in Gran Bourg will not happen again, when we waited from 9:00 in the morning until 10:00 at night, and they just closed the door in our faces, calling us crazy old women. I know we aren't crazy. The Mothers of the Plaza de Mayo investigated, as did we, and they support us. We're going to keep at it.

Recorded radio interview with commentator and Alejandro Gómez, just hours before his death.

VOICE OF RADIO COMMENTATOR: How are you doing?

VOICE OF ALEJANDRO GÓMEZ: We're doing badly, because we understand that the police have gone to clear the blockade in Cornejo. That's where the truckers have also made a symbolic road blockade. We helped them to block it with trucks, vans, and all kinds of little vehicles. This is on Cornejo road. It's shut down—200 or 300 meters farther than Olmo Road.

First, two police officers came, saying that if the road wasn't cleared… They said they came as volunteers to talk with us, and later it would end with General Mosconi. I came here, on the radio, to try to get people to go to the blockade to help. We have information that the police are on the way with highly-armed military police—with rubber bullets, tear gas, enough to punish many people. The latest news we have is that they are at the station. It took so much to get the work subsidies that we have, so if people are working—if you're listening to the radio now—drop everything and go take care of your *compañeros*, because there are many *compañeros*. They're your sons, your sisters. Everyone is at the blockade, and all we're asking is for you to go and help the people.

We will wait for you there. That's all. And I ask Commander Hidalgo that, if he has a family, to put himself in our place and try to hold off, to wait a few more days before repressing us. That's it. Thank you.

Neka and Alberto, MTD Solano (an unemployed workers' movement)

The government is attempting to criminalize protests of all kinds. This is a strong statement that reflects new forms of institutionalized repression aimed at ending political action and countering new strategies of resistance, such as occupations. Part of the government's current strategy is to achieve a social consensus and alienate the movements. This is a reaction, in particular, to sectors of society that are working to become more autonomous. These sectors are their new concern. The government is trying to placate people in order to annihilate all types of struggles and movements. In my opinion, that's the current form of repression.

When institutional forces assassinate *compañeros* in the streets, the conflict is clearly with the state, the repressive forces, and the institutions. For example, when they exert direct violence, like the *compañeras* who just left talked about, the conflict is very clear. Now, what they're doing is subtler, they come around and try to buy off *compañeros*, and try to infiltrate the movement. People's anger becomes focused elsewhere, away from them. The *compañera* just now mentioned that there was a lot of resentment against the *compañeros* who sold out and tried to co-opt our movement. I think that each of the different types of repression affect the movement—and our relationships within the movement—in unique ways. This new type of repression also causes different emotional reactions than direct state repression. Maybe we don't feel the same kind of sorrow that you feel for a murdered *compañero*, but there's a pain and loss of trust that one feels because of infiltration and dirty work. They are different experiences, but each experience causes us to reflect, evaluate, and reconstruct ourselves, and pushes us to continue moving forward.

We've suffered from different types of repression. For example, they have assassinated *compañeros*, they have burnt down *compañeros*' houses. There was a more physical hand-to-hand confrontation right here in the neighborhood. In the current context, I think the repression is much more subtle. There's been a sort of fine-tuning towards a much stronger form of social control, which you can see in the attempts to regenerate the society's trust, so that people will stop struggling and building the movement.

If we look a little closer and examine different provinces, there's actually been an increase in militarization. Examples can be seen in the provinces of Salta and Misiones, in the border regions, and also in some neighborhoods. I believe that the government has been able to install military control in different provinces by promoting and playing off of a media-generated message of insecurity and fear. Where we live, for example, we now notice more police, and many more repressive forces stationed in more locations than ever before. At other times, they were more concentrated in the streets, and were a stronger and more brutal confrontational force. Now they're in very strategic places, like on the trains going in and out of the poorer neighborhoods.

Gisela, Elipsis-Video (an independent documentary group)

These are very difficult times. About a month ago, the police began to violently evict people from all sorts of places, including their homes and popular assembly meeting halls. There are still many eviction orders pending. This happened recently at Padelai, a self-organized childcare and family center, where more than 160 families lived. All of the residents were violently evicted and thrown out into the streets. Now people are organizing constant watches of the occupied, self-organized places to resist potential evictions.

The elections are the primary reason that so many of these eviction orders are being carried out. No politician wants popular assemblies—groups that could hurt their campaign—to meet. Therefore, if you receive an eviction notice, it's because the government wants to wipe out all types of meetings where there are large numbers of people with new and innovative ideas. In fact, law prohibits public meetings the weekend before and the day of elections. I don't believe that they'll be able to prevent such gatherings during this election.

Mario, Unemployed Workers Union, Mosconi, Salta (an unemployed workers' movement)

During the last few days that we've been in Buenos Aires, we've asked for our ten imprisoned *compañeros* to be freed. They've been in jail for more than thirty days, and so far, there's been no evidence presented or formal charges made. The only reason we can come up with for why they are still being detained is that they're working with social movements, and that we're protesting against the national and local governments. To date, we unfortunately haven't received any response from the courts, the executive branch, or from representatives of congress.

The root of our problems is that in the 1990s, the government began a policy of privatization and started turning over all of the state's national businesses to private corporations. This is especially true in the case of YPF [a petroleum company] in the energy sector. In the San Martin region, 90 percent of the population, or around 150,000 people, work for the YPF. We were stripped of everything we had without any kind of prior consultation from the authorities. There was no discussion about the social effects. We were evicted and thrown out onto the streets like trash. Unfortunately, despite all of the work fighting against the evictions, especially in 1986 and 1987, the privatization policy came into effect in 1991. This was totally contrary to public opinion. On top of all of this, the debt from the previously state-owned company got passed on to the ex-workers of the company—those that were laid off. The company had a debt of $560 billion, and now it's said that it's the workers' debt.

We believe that we have a deficit of work. We don't have any. Everyone is unemployed, and there hasn't been any assistance for unemployed workers to reenter the workforce through any of these newly-privatized businesses.

We've been plunged into this social crisis, and what makes it worse is that the now-privatized company continues to plunder our natural resources, especially in the San Martin area of Salta. This area has the second largest gas reserve in the country, and the third largest hydrocarbon reserve in South America. Lamentably, the legal decree, number 546 of the Nation, by current president Kirchner, gave away local ownership of hydrocarbons. [This law takes the provinces' rights to resources and allows them to be privatized.] This is another reason why we condemn and oppose these privatization policies.

The YPF hasn't responded to our concerns about the people who have been jailed or other critical social issues. People are dying at earlier ages. For example, in our region, the average life expectancy is fifty-eight years old. One of the reasons that people are dying younger is that the water we drink isn't potable. There are serious environmental problems in the region and the province, due to the well-known fact that these petroleum companies burn gas fumes. This is causing serious problems. I have petitions here that propose different possibilities.

Although we're rich in resources, we're completely unprotected. The region of San Martin generates 75 percent of the gross domestic product of the province. It turns out that we're one of the provinces with the richest resources in the country, but unfortunately our people are suffering from the worst poverty I've ever seen. In this region so rich in natural resources, we haven't had any response or support from anyone at any level of government over the last fifteen years.

Claudia, lavaca.org (an alternative media collective)

We need to talk about impunity. For example, a woman who was the leader of a prostitutes' union in Rosario was killed this week. We're talking about things that we aren't supposed to see. This kind of repression is like guerrilla warfare—it strikes and then disappears. Every month there are episodes of violence, tear gas, arrests, or attempted murders. I think that it is important to be very conscious that all of these little battles are strategic. None of these violent repressions are small isolated events or just anecdotal—they are truly deep fights. They are tests to see how deeply they can sink in the knife, in order to take one person or the whole movement down. I think this is important to understand. However, also be aware that all the movements that are facing the most repression (in one way or another) are the smallest ones—they are the ones who are not pontificating about taking power through armed struggle. This is proof that what is truly revolutionary, and what therefore worries those in power the most, is not a group that says, "I'm going to take a lead pipe and go take over the government building," but it is those who are working for power block by block. It's clear that daily repression is also happening block by block, each and every day.

Nothing stifles creativity as much as fear. We have a saying, "When you're scared you can't even play the game." You're so scared about how things will turn out, you can't do anything. A scared person doesn't even leave their house because they're worried about what others will think. It can be the most frivolous things. In the midst of everything else, even facing death, there's the fear of losing yourself, putting your foot in your mouth, not knowing who you're really working for. There are all of these nagging fears. If you do something, you're worried about what others will think, or that they're going to come after you. Because of all these fears, you become less spontaneous in some ways. I think that any kind of propaganda, which plays off fear—whether used by the left- or right-wing, coming from within the system, or from those supposedly against the system—this kind of fear is just as harmful to our new movements. Fear conspires against any possibility for change, because people start to believe that things can't improve. Of course there's a real possibility that threats will be carried out, so sometimes the fear is justified. Without a doubt, the system has the advantage because it has the criminal justice system, police, colleges, and access to the media. It has a mountain of tools to use so that fear doesn't remain just a threat, but becomes something concrete. It becomes a part of your life—it marks you, leaves a wound, you see?

The left-wing parties might not have the same political power. I understand that there's a difference between the right and the left, but they're the same with regards to political creativity. Therefore it's necessary right now to be able to somehow construct another way for the people—not only to fulfill their desires and dreams, but also work to change their realities. I think that in order to achieve this creativity, we must become more clear and focused, and eliminate all of this white noise and distraction about fear from our speech and communication. Fear is something very concrete here, because the police are on every corner—but there is also a "police of the left," those who have very closed minded opinions about how people should be.

Daniela, MTD Almirante Brown (an unemployed workers' movement)

It's very difficult to talk about repression here in this neighborhood, because repression is obviously something very complicated and also something people are scared to talk about. This was demonstrated on June 26th, when we lost a *compañero* who was very close to us in our neighborhood. People were left immobilized. The police killed him. There are photographs and everything.

"In memory of the compañero Dario Santillan assassinated by the police of Duhalde on the bridge of Pueyrredon 10 months ago."

Kids around Dario Santillan's memorial in the MTD Almirante Brown.

We try to focus on the neighborhood level more than anything, because it's very difficult for people to mobilize on a larger scale. We keep trying to work on this level, so we don't lose the benefits of organizing. The government is very scared of us when we organize—when we join together and think about what we are going to do in the future. We'll try not to lose all this. We don't want to lose this organization.

Ariel, Partido Obrero (Trotskyist Party)

Why is there repression? Well, the state represses an organization and makes an example of it, not only for the sake of stopping that organization, but also so that the masses of people in the street and the rest of society understands the danger they face in organizing within this repressive context. In Argentina, there are 20-million poor people. Imagine if one million of them got organized and went out to demand unemployment benefits. Imagine all the government representatives were fired, and that a governing assembly, made up of all of the organizations in the struggle, took power. They could organize a strike until the government stopped paying its foreign debt, for example. They could even get rid of Kirchner, Duhalde, all of these sons of bitches... Well, it would be a huge qualitative change, right?

We, the people of Argentina, sometimes pay too much attention to the superficial. Sometimes we're not very observant when we're standing over a bubbling volcano. It's quite possible we're in a pre-revolutionary situation, which doesn't necessarily mean we have a fatalistic perspective, but that destiny assures that we will reach our goal—class war. It's a struggle that we could win or lose. Today, there are many social sectors in Argentina in which people are fighting to transform our society and bring about measurable change once and for all. I think that's what socialism is all about.

Compañera, MTD Allen (an unemployed workers' movement)

This is a warning to the government. There's a new society that's being formed, with different values. There can't be change, the government can't move forward, because this new society will destroy them. At any moment—I don't know when, but sometime—there's going to be a very strong fight against the government. It will be a strong fight because we'll keep advancing. However, there'll be a moment when they say, "We'll only allow change to happen up to this point, no more. We won't allow the people to advance any farther." What's going to happen then? We're not sure, but I think that at some point, it'll come to this. Right now, the government is trying to get us to agree to stop blocking streets, and there's a new law against blockades. It's like the government directly saying, "You don't have the right to protest."

The heart of the matter is that the new society being formed is a different kind of social group, with completely different values. I think that's what worries them the most.

Paula, feminist and GLTTB collectives

Repression within a capitalist system, as we all know, can be economic as well as political. The eviction of popular assemblies represents both of these types of repression. On the one hand, the government is taking back the buildings that the assemblies had taken, which are private property. The neighborhood assembly, Cid Campeador, even took over the Mayo Bank. A bank! Can you imagine a better symbol of capitalism? So, on the one hand there's this: under capitalism, the law must protect private property, and this law must not be broken. On the other hand, this is political repression, since people were using the space for an assembly, in order to create new forms of doing politics.

Mural depicting Mothers of the Plaza de Mayo confronting the police.

Capitalism does allow for some political play, in regards to the representation of the bourgeois through the political parties. Anything that's outside of this kind of politics is a threat to capitalism. For example, I don't think that any government, no matter how right-wing it is, wouldn't support the Workers' Party participating in elections. I think that this is part of the accepted political game. Now, an assembly is a very different thing, because there is no institutionalized control mechanism. Therefore, this is something new and threatening. According to the government and the state, in general, the MTDs are a big threat. The unions in Argentina maintain a disciplinary control over the working class. It's been years since there has been a general strike in Argentina. However, the MTDs are different. MTDs block streets, argue about politics, propose a different kind of society, and the MTDs are based in very marginalized and poor zones. They really are a threat.

Christian, Attac Autónomo (an anti-capitalist collective)

Look, no matter how many acts of repression the government commits, the people aren't going to quit. Never. That's part of what gives us more strength to keep struggling. If we, as an organization, a collective, and also as individuals...if our struggle was having no effect on the system, they wouldn't be repressing, threatening, or persecuting us, right? This is the other side of all of this bullshit—the fact that our struggle is generating change. Those in power don't want change to happen. Do you understand? People start to act from where they're at. At first, perhaps they don't really struggle very hard, or they have a certain way of struggling, but don't yet have a larger vision, or don't know exactly how to make change, or why. Later, learning from the experiences of the *compañeros* who are here, they take this vision back to where they're from, and this helps them to get more active. That's how learning happens, right? Sometimes I say, "Wow, that's crazy!" about how we are able to have an influence on someone else.

Neka, MTD Solano (an unemployed workers' movement)

Repression and dictatorship with physical "disappearance" and annihilation have a strong history in our culture. I think that destruction, murder, and crime play out in different ways in life. When they erase the possibility of thinking, producing, and creating, I think they're also destroying and annihilating people. One of the strongest ruptures from those times is resisting that erasure, and I suggest that we must be creatively facing the present-day criminalization of resistance.

I think the path of dictatorship and crime are continuing in other forms—with other faces, but continuing nevertheless. I believe that all the institutions are in the service of its continuing. Resistance has to do with this, and the criminalization of resistance also has to do with this. For example, the media campaigns intended to isolate people—first to identify people, and then to isolate and demonize the movements of people who are resisting. It is a very powerful weapon in times of criminalization. To back up this criminalization, there's the whole judicial and legal system. For example, there are new laws proclaiming which types of actions are permitted and which are forbidden. From our point of view, many of the laws prohibit legitimate action. Sometimes it's necessary to break a law and block a street in order to defend something that's rightfully yours. This could be your work, your right to life, health, education, or the right to be able to create these necessities and run them autonomously. More than just the right, we must have the possibility to be able to create things—like through this group—but these types of actions are being criminalized through laws.

Perhaps the question I'd ask is, "Is it inherently dangerous to resist in order to radically transform this society?" I think that's the key question. When they attempt to criminalize, persecute, and disappear people, I think it has to do with this question: "To what degree are you a danger to the system and its plans and designs?"

Gabriel, Ava Guaraní Community (an indigenous community)

The eviction happened on September 16, 2003, around noon. First, a security guard from the company and a policeman from the provincial outpost came to survey the community, then left. At the time, there were around 170 of us indigenous people who were working in the fields, on our land.

That night, they became Rambo-types, and handcuffed all of us as if we were animals. They shoved us like we were mules and threw us to the ground. They hit us and fired shots in the air, and they tortured some people. Those who escaped notified the neighboring villages and the media. That's what happened.

Ah, the company? Well, they use very advanced mechanisms for their personal benefit and to directly line their pockets. They indiscriminately clear-cut thousands and thousands of hectares of land, they kill off nature—armadillos, wild peacocks, iguanas. They kill off everything that lives in the mountains, and in many cases the indigenous people live off of these animals. Not only do they kill the forests, but they also kill all of the animals. This is all for their own benefit, because there's no longer any work on the plantations, since there are only machines doing the work. The company doesn't generate jobs, because the machines are doing all of the work.

So who benefits? The company can employ just eight or ten people for a job that a hundred people used to do, and they're just short-term jobs of one or two months. The workers have to wait almost a whole year just to work one or two months. Meanwhile, the land is being completely destroyed. The companies leave behind pollution. They contaminate all of the rivers, and this affects the fish. How are people going to fish? Only hunger goes fishing, because the people bring hunger to the river, and leave just with their hunger and no fish. This pains us. The businesspeople and the "democratic" governor we have in Salta are selfish and egotistical. Why won't they return our lands to us? The land is ours. It contains our ancient cemetery as proof. But they are the authorities, and they are arrogant and overbearing. What do they know? They use the police for their personal benefit, to repress us, to subjugate us.

Group of compañeras, MTD San Telmo (an unemployed workers' movement)

COMPAÑERA 1: They feel threatened because we really want to advance through doing things for ourselves. What they want is to give things to us, but only what they want to give. Aye! I can't talk about the government.

COMPAÑERA 2: I don't know if they see themselves as threatened by us, because really all that we want is good things for our children. What we want is a better future, a future better than what we had. I don't want my children to be hungry from one day to the next. I don't want them to have to stop going to school because they have to work.

It seems like the government likes to exploit us, and we need to struggle to get the most we can. You quickly understand that we're either with them or against them. I prefer to be as I am, not with them. Even though, if you look around, you can see that those who are close to the government have money from one day to the next, I still choose not to work with them. I often used to get up and not even have enough to get bread for my children. But, with government... I'm twenty-six, and it never interested me to work with the government. This government doesn't interest me.

It also seems like they like it when we have to ask them for things, to relate to them in that way. But when we do go and ask for things nicely—like they want—they refuse to hear us. So we have to go out in the street and shut it down. Make *piquetes*. Cause disruption, "*quilombo*," as they say, so that we can have a bit of dignity for our children. I don't know, that's what I think. I can't speak for my *compañeras*. What I do feel is the true though, is that we have to get into the middle of things to get anything from the government. If not, they just toss us poor people aside. We have to get in there and fight for what we need.

COMPAÑERA 3: We all got together, all of us *compañeros*, and agreed that we should take over a space. When we did, there weren't that many of us, but we knew we would need a big space for when we began the popular kitchen. The place we chose had been abandoned for years, and the idea was to open it and use it as a popular kitchen, as well as a space for the children. It seemed wonderful. Most of us live in hotels with our children, so there's never any space for them to play or study. So we decided all together to take over this place.

We were only inside twenty-five days when the police came and surprised us with a violent eviction. They came really early in the morning, without a warrant, and threw all of us onto the floor. The children were all there, crying and asking why we all had to be on the floor. They held us all at gunpoint. At one point, they tried to separate us from the children, but we said no, and refused to leave the kids. They held me and all the kids at gunpoint—like I was going to assault them or something. While this was happening, even more police were coming in, entering through the windows and every other opening. It was like ants coming in from all directions.

And, well, I couldn't do anything and felt awful because of that. I wanted to call for help on the phone, but they had cut the wire. I was left without communication. Then I saw a few *compañeros* in the garden and began to communicate what was happening. I kept asking the police to please let me take the kids out because they were so upset, but they refused. It was at this time that all of the *compañeros* began to arrive. In the end, there were four compañeras detained and taken to the police station. I felt so powerless, because I was just looking after the children. It was crazy, them treating us as if we were dangerous criminals, when all we want is to do something good for the kids; give them things they need, like a plate of food and glass of milk. I felt so bad. To the police and the government what we were doing was nothing, but for us it was really valiant.

COMPAÑERO 2: I now agree with the *compañera* that they feel threatened by us. We're a small group and we're unemployed, but what we're doing is questioning all of this by what we're constructing. Right now, really, we're not threatening them much, but they still don't want us to organize. They know that if we organize together we'll have more strength.

Carlos G., Zanon (an occupied factory)

Here, in this conflict, we've always been attacked. Always. We've had five eviction orders and eviction attempts, and we got rid of each one through organizing the support of the community and movement. Each time they tried to evict us, there were 270 of us inside the factory, and within half an hour, a thousand people had gathered outside. There was no way the factory would be evicted. The factory belongs to everyone, like we always say.

It really takes a lot to resist all of these eviction orders, especially when there's no specific date. One of the things that we organized was a caravan, which we called the National Caravan in Support of the Factory. We made different sorts of flyers explaining the occupation [showing flyers]—like this one that shows a big event we put on, and this one that was for the community to explain what "under worker control" means, and this which was for an action that we did on the 29th of June inside the factory, where different social sectors from all over the country came to show us support and unite against the potential eviction. We went all over with these different pamphlets. This one says, "Defend Genuine Work—No to the Eviction of Zanon."

This is how we organized. And more, before the threat of a recent eviction, we announced on our radio program that our struggle is one that radiates outward, and we asked everyone to come out to the factory on Tuesday. From there, others took up the call for everyone to come out to the factory on Tuesday, and it became a huge movement. Indymedia wrote to us to tell us that, apart from the demonstration here in Neuquen, there were cyber demonstrations where over 7,000 people participated, showing support for the workers of Zanon. Thousands of people visited their site to see what was going on with us. The solidarity was impressive. Apart from the media, there were people from countries all over the world coming to visit us and show support—from independent journalists to all sorts of people. There were people here from Mexico, Germany, Switzerland, Spain, England, Sweden... There were at least eight countries represented, and all to report on and support the Zanon's workers.

The chief of police here in Neuquen was using all sorts of intelligence against us in the factory, including tapping our phones. Because of this, they had a good idea of what we were doing, and they also knew about all the support we were getting inside and outside the factory. It was this that made them decide not to evict us this time. They knew that they couldn't do it because of the support we have. They didn't try to bring even one uniformed cop near the plant. The police that were brought in to help the local police evict us went back to Buenos Aires.

We all felt such an amazing feeling of euphoria, because we had won. In many ways, each step that we take gives us this—gives happiness to each one of us. It makes us jump for joy, really, together we were all literally jumping. When the judge said there wasn't going to be an eviction, we were all jumping together with such happiness that you could feel the life of our joy as a physical sensation. This all happened on Tuesday, and by Wednesday we were all working again, because the idea of all of this is to work, and we are working. And well, to this day we continue working and bringing Zanon under worker control forward.

At the feet of a policeman, the daughter of a jailed *piquetero* holds a sign asking for her dad's release.

"Today is exactly three months since we have been deprived of our freedom," Elsa said on December 31, 2004. At the time of the interview Elsa, Selva, and Marcela are in jail for participating in a protest. This interview was done inside the jail by lavaca.org.

ELSA: I'm one of the people who was detained for demonstrating against the municipal government. We were petitioning for work, genuine work. We were out in front of the municipal building for eight days without any type of response from either local or national government. The only thing that they said to us was that the only way we could get work was to go to the company and ask for it. So that's what we did. 250 *compañeros* went to Termap and waited there—non-violently, because at no moment were we going to start any type of violence, break anything, or confront anyone.

It was there that we had to face the army, which the government used to try to make us leave. They prevented people from bringing us food and warm clothes while we waited. Then the security guards from Termap soaked us with water hoses. All 250 of us were drenched from head to toe. We were there until the next day, when they permitted our families and friends to bring us food and dry clothes. Our friends and families were the ones who ended up suffering the worst repression from the army. It wasn't the 250 of us demonstrating, but the group that came to show us solidarity. They beat them, kicked them on the ground, and did horrible things to them. Really, the repression against them was much more intense. It looked like a pitched battle.

MARCELA: I receive the little bit of government subsidy (that was won by the movements), and have for seven years, but I don't want to. I want genuine work and for the subsidies to no longer exist. I have six children. One of them is nine years old and has been in school four years, which costs a lot. Every day, it seems like things get more expensive, and we keep having to give up important things. We live far from downtown, which makes things really difficult. I also help my family a lot since my siblings are unemployed too. All of these things have pushed me to organize.

SELVA: I went out to protest because I couldn't pay for my son's studies anymore. I went out because my son couldn't play sports anymore, because I couldn't afford the shoes. I went out because I don't have enough money to put bread on the table at the end of the month. In times like these, I end up giving my son a glass of tea without milk, instead of food.

My kids have a skin disease that sometimes makes us choose between buying medicine for their skin or food.

SELVA: In the jail, there are all sorts of rules for people visiting. Visits mean nothing to the jailers. This even includes children visiting. They strip them before they can enter the jail. They take off their clothes in front of people that aren't their mother or father. I said to my husband that if they're going to take off our children's clothes in order for them to see me, then I'd prefer they didn't visit. All these years we've tried to do the best for them, to take care of them physically and psychologically, especially now as they try and push us over the edge. Bettering the conditions of the visits and the prisons was one of our demands of the hunger strike.

MARCELA: From the beginning, when they first detained us, I have considered us political prisoners. We're not social prisoners, as some people claim, because social prisoners are in jail for things like stealing, so they can eat. We're political prisoners, because we went out to demonstrate and demand things from the government. We're political prisoners because we went against their model. We went out to protest against their model of politics that doesn't give work to anyone, and the only thing it gives you is a small subsidy and a bag of food.

Madres of the Plaza de Mayo participate in a protest.
"The lack of work is a crime."

ELSA: We're political prisoners for standing up for the clear right to not be put in tiny rooms of two-by-two where they say, "Here, be silent." Today, the politics of this country doesn't like it if you demand things. There's no way that this government can say that we're moving forward in Argentina when we have 250 families that are dying of hunger. Let's be real. They can't say everything is going well with their negotiations with the multinationals, when the multinationals are taking all that's left of our natural resources.

MARCELA: We're in jail by chance. It could've been anyone. If we'd been getting by, then they would've arrested other *compañeros*. It wouldn't have been us. It's gotten to the point that if a person goes out just to demand some bread, they're considered an instigator. Do you know there are people in jail for the same thing we are, but they weren't even out protesting that day? And yet they are in jail.

women

Daniela, Marta, and Ariel, MTD Almirante Brown (an unemployed workers' movement)

DANIELA: Historically, women have been subjugated by the system, as well as by society, in general. Now there's a change in the movements, and women are more and more the protagonists. Women play a leading role in the movement, and really have from the beginning. They were the ones to first initiate the movements. The movements were born from women. The husband stayed home depressed and the woman went out to get food for her children. For all of their lives men had the role of going out and fighting for food, and when they suddenly had no work, they got depressed. So women went out to fight. Women made up the movement, make up the movements, and really are the stars. Later they brought in their husbands. For example it was Turu's [Ariel's] mother who brought him into the movement. This is an example of how things can happen when women begin to be recognized in the family, they begin to bring in their sons and husbands.

I believe women have a very important role here—of course men do as well, but the role of women is fundamental. There are many things we have to do. What's at stake isn't only our own lives, but our children's and the entire family's, and that is very important.

ARIEL: Yes, it's true. When a man is unemployed and he goes out and looks for work—odd jobs, looking for whatever resources he can find—and doesn't find anything, well, after some time he gets depressed. Even if he says he'll do whatever odd job, like cut the grass or some other dead-end job...

Women were the first to go out in the street and fight. It's women who began the movement. They still maintain this initiative. For example, sometimes in the assemblies we feel like we can't do much, or maybe it's a cloudy day, or there are fewer people in a particular work group, and some of us feel like things cannot be done...it's the women who are there, reminding us that we have to work. We have to do it because we need this or that... And it's the women who come whether or not it's raining. They come and cook for the popular kitchen whatever the weather, because it's necessary. Women suffer more when our children don't have anything to eat. At the end of the day, when the kids are hungry they ask mommy: "Mama, give me some bread. Mama, give me this." Not the father. The father comes home, watches a little television, and goes to sleep, but the women see the hunger in this neighborhood, in every neighborhood, and what happens is profound. It touches the women first.

DANIELA: What these organizations give to women is so important. The system makes us submissive and unaware of our own power, especially the young women. We are taught that our role is to be in the house, in charge of the kitchen and the babies. We're told our role is as a non-thinking housewife, without opinions. In our movements, in these organizations, women begin to acquire other roles, begin to have a voice and express what they feel. I believe things are changing, changing on the level of everyday life. A woman who is a *compañera* of the MTD is not the same as a woman outside of the organization, and others are going to notice the differences.

It seems to me that in Argentina there were organizations—for example, in the 1970s—which were composed completely of men, and women didn't participate very much in the struggle. They went along, but weren't really involved; they didn't participate. And now it's really powerful, both women and men in the movement are more free to

Zapatista woman

express what they feel. I believe this is something extremely new. You go to movements now and they're full of women. There are men too, of course, but the majority are women, and they go out to fight, and are deeply respected. Women feel good, as well, because we're somewhere where we can express ourselves—where we can say what we feel. It's so great to have such a place.

ARIEL: In my house, before, I would come home from work and find everything ready, my meal was on time, my clothes clean—I took a shower and everything was prepared. Now when I get home I don't have any of this [laughs]. Sometimes I get home and my *compañera* says, "Oh good, you're here. I have to go out." My wife is in another MTD, in the Don Orione neighborhood. I go there a lot to support the work of the movement, but I grew up in this neighborhood, Cerrito, which is where I joined the movement. I've lived here for twenty-six years and only lived in Don Orione, where my wife is a militant, for five. Sometimes I get home and she says, "I'm off now. I'm going to work in the popular kitchen." Or I might want to go out in the morning, but instead I have to stay in and watch the kids. Maybe while I'm with the kids, I notice that there are clothes that have to be washed, and I may pitch in and do some because I understand that it's important that she is participating in the popular kitchen. I may also go to our movement bakery to make donuts, because tomorrow there's an activity where we can sell the donuts to help fund the popular kitchen. There are all sorts of activities that we share now that we never did before, and so many things we now do together. For example, Tuesdays are the inter-neighborhood assemblies, and if it's my turn to fetch the children from school, but I also want to participate in the assembly, she might get the kids. Or the other day, I was in a meeting at the kids' school, which I hadn't done before because she used to be in charge of that. Now I go to the school meetings because my wife works in the popular kitchen. I do so many things now that I didn't do before. I used to come home and ask, "how did the kids do in school today?" because knowing that was her job. Now I'm a part of it and am much happier. She is also happier, which makes me happier.

Claudia, lavaca.org (an alternative media collective), Paula, feminist and GLTTB collectives, Mabel, Asamblea Palermo, Neka, MTD Solano (an unemployed workers' movement)

NEKA: Since the movement began eight years ago, I've reflected a lot on my situation as a woman in relationship to both my *compañeras* and *compañeros*. In the beginning, the movement was 90 percent women, but now—though we're still the majority—there are many more men participating. We've begun to collectively reflect more on the role of women in the movement, and have noticed that there aren't always empowering places for women, even though we're building a new and totally different subjectivity. This is something we're paying a lot of attention to now, so we can change it.

We came from an experience of submission—not only in the home with our partners and families, but also at work, in the neighborhood with the politics of clientalism, and in situations of sexual abuse and domestic violence. As we organized in the neighborhood, we saw more and more need to reflect on all of this.

Today we're beginning to come together in groups, not with the whole MTD, but within it. We're searching for what it means that we sometimes remain in relationships of domination, though we're also making such changes in our social relationships and creating new subjectivities. I'm not talking about relationships with men or children, or thinking about sexual differences, but a stronger question—a more integral reflection on all areas of life from the woman's viewpoint. In the movement, we discuss and search together from a basis of confidence and trust. This is key to our social creation and has been developed over the years together in the movement.

With regard to issues such as abortion, sexual abuse, and rape, I believe that in these neighborhoods—at least in Solano, where we live— these experiences are deeply connected with the idea of death. Most of us come from other provinces where the culture is very traditional, especially with regard to politics and religion, and often ideas that are sometimes very backward become ingrained in us. These ideas are combined with a great many other things, such as guilt and the idea of sin, and this again relates to the idea of death. We spoke about this in a workshop on women at the *Enero Autónomo* gathering—this question of the legality of abortion in our neighborhoods—and we grounded the question in the need to understand how these situations are experienced and their root in how we feel physically and psychologically. Among us, there's no movement per se for abortion services, but we're interested in the topic of what is illegal and what is humane. We're fighting with the state, with a system of domination and authority that decides whether or not you can have an abortion—a system in which you're an instrument, a tool, an accessory.

There are many other questions—many profound questions—but for us this whole conversation is a step, a change from how we lived our lives before, and we are confident that we can be different in the future.

CLAUDIA: What Neka says is very interesting and it's also what I hear a lot in different neighborhoods—that they're not interested in legalization. When it comes to abortion, only the feminist movement wants to legalize it, and there hasn't been even the tiniest bit of progress in that direction in the law.

MABEL: But it's being discussed within the women's movements—the idea of de-criminalization and legalization, and it is much more inclusive to speak of free abortion, than de-criminalization and exclusion.

CLAUDIA: When I was at a workshop on de-criminalization, a woman said that she wanted to leave the pain behind. To me that was really profound, because it shows how we're responding to institutions, and understanding how to handle the pain within all this—the guilt, the questions, what is and isn't death. I see both sexes as involved in this system.

NEKA: There are so many necessary elements of this transformation that we are a part of. For example, in the movement when we discuss the role of women… If you were to ask, "What is the role of women for the *compañeros* and the *compañeras*?" It would be a really good discussion, though superficial, because the ideas must also confront practice. What happens when we leave the assembly and go into the street, and all the women sing political chants that degrade women's bodies and humanity? Or the way we relate in concrete practice with the *compañeros*, which is often unequal—sexually as well as in other ways. It isn't just about inequality, but degradation as well. When we walk down the street, they look at us because we have big breasts or because we have a big rear—always making the relationship one of objects, rather than people. Every day is a challenge, and to begin to unlearn this, and to begin creating ourselves anew is a process.

CLAUDIA: In addition to what Neka is saying, the ratio of women to men in the movement has decreased a lot, especially since the first *piquetes,* which were made up of a vast majority of young and older women—women who put their bodies on the line. Though this issue was roughly equal in the beginning, it is being discussed more now. For example, on the early *piquetes*, when it came time to negotiate, sometimes women would send men as the spokespeople; the voices for the movement were not women. It was, and is, really difficult to overcome this imbalance in the perception of power.

NEKA: We're trying to create new relationships in practice, and are doing so in a concrete way. This idea came up in the women's discussion group—that we should create our relationships and selves anew in practice, and not just discuss it. We also discuss core issues, like our experiences with our *compañeros*. Really, we're learning to act and be together differently. The key is figuring out how to live by our principles in specific situations.

As far as abortion goes, it's like Claudia mentioned: it isn't so much the issue of legality or illegality. There are just more pressing things we're worried about, and legality, at this point, isn't one of them.

MABEL: There's also a different concept of maternity.

NEKA: Totally, yes. In many cases there's no choice whether or not you become a mother.

PAULA: My personal view is that legalizing abortion won't change the situation. It may change some things, but not everything. This is mainly due to the powerful cultural pressure exerted on women. To have an abortion is a terrible thing, whether you have the money to have one or not. It's a horrible experience from a cultural point of view. It's also awful because someone is messing with your body.

MABEL: I disagree.

PAULA: I'm talking about me—my personal experience—not other women. It seems that we're living in a culturally violent atmosphere, and this generates a serious debate in society around any concept of abortion that isn't religious or traditional. Maybe legalization would be a step, but the way we live now—even if you don't come from a religious family—no one is happy to have an abortion. It has to do with the old-fashioned cultural norms that exist in all classes.

MABEL: I think that what's important isn't the abortion, but its illegality—that you are doing something illegal, which creates many ghosts. I believe, for example, that if a forty-year-old Swedish woman has an abortion, she doesn't think she's taking a life.

PAULA: Well, but that's a different culture.

MABEL: But what I want to say is that if you compare us with societies where abortion has been legal for decades, where abortion is decriminalized and legal and is a right like other rights, I don't believe that it's as traumatic a situation.

PAULA: But culturally, the Swedish society has been a secular society since it began. Its culture is very different from ours. It's not traditional. To not penalize abortion and to allow it in a public hospital isn't determined by the state characteristics, but by the culture as a whole. In Argentina, to go to some guy and put a thousand pesos on the

Two workers from the occupied garment factory, Brukman. One is holding their paper, which reads: "Brukman is the workers'."

table for an abortion calls up all kinds of fears—not only that the police could barge in at any minute, but fears like being unable to have more children, or not knowing if it's the right thing to do. It's a sensation springing from cultural violence. It's still very powerful, even though I don't think I'm taking a life.

NEKA: I don't believe that it's traumatic only in the moral sense—that it's simply a question of guilt because society condemns abortion. I think that any intrusion of your body is a violent act, whether it's an operation on your leg or ear. I mean, many people, especially in our neighborhoods, die from those kinds of operations.

PAULA: It's a reality that many women die. Apart from that, I have no doubt that if you did an interview on the street and asked if people thought abortion should be legal or not, it would be a very profound cultural question, not only a legal question.

MABEL: It seems to me that however the debate on abortion is started, it's important. I accompany *compañeras* that talk about legalization in various venues, but I think there should be a sharing of the experiences women have in Latin American clinics, independent of whether it's authorized or not. Dealing with the trauma of abortion is opening another door, which is important. What other way is there? To accept the pregnancy, even if you don't want it? To me, it's more violent to have unwanted children.

CLAUDIA: There are many new issues coming up in the movements, and many are related to the participation of women. There are many women participating in all of the movements—from recuperated factories to the neighborhood assemblies and the *piquetera* movement. As a result of so many women participating and leading in the movements, many new issues are arising. There are a many women in the recuperated factories—for example, in Aurora they are the majority, walking picket lines in 14° F. Women are in the forefront of the resistance against capitalism, and through this process of struggle our identities are being transformed. This is still not talked about a lot, but it's true. Many ideas are new and it's not as if there's "a" direction—it is all a process. One thing that's clear, though, is that the feminist discourse of the past no longer works. It's old, and it needs to be revised to speak to our present conditions as women.

NEKA: I see various aspects of this, and that in some cases, in some movements, it's almost a forced situation—it's a sort of fashion, the topic of strong women. What is more interesting is what we do as far as work in relation to our everyday practices, and how we try and work in a democratic way. An aspect of this that I feel is interesting is how we are beginning to see changes with, for example, the daily tasks that we do as men and women, and as couples in the movement. There may be little modifications in behavior, but it's better than nothing. For example, with me, it wasn't that I was at all *machista* before, but it was assumed that the woman in a relationship would wash the dishes, or cook and serve, and clean the clothes. But now there are changes in this, and we're more conscious of these sorts of dynamics. I believe we're taking steps forward. Before, if a couple was in the movement, it was the woman who stayed home with the children while the man went out into the streets. There has been a change in this—now there are both *compañeros* and *compañeras* who look after all the children. I believe this is a real transformation. We talk a lot about all of this and feel we are collectively taking charge of our history, doing so in solidarity with one another. Another thing that is discussed a lot is that we see the children as all of ours, and not so much belonging to anyone; they're all of our responsibilities. Before we came to these sorts of conclusions, if a baby was fussing in meetings, someone would say, "Take care of your child." But now, whoever is closest and most able helps the child.

Eluney, Etcétera (a militant art collective)

I have no doubt we're living in a macho society. This is something we have to work on as women—not allowing ourselves to be dominated all the time. It's clear that there are serious attempts to dominate us, as well as restrict our freedom—much more than men. It's we women who must respond to this, and do so in such a way that doesn't either marginalize or exclude us. There are so many things to change.

Men usually organize, command, or initiate things in ways particular to their gender. One of the changes that's been taking place over these past few years is that women are bringing in other ways of relating and connecting. Women simply have other ways of relating and doing things. I don't know where it comes from—if it's a question of genetics or if it's culturally nurtured. I don't know, but it exists. There are many men who say, "I don't want to discriminate against you because you're a woman, so I'll discuss issues in the same way that I discuss them with a man."

These ways are often very aggressive, and have a sort of violence in their interactions that women want to escape. It seems to me that a certain level of militancy is necessary to bring these things up and think about how to change them. We're not asking for the level of discussion to be lowered, but for certain practices to change. It's about creating another way of relating and generating discussion, one that comes from another place. This is something women have to learn. We have thousands of things to learn, from ways of organizing to ideas of *compañerismo* and solidarity. The role of women is something that's been coming up a lot since the popular rebellion, and it's something that must be heard.

Women's position has become much more recognized and respected since the economic crisis and rebellion. Before, women were always given the blandest work or pushed aside. At the time of the economic crisis, with all the suffering we felt and lived, it was the women who maintained the home, didn't abandon the children, and who gave up their other lives to sustain the family. Women will sustain their children and families with anything—with their bodies, minds, and claws. I believe that for this reason, and more generally as well, women are beginning to be valued more in many places—from the MTDs to the neighborhood assemblies. As a whole really, it seems that there's been a change in the question of gender. I knew crazy feminists that were fundamentalists, extremists, and their proposals didn't appeal to me. But now there's another, more profound type of reflection that is much more interesting. There's a lot of discussion and action around gender and women's rights, because they are among the most violated rights, yet one of the most basic and elemental. Poverty, inequality, a great many things are discussed, but the rights of women are also extremely important and haven't been discussed for a long time. Now we're beginning to see that it's something very basic to not feel respected. Maybe now that we're thinking about respect differently, the topic of women will come up. Now all of this is talked about a lot. The other day, a friend said it was a fad, but I think it's more like something we used to let slide and now are more conscious of.

**Woman working at Grissionopolis,
an occupied factory.**

Elvira, Fénix Salud (an occupied clinic)

For International Women's Day, we decided to have a women's meeting within the recuperated factory movement. Invitations went to movement women, most of whom had never met until then, because well, because of machismo. Another *compañera* and I had talked about why there was always masculine participation in everything, and why there hadn't been a meeting of women in the movement, and she proposed calling a women-only meeting on International Women's Day. The meeting was last Saturday, and it was spectacular. There were eighty people there, and we decided to continue having meetings, because we didn't have time to cover everything we wanted. We're all coming from such different places, as far as process and experience in our recuperations and occupations. For example, here in the clinic we began this process just recently, but there are people who've been working for years in a cooperative or recuperated workplace. It's really good that we're all coming from different situations, because we can share our various experiences and learn from each other. For example, someone who has years of experience in a recuperated workplace can listen to someone who's new, and it might give the new person lots of energy and inspiration, and remind the more experienced of their beginnings. It's really good. It was so good that we decided to meet once a month.

Within the recuperated workplace movements, there are many factories. The majority of them are factories, and there's still a very macho mentality. This feels like the time to make a small beginning—to begin to meet with people from other places where similar things are happening. And use this is a chance to learn from one another, and support one another, especially in circumstances where people are being messed with. It's a process of sharing from our experiences, and then finding ways to change the situation. I believe this will be really rewarding.

Gisela, Elipsis-Video (an independent documentary group)

Women fight everywhere, however they can. There are recuperated factories that are women's factories. Women and men are in the struggle in the same way, and they occupy equal space. I don't believe there's any type of difference now. Maybe a woman has more duties within her family, but she's participating in the struggle from within her family.

This is something important [her baby on her lap bangs on the table]. It's very common now to see children in marches, demonstrations, and on road blockades. You'll find many children in every demonstration, which wasn't true before. Now the entire family demonstrates together, and it's a really nice way of participating.

Paola, Barrios de Pie and La Toma (an unemployed workers group and occupied building)

The womens' group of la Loma

For me, it seems very different to be a woman, rather than to be a man, and participate in an unemployed movement or assembly. In part, this is because women have more responsibilities than *compañeros*—social duties, societal expectations—so a woman can't be out all day. If she is, people assume that she isn't taking care of her house and family. I don't have children, and I think the *compañeras* that do have an extra load because of family pressure. My family doesn't participate in the movements, so my house is "normal." My mother even asks me why I can't be normal, why I have to go out every day, why I can't be like other girls my age, why I don't get married and have children. It gets complicated. Things are more complicated for a woman, than for a man, because of the deeply rooted machismo in society. This is something that is present everyday, even with *compañeros*, because machismo is unconscious. Sometimes we fight about this in the movement. Why is it that the women have to wash the pots and the men grab the shovels and go out to the garden? Are women weaker? No, it's because that's the way it is. A man can't wash a plate, but he can grab a shovel. It's shameful for men to do the dishes. Shame and machismo are huge. There's a constant argument about this and I believe it will change with practice. Through talking and arguing, it'll change. Those who don't participate in the movements, they think it's really crazy. They think that a women's place is in the home, being tranquil with the children, which, of course, isn't the same for the man. We're talking about centuries of domination, of macho ideas that must be discarded. We must break with machismo every day. For example, in the road blockades we have security. The *compañeros* that are in front, whether or not they carry sticks—they're in front as defense, in case the police move in on us or something else happens. Sometimes there are *compañeros* who say women don't have to be in security, and this is a big fight because I always ask, "why not?" The police are going to sock me, too. Am I going to hurt more because you have bigger muscles? Everything is a learning process. It is a constant learning process. Some might say I can't be a part of security, but I'm going to be, whether they like it or not. It's difficult, but it has to be done every day.

Inside the movement, we discuss the issue of women specifically, which can also be problematic. To give you an example, in the neighborhoods the majority of those who work in the popular kitchens are women. In fact, most of the popular kitchens were started by a few women who did everything. Eventually they brought their husbands in to work, since the men were at home all day not doing anything. You know what happened though? As soon as the men showed the littlest interest in what was happening in the popular kitchens, the women instantly shut their mouths and let the men take charge. So we have a lot of work to do to break with all of this. Especially to break this within the *compañera*. If the husband comes to work in the popular kitchen and collaborates, it is as an equal, and the woman must speak up and give her opinion, even if it is the opposite of her husband's. We're working a lot on this. It's a huge social issue. In some meetings, there are more women than men, but it's always the men who speak more. It's a lot of work to break with this. Machismo is so deeply established. There are *compañeros* who've fought next to you on the streets for years, but sometimes they'll tell you to go wash the dishes. It's typical. It's a common joke. And we have to fight this every single day.

When we first began occupying this building, La Toma, there was a group of young people eighteen to thirty years old who did night security, and maybe fifteen or twenty of us stayed during the day. At night, there were always more men than women, so this group became a kind of secret meeting place for guys to talk about women. It took a huge effort to get this to stop. Those women who stayed—we really broke the balls of the men who talked about girls like this. They did it for at least three weeks until one day we said enough, and made it stop. Another thing that was common was that the guys who stayed would play ball every night and never invite us because it was "a man's game." Now, after a process, we say, okay, let's play something we all can play. It was natural to have separate women's and men's groups for recreation, but we've changed that. I don't know if it was learning, exactly, or telling them to "stop busting balls," but regardless, it doesn't happen anymore.

In La Toma, most of the *compañeros* come from militant backgrounds, or from the assemblies that supposedly aren't macho. But still, they used to get together as a little group of guys, away from the five or six of us women. And we fought to end that, because that was machismo. Now they don't do it anymore. Now we all meet together and talk about everything.

Group of compañeras, MTD Allen (an unemployed workers' movement)

COMPAÑERA 1: There are many women in the movement who are no longer married or are separated. Many of us find that here, in the movement, we're able to discover the best and most real ways to contribute to our families.

Organic garden of the MTD Solano.

COMPAÑERA 2: We all work in the movement, but it isn't anything like the work we did for the municipality. We have a nursery school and popular kitchen here—milk and breakfast for the kids, and an independent, self-organized healthcare system that everyone can use. All of this is such a huge help for each of us. If a child has a fever and the medicine costs a lot, we organize creative ways to take care of that. These are things that you just don't get outside the movement. I'm really happy to be part of this. It helps me fill my needs in so many ways.

We feel that all *compañeros* are truly equal—not just by circumstance, since we all get the *planes de trabajo* [unemployment subsidies]. It's different here. We've learned how to fight, and we've discovered together that "politics" is always the same, but what we're doing is different. We can think, we can express how we feel, we can articulate our needs, like full human beings. We are different.

COMPAÑERA 3: Within the movement, we collectively choose how we're going to work and what we're going to do. Because we do this together, and it's ours, our work becomes dignified.

COMPAÑERA 4: That's how I feel, too. I have a little baby, Máximo, who's only a year old. If I worked for the municipality, I'd have to clean the streets from midnight until 4:00 in the morning. Then who would take care of Máximo? Would he be safe? And if I were to bring him with me, something could happen on the street. At that hour of the morning things happen, or he could also get sick. Now I know that if I bring my son here, [gesturing around the MTD's common space], there's a nursery school and women to take care of him, so I can go to work.

COMPAÑERA 1: I worked on the street selling different things, and I had to bring my son with me while I did it—no matter what the weather, every day. The only positive thing was that my son was with me. Now he is taken care of in the MTD. Of course, there's always a risk that the person taking care of him in the MTD is untrustworthy, but I added things up and this way we win. No one is required to bring her child here. If my son comes here, I know that in the morning and afternoon he'll have his snack, and at noon, if he's here, he'll have lunch. I feel more like a mother. Well, to really feel like a mother, I'd have to be with my son. You know how it is…you want to see him grow. There was a time when I was afraid I wouldn't see my son learn to walk, or that he wouldn't be able to do it. These may seem like little things, but for a mother, seeing her son begin to walk is huge. They are things I wouldn't want to miss. Not just walking, but all the little things they do growing up. But to grow, they have to eat—that's essential for us—that our children eat, and eat well.

Myra, Asamblea Colegiales (a neighborhood assembly)

The issue of machismo is deeply embedded in everything, and that makes it hard to deal with. We don't talk about it. I see it, you see it, but that doesn't mean it's going to change. We never discussed it before, but now we've entered a time where we're talking about a lot of things that used to be taboo. I think one of the things that happens is that we prioritize, and machismo is low on the list. There's still a lot of machismo at the social level, even though it's mostly absent the neighborhood assembly I'm a part of.

Machismo has to do with the way you're raised. There's a hierarchy of prejudices, and machismo is near the bottom. People are totally prejudiced against homosexuality and transsexuality. It's terrible. It's a disgrace. It seems to me these are subjects that we are really behind on. For example, I've never seen a transvestite participating in my neighborhood assembly. I think maybe we haven't created enough space. No, I don't know if it's that, but they don't participate in our assembly. Ever. There are sectors in society that are very marginalized—not just the poor, but transvestites, prostitutes. Capitalism tries to force us to accept the marginalization of ourselves and others.

What can be done to reverse it? Of course, other economic forms can be created. I'm not speaking of absolute communism. I'm talking about other forms. Men, women, humanity in general—we have the ability to create. Why not create another form, another way?

protagonism

Paula, feminist and GLTTB collectives

The best part about the assemblies is that they let people do politics in a different, nonpartisan way. This new relationship has given way to very deep changes in people's subjectivity.

The way people get together in their neighborhoods now and talk about things, the way they listen to each other and value every person's opinion equally, is profoundly important. In political parties, it's not like this. In political parties, some people's opinions are valuable and some aren't. I believe that we are constructing a new way of being political, which is really positive.

If the assemblies disappeared, it wouldn't be so terrible. I say this because there's something happening in people right now—a real change. And this is really important for building whatever kind of future—it doesn't matter what kind exactly. I think the most important thing, with respect to the neighborhood assemblies, is that they've created a profound change in people's subjectivity. People who believed they were never going to do anything again, all of a sudden did. This is especially important considering our society, which teaches us that nothing done collectively matters, and that the only important thing is the individual. Just the fact that people have started to realize they can do things collectively is really important. They feel like if they can gather ten, twenty, or thirty people together, they can do something—they can change something, even if it's small. This, just this, is really important. This change is an extremely deep subjective change, because people are questioning this individualism that has been so entrenched in us since the end of the last century. While the neighborhood assemblies aren't everything we'd like them to be, I believe much of this change is related to them.

Daniela and Marta, MTD Almirante Brown (an unemployed workers' movement)

DANIELA: More than anything, what has changed is our human relationships—both within ourselves and with others. For example, when I met Marta, she was a very closed person, and so was I. I'm pretty shy, and it's always been hard for me to relate to people. The MTD has opened doors for me and for many others—other possibilities and ways of relating. Older people in the movement are now relating to younger people differently, and we're also relating to older people more, and in a really different way. This new way of relating and creating new relationships seems to be based in human values—in our taking them back. Through this process, you get to know really interesting people, and they become your friends. We're now equal to each other in the street, in the neighborhood, wherever.

MARTA: Today, if you go walking down the street in another part of town where people don't know you, or you meet people in an elevator, they almost never say hi to you, or they'll push you on the bus and not say anything. In contrast, here in the popular kitchen or at the assembly, the old women, the "ladies," come over to you and really talk to you as a person and an equal. They ask you questions and want to chat. A really beautiful trust has been created here. People are comfortable with each other. They tell you about their problems, what's going on with them at home, and with their children. We sit at the table together—in the movement and in the neighborhood—and have beautiful conversations. You go over and hug an older woman and ask her, "how's it going *compañera?*" And you give her a good hug. In other places, you don't see this kind of thing. Sometimes I'm sitting down eating, and I worry that a *compañera* doesn't have a seat, but she says to me, " No, no, you should sit and eat, too." We're talking about a seventy-year-old woman, and she's worried about me eating standing up! She gets up and says, "Here is your plate, but let me serve you." She wants to serve me, not because it's an obligation, but because she's a friend.

Martín K., Asamblea Colegiales (a neighborhood assembly)

Participating in the neighborhood assembly has changed my idea of what it means to think. Our culture, based so much in the individual, has made us believe that one person comes up with a new thought, names it, and it's theirs.

In different places—not just in this country, but throughout the world—I'm thinking of people in movements in South Africa, Ecuador, all of us that were in Porto Alegre at the World Social Forum, and so many more in different places all over the planet. We all feel the simultaneous need to change the way that we exist in the world in relation to politics. We need a complete transformation in our ways of being in the world.

This struggle is revolutionary, but not the way people meant revolutionary in the 1970s. It's something else, and we still haven't named it, because it's not a revolution in the sense of bringing down the state. We have to create another world, build another world—think of how to organize this other world, using a different logic. The logic of the state and the politics of representation are so entrenched in the market that, together, they have taken away our tools for social change.

We're creating new ways of relating to one another. No one knows exactly how to do it. It's a collective process. No one's going to come and tell us how to do it, and it's exactly this process that is so beautiful.

Recently, my wife and I separated. I believe this came in part from my starting to experience relationships in a different way. This transformation has to do with going from a type of passive satisfaction—a comfort in waiting for someone else to give emotional things to me—to something more active, and trying my hardest not to wait for someone else to do it. It's this idea of taking an active role in things, in our relationships, and the construction of our world in our every day life, that has affected me so profoundly.

I believe that there's more creative protagonism when there isn't so much focus on the individual. I say this, in part, because the person I am today isn't who I used to be. I'm still getting to know myself, and undergoing an existential transformation that's teaching me a different way of being in the world. I changed my relationship with the world, and because I'm basically in another world, I live differently, I see differently, and I can understand society differently. This is partly because I've had the experience of trying to live in the world in another way for a year and five months—the time since the rebellion and emergence of the neighborhood assemblies and other movements.

In my case, this transformation took place on a personal level. This is true for a lot of people in the assembly. There aren't statistics, but many people survived the crisis and began to think about how to rebuild their lives in a different way. It's really incredible.

I feel like a different person. Happy, although still with uncertainties and the challenges of someone who is trying to think and be self-reflective in this day and age.

I have a lot of faith, because I hear other people saying the same things I say all the time, and I feel like I'm part of an era of change. When people feel like there are others who feel the same as they do—especially when coming from different situations and places—it helps us feel more comfortable. It really is an amazing feeling. This new political action is based on trust and it wakes up people's emotions. I believe that this is the revolution that's happening now. You can see this all over—from the e-mails we send in the assembly to how we conclude the assemblies.

It's also true that there has been a backlash—violence, the capillary fascism. But we're here, living at the crossroads of different possible worlds—thinking, feeling, creating, and doing what we can.

Liliana, Brukman (an occupied factory). She's standing across the street from the factory, where works had recently been forcefully evicted.

I feel flattered, because I've been told that we're fighters. But inside right now we're a little bit tired and worn out. We're workers, not delinquents who have to be fenced in and guarded by police. I think that there are more police here than in a jail. I believe that many of us feel that if we have to give our lives, we will. If we have to give our lives, if that's what the government wants, then we're valuable. I sometimes think that this—our lack of fear—worries those who are in power. It bothers them that we keep struggling. They don't want us to be an example for others.

Emilio, Tierra del Sur (a neighborhood assembly, occupied building, and community center)

We're historical subjects. We're not the passive subjects that the system tries to make us anymore—the same system that pushes us to vote. We're no longer marginal subjects—empty and excluded—but are now historical subjects, active subjects, participating subjects. We're actors in our own lives.

Compañer@s, MTD Allen and MTD Chipoletti (unemployed workers' movements)

·COMPAÑERA 1: There's a good story about an older woman in the movement that reflects how the system affects people. The woman is Mapuche and speaks Mapungú [the Mapuche language]. She spoke in assemblies and gatherings, but usually very little. Then a teacher from our little school suggested she start teaching Mapungú to the students. She was so emotional, because she'd never imagined that she could pass knowledge on to others. It's quite a feeling—for her and for us.

COMPAÑERA 2: It's not just about moving from a position of powerlessness to one of power—at least in the sense that someone can start producing subjectively. The movement...or the spaces that the movement creates, are in some ways the spaces where you can transform your own existence and have another way of interacting with people. The movement is something collective, it helps make everyone feel special, and somehow, everyone finds a place.

COMPAÑERA 3: I was working until just a few months ago—totally exploited, going crazy in the little spare time that I had. Then I decided to join the movement. At first, I had to escape from work to go to marches, to be here in the movement space and participate in discussions. It was a huge qualitative change, because you get used to theoretical abstraction. And when you find yourself in the movement, all the previous social constructions fall down—all the mental structures that you carried. You start to create and learn from little things that happen—little things that are really big things. It's a really big change that I'm not sure I could recommend to everyone at this moment, because of its intensity. This type of conceptual change may be necessary, because there's no other option. Really there's nothing—you don't have any money, you have to scramble for the littlest bit by doing odd jobs, and obviously you're staying within the system. Now I couldn't spend eight or ten hours working for a multinational corporate supermarket.

You start to feel tons of new things. You feel much happier, more dedicated, and the best is that you feel like part of something, you feel integrated. Really, when you start to be engaged, the feeling just grows, and tons of strong new feelings come up. These are just the changes that have happened until now. Surely, there'll be thousands more to come. You can't be a futurist—you have to see how things go and keep evolving. The idea is to keep learning from our collective experience.

Ricardo, Esperanza (an occupied sugar plantation and refinery)

I feel really fortunate to have participated in the takeover of the refinery. One of my roles was to act as a part of the new overnight security. During the day, I didn't participate, of course, because I had to rest and save my energy for the nights. At night, I would take my backpack and go, meanwhile, everyone from the refinery kept working. It was a beautiful experience. We've really made something of ourselves from the experience of taking over and running the refinery. During the occupation, we used to say that beyond giving us our sustenance, the refinery was our second home.

I'm not sure that, at the time of the occupation, we noticed the extent of the impact we had on other towns. People's excitement, the powerlessness, the anger, and then the effervescence, everything was inside us... At first we felt like we had no power to resolve our most extreme problems. You don't always notice these things at the time.

I participated in one of our more extreme actions, which involved locking the bosses up inside the offices and not giving them food. We told them that they were virtually in jail, though they were not completely deprived of freedom, since they could leave under certain conditions. Our concept was that not letting them leave made them suffer like we suffer. We probably didn't realize the magnitude of what we were doing in those moments—at least not for a couple of months. Later, when we would go to other places to speak about our experience, people would say things like, "How cool that you threw out those guys at Esperanza." We've since realized the gravity of what happened, but at the time, we didn't have the slightest idea what we'd done. I have a great memory of when we were in the occupied refinery one night, at 2:00 or 3:00 in the morning, and I saw people taking such good care of the machines. It was like taking care of our homes.

I think that it's really different working without a boss. The difference is that you take real responsibility for things, and for each other. If I'm a machine operator, I know my own strength and I use the machine as efficiently as possible, while making the best use of myself—the best that is humanly possible. I might work an hour longer than I have to because I'm producing for my own benefit, and for the benefit of many other families. On the other hand, a boss uses you, he tells you what to

Celebration, and protest against eviction of neighborhood assemblies and occupied buildings that are used as social centers and for housing.

do. He never speaks to you about productive capacity as it relates to us. That doesn't matter to them.

Now we know that something besides just a strict administration can function—that the same workers who're responsible for their own work can also be administrators. We have highly-trained people.

Nelly, Clínica Medrano (a recuperated clinic)

Personally, before the takeover, I was on the verge of a serious depression. It came from the lack of solutions to our work problems, and all that resulted from that—taking care of daily needs, like paying rent, and finding food. This gives you a sort of crisis mentality, a sense of immediacy that creates a lot of stress. At first you get stressed out, and as the stress builds up, you start to get depressed. This situation is created when you can't find any way out. That feeling and experience is so different from embracing a common project—one that's yours, along with all the workers around you, all your friends.

Now we work together and explore ways to see beyond differences that we have, because real differences do exist. That's why we have the assembly, and because it's our own project, we need to meet together. This collective process revives you and helps you gather the strength necessary to confront other challenges. It's really a big challenge.

I remember some really wonderful moments, like the inauguration of our new clinic, after we recuperated it. Another time was when we threw out the goons the previous management had hired to intimidate us. Then we were really on our own, and the clinic was ours. We all spent that entire night together in the clinic. After that, we took turns staying the night, because we didn't want to abandon the clinic.

The inauguration was phenomenal. We'd struggled so much, and suddenly we got what we wanted. It was a beautiful moment. The clinic was ours. There was such a feeling of unity; everyone uniting around our common objective. Everyone was so full of emotion. People outside, as well—neighbors and supporters—we could see that they trusted us. There were people who would wave to us, people we didn't know, and some would come in the clinic for a little while to show their support. This affects you deeply.

I was never into politics before. For me, all of this was a totally new experience. I studied and then went home. From home to school and back again. On the way from school to my house I didn't see anything, except maybe when there was a strike, or a road blockade, and even then I wouldn't really understand what was happening, or even wonder why. I was one of those people. It didn't interest me. When I got here, I started to see things differently. Now I even feel like a different person. Now, every day when I listen to the news and hear what's happening in the movements—and not just the movements, but also all the political problems in other countries—I start to relate them to what's happening here. I've started to see different points of view and compare situations and draw conclusions. This is something that I didn't do before.

Natalia, La Toma and Asamblea Lomas Este (an occupied building and neighborhood assembly)

I used to believe that if I just worked hard and got my college degree, things would work out and I would get something in return. Now I have come to understand that a career is relative. What feels most important to me now is relating what I learn to other experiences—life experiences, personal experiences, as well as a potential career. La Toma is a place where I can use the things that I learn, rather than have learning be my only objective.

I feel like I'm doing something important now. I'm not studying incessantly or focusing on trying to get a high-paying job. This [looking around La Toma] is what's important to me. Without this, the other things don't make sense. Now I've come full circle from my previous activities. College makes sense now, thanks to my participating in La Toma. Now I really know that this is what I want to do, this sort of thing, and my life is dedicated to continuing in this direction.

We try not to aim too high or think too big, because we know that it's a long and often difficult process. But it's worth it. For example, when we see one of the older boys helping a younger one to read, it's an enormous joy. I can't even explain how it feels. You have to understand the history—these are boys that used to live and work in the street. Many of them would hustle right here at Lomas' train station. We began to form a relationship with them. In the beginning, they would steal from us, hit us, and sometimes spit on us. And now, seeing this sort of connection with others is incredible. What we see is that if we can get there together, with even one young person, then that's enough. All the hard work is worth it.

Group of compañeras, MTD Allen (an unemployment workers' movement)

COMPAÑERA 1: When we go out on a road blockade, we really feel our strength and unity as *compañeros*. When you begin to take note of this unity, your chest fills with happiness—a joy in knowing you're not alone. We also realize that if you go it alone, you don't achieve anything. It makes you really happy to know that you're not alone, and this helps a lot. We know that we're together with our friends—we're all there together—and all have the same needs. There's no one marching behind anyone else, but we're all in front, and we're all together.

COMPAÑERA 2: It's nice being together on the road blockades. When you go to the bridge to shut it down, it can be pretty intense. You don't know what you're feeling. I can't express to you what I feel. I don't know if you've experienced it—it fills you with pride and you think, I'm fighting for what's mine, for what I believe is right. And to have a community like this gives you that much more strength to keep struggling for what you believe is just.

COMPAÑERA 3: I think that egoism is one of our big challenges, and one of the most difficult things to change. Even though I think it's one of our biggest barriers, we see it as a process that we're all involved in. This is also a process that's developing every day. Every day, we have to make decisions—sometimes they're made in the most solidarity-inspired way, and sometimes there are lots of holes in the process. This is one of the things we have to work on.

COMPAÑERA 4: I don't have family here, but this is my family—the movement. I always say that, here's my family.

COMPAÑERA 5: One day, my partner left me, and I was left alone with my son. I wasn't afraid though, because my son wouldn't want me to be. The only thing I had is here [gestures around the MTD space]. I bring my children here, and when something happens to me, I come here to talk about it, to see what kind of advice *compañeros* will give me. I always have a place to go. My family is here. I don't depend on anyone in the same way that I did—not on my job and not on my ex. I feel different now.

Group of compañeras, MTD San Telmo (an unemployed workers' movement)

COMPAÑERA 1: Here, we're all equal. No one is seen as above or having more value than anyone else. We work in different groups and on different projects in the MTD, but we all start from the same foundation of trust, and this makes everyone feel really good. For example, if for some reason you arrive late because you've had an emergency, no one demands to know why you didn't come when you were supposed to. Part of why you feel so much better here is that you know there isn't someone in charge of you, interpreting everything and putting a spin on it. If you're late, you don't feel like you're no good. Here in the MTD, if you say, "I couldn't get here, friends, because I had to go to the hospital," or whatever, your friends understand and support you. It's better not to have someone in charge of you. Working together, and doing things based on your own desire are the most beautiful things there are. This is a special place for me. In other places, it's like, I'm not going to get there because they're going to suspend me, or I got there late and now I have to leave. Here, you know that whenever you arrive, there isn't going to be a problem, and you chat with your friends who say things like, "So, you had a problem, and it was a problem." This feeling is really wonderful. You don't feel alone, but rather part of a caring group. It's another way of organizing.

COMPAÑERA 2: It's like being at home. We try to act like a family.

I think I've changed a lot since I began participating in the MTD. We talk about this a lot here: how we have changed and what's different. Here in San Telmo, a lot of workers live in hotels, where we pay day-to-day. The living situation in these places is really hard. We're all families with lots of children. We talk about this a lot, how difficult it was—and still is—for women and children without resources. We also talk about how so many of us women were in really complicated relationships before we began participating in the MTD. Being in the movement has helped many of us see our relationships and ourselves differently, and things have changed because of this.

Many of used to fight with each other a lot before we were in the movement. We really had so many more problems, and couldn't see our way out of them. Now that we're in the movement and working together, we're learning to coexist, and we have fewer tensions and feel better. It's a learning process. We still fight with each other a lot, but together we continue to learn how to solve our problems. We try to talk without getting mad. We're also learning that there can be differences, but we don't have to kill each another over them.

COMPAÑERA 1: I have an example of this. Another woman and I were having problems in the hotel where we both used to live. We'd argue every time we saw each other. Later, I started coming here to the MTD, where my kids could get help with their schoolwork. When I saw that this woman was also coming to this place, I thought, no, I'm not going to work with this person. I figured we were going to fight and carry on, and have bad blood between us, and then one of us would have to leave. But then I thought that I would try to get along with her for the sake of my children. Many of the *compañeras* helped us, and now we're friends and we get along well. Whenever we have a problem, we try to talk about it and work it out. I don't think we'll fight anymore. I've learned other ways to communicate with the *compañera*.

We learn to love and respect ourselves here. This is a really big deal when you think about how most women think of themselves—especially those outside the movement. As women, we're learning a lot of things, the guys as well. There are a few guys that work here, and we all get along. They're really good friends, very supportive. When you have a problem, you can sit down and talk to them, even though they're men. They'll help you, and sometimes they'll give you advice. We're a family and we're slowly starting to get to know each other—opening up to each other and stuff. So that's all, the MTD San Telmo is really nice

COMPAÑERA 3: We have an after-school program to help kids who don't do well in school. I work with the youngest kids in the MTD, and my friends are with the bigger kids. We all work together to teach them. I love it. This is something I didn't know about myself before, or I wasn't able to find in myself. I'm not someone who has patience with kids, but here I am learning to have a lot of patience. I have two boys that I'm not very patient with, and I realize that. Here I have more patience and am learning more patience that I hope will transfer to my relationship with my own kids.

Carina, Argentine World Social Forum mobilizing committee

I changed. For me, it wasn't a political awakening, because from a practical and theoretical point of view, I was always involved. But what I did have was a really skeptical attitude—a typical sociological point of view.

For me, there was hope after the nineteenth and twentieth. Although it was difficult economically, I didn't have this hope before. What I had before was lousy. It made me sad to feel like the only person who was going to save me was myself. I was thinking about things like: what do I do with my career if I should leave the country? Or if I don't leave the country, how would I find work? I felt like the only thing I had left was myself, my friends, and the possibility of building a family. I needed to put my energy into some type of cause and I couldn't find the cause. I moved through a lot of spaces—from political parties, to the world of NGOs. At the same time, I saw lots of other people who were also searching and couldn't find the way.

Now I want to stay in the country. Two years ago, I thought about applying to do research at a European or Yankee University, because I thought I would like reading and researching in another place. And now I want to stay, which is important. I'm from the class of people who can choose to leave. We can choose another type of life abroad and have better economic opportunities. If the country doesn't offer me anything, then I can read and research, because, as a last resort, these are noble things. Given that I can't do that here, what part of the world should I do them in? That was the question. I had a strange feeling thinking about that question—a kind of sadness because I had to leave. But why? It's one thing to say, I'll go have an experience in another country and come back. That was always my idea as a last resort, but I felt like, in some way, my country was kicking me out—that the social situation was driving me out, and I couldn't be happy under the circumstances I was living in because I couldn't find myself. I couldn't fulfill my desires. Now, I feel like this is a place to stay and work. In spite of the problems—not just economic, but everything else that I told you about... Because of the old politics that are still practiced, there will always be favoritism and there will always be problems. But in light of all of this, Argentina is where I want to stay and continue being involved.

In terms of the process of changes in subjectivity, the interesting thing is that this is a social education. Imagine if the assemblies disappeared. We've still had the social training of the assembly. The nonhierarchical structure and self-organization are things you can use in the future, and in other political experiences. In this sense, I'm not a pessimist. I can be more pessimistic in the short term—in the sense that I would like the assemblies to be stronger. But in the long run, what I know now is that the crisis of the 1990s brought about lots of social education. We'll learn from all these experiences of self-organization, and the next time we need an assembly, we'll have had all the experiences from the assemblies of nineteenth and twentieth.

Ezequiel, Asamblea Cid Campeador (a neighborhood assembly)

I'm much more patient than I used to be. This is especially true, and necessary, with the processes in the assembly, because if you can't be patient with the assembly process, you won't survive more than two meetings. They can be really slow-going, and sometimes anger-provoking. It's a very slow process that doesn't always produce immediately visible results. The process itself changed me. I am much more patient and tolerant of others now than I was before. I feel like a different person. I think it also made me a little more generous with others in terms of valuing their efforts, even if they don't do things the way I would. I realize now that the gradual changes that happen in the assembly can only be made in an environment where people are generous. For example, I remember this one incident involving a young woman, Jackie, who had participated in the assembly from its inception. She was very young—she's probably around eighteen now. In the beginning, she stayed in the corner and never spoke. She went to every assembly—she never missed a single one, but she just sat in the corner, observing in silence. Then, recently, she jumped in to speak—I would say some six or seven months after the assembly was launched. She lasted six or seven months without speaking and then started to speak very gradually, a little at a time. One day, a very controversial situation arose, and she felt the need to say how she felt, and that was the first time she spoke. Over time, as she built more courage, she spoke with more confidence and conviction. She was a good speaker. It's easy to clip someone's wings if, for example, in response to a person's first attempt to speak, you treat them badly, if you lack the patience to listen to what they have to say, or you think what they're saying is foolish. Then they can become really demoralized. If one does behave generously with others, that dynamic can be easily truncated.

This whole process also involves a certain amount of self-examination and reflection about all the trash associated with power that we've internalized—the echoes of authoritarianism we carry within us as tics of the old politics. No matter how hard you try to think them away, they're lodged so deep inside you that you have to work constantly to remove them. Even though we work hard to remove them, we find again and again that there are still remnants. It's a huge task to figure out how to deal with these aspects of yourself. I'm not quite sure you can ever really get rid of them entirely. Maybe the best thing one can do is to learn how to deal with these things so they don't disturb others or the movement, generally.

I'm convinced that we're all transforming. However, it needs to be said that this is not something linear, and that in this case, it's a very difficult process. I wouldn't say we're entirely new people, but we're definitely a lot different from what we used to be.

Candido, Chilavert (a recuperated workplace)

I'm Candido Gonzalez, a member of Chilavert, a workplace that was reclaimed by the workers. Our print shop was not only retaken by the eight workers on the inside, but by an entire society committed to us, one that has grown tired of our governing body's inefficiency and tired of waiting for change to come from the top. So, together, we've begun to change from the bottom.

I am a printer with more responsibilities than I had before we took over the factory. Not just responsibilities with regard to the print shop, where we all assume additional responsibilities. Now we have more moral duties to help other *compañeros* take over their own factories. This is a chain, the movement of recovered factories. It's a chain we add new links to all the time. The last link added is always a little wobbly, and that link needs and receives reinforcement through the unconditional support of other recovered factories—whatever help they need, including resisting the police, if necessary. If there's one thing that all the recovered factories agree on, it's that we're not alone. It's about all of us—really all of society—other recovered factories, everyone. Once you feel and receive this commitment, it's as if it's branded on you by fire. You feel like you have more power than money. Your moral duty is much more powerful.

Martín S., La Toma and Argentina Arde (an occupied building and alternative media and art collective)

From the very beginning, within all this constant social change and social construction, something really powerful began. It was as if a barrier ruptured and issues of prejudice got ripped apart. Now it feels like anything is possible. This is something that those of us here in La Toma are feeling and saying out loud.

Out of this experience, a group of many people who knew each other from one place or another was formed. And now, being here and sharing—not just the many hours daily, but also many activities together, and sometimes even having to hold back on certain things—has made our relationships very special. We see this as we spend time together doing guard duty on the night shift, celebrating birthdays, preparing collective dinners, or whatever. The truth is that being here and being together creates an emotional need to be here. In the summertime, especially, we all want to be here all the time. There was a time when we used to say that we better start getting used to the idea of being away from La Toma, because if they evicted us, we would all end up in a psychiatric ward.

Politics of Affection

Group of compañeras, MTD la Matanza (an unemployed workers' movement)

COMPAÑERA 1: We're really forming a community here. Inside this space, things feel different. They're distinct from the outside. Something really special and unique has begun to grow here. At first, it felt like a space that was completely separate from the world, but gradually we're starting to feel like part of the world.

We're all a part of the process and growth of the movement. We're constantly thinking about daily and future tasks, and the feelings they evoke. We are constantly doing things, as well as reflecting upon the meaning of these things and what we're creating here. I believe this has something to do with the distinct community we are creating. It's as if being here is one thing, and going outside is something else entirely different.

COMPAÑERA 2: That's what it's about. We all arrive here from the outside, having been beaten up by the outside world. You arrive in bad shape because, well, it's difficult out there. Without work, it's hard to get ahead. Whereas, here, you may have a problem, but it comes out of work we're engaged in, rather than your lack of something. If you have no sales, then you won't have any money to buy food that day, or the following day. Nevertheless, you enjoy yourself, and you're at peace. It's a different affective flow. It's easier to overcome all the problems you might have—which are more or less the same as before—except for the fact that now you're in a really different place, a different situation and community. You have more possible solutions, because as you examine the problem from a different angle, you see many possibilities fan out before your eyes. That's what it's about. You're constantly exploring how you will work tomorrow, and you're simultaneously thinking about what you are going to do the day after tomorrow. And it's good—the possibilities look good.

COMPAÑERA 3: It seems to me that it has something to do with shedding the idea of placing blame or guilt on someone. When you're alone and unemployed, you take complete blame for not having a job, believing it's due to a personal defect, or your not having studied enough to be able to get a college degree, or any number of things. For me, beyond the affective experience, coming here and meeting people who were in the same situation, and who've joined with others to begin to do something about it...well, it seems all a part of the process of eliminating this sense of self-blame or guilt.

Zanon factory workers sing and celebrate at a march.

Martín K., Asamblea Colegiales (a neighborhood assembly)

It's about being able to create a new relational mode. What happens is that no one knows exactly how to do it—no one knows. It's a collective process, it's not like someone is going to come over and tell us how. One thing we have called this is "affective politics," politics of affect, politics of affections.

The feeling shared by those of us who want to engage in politics is that there's no political scene—that there's no place to make the move.

That's the impression. This is why assemblies are held on random street corners. Since there are no institutions—not even a club, church, or anything—the assembly meets on any corner, and in the street even. When this new form of politics emerges; it establishes a new territory or spatiality. At first, it's defined by a single moment in time and space, with the first minimal number of coordinates necessary to build a territory. And how is this sustained? It can't be supported through ideology. In the beginning, the assembly consisted of people from all walks of life—from the housewife who declared, "I am not political," to the typical party hack. But there was a certain sensibility. I don't know what to call it—something affective. There was a sense of wanting to change things, a desire for transformation. And that generated a certain kind of new interpersonal relationship, It generated a way of being and a certain sense of "we," or oneness that is sustainable. I think this is what makes things self-sustaining in the assembly. It seems to me that other forms which were more ideologically based, such as "we leftist revolutionaries," ended up fragmenting the assemblies and alienating participation, because they were more closed. In general, when the assemblies were more relational, they were more open, and people came and participated because they had a certain sensibility. In this respect, the new politics need to

Murga, a traditional dance, during *Enero Autonomo.*

have some affective quality. Call it whatever you want to call it, but it needs to create a particular affective space. It's as if we live in flux, moving at a certain speed, like little balls bouncing all about, and then suddenly, the assembly is our focus. Our intention is to momentarily pause time and space, and say, "let us think about how to avoid being dragged and bounced about, and simultaneously attempt to build something new ourselves." For me, that is what the new politics are all about.

Speaking of affective politics, we are talking about a lot of different things for which previously there were no words. It's a new language, and this new language constitutes a new space.

Neka, MTD Solano, and Claudia and Sergio, lavaca.org (an unemployed workers' movement and an alternative media collective)

NEKA: This experience draws you in and makes you commit right from the start. Something that made a profound impression on me related to the idea of affective politics, was listening to Luis Mattini speak on his participation in the struggles in the 1970s. He was giving a self-critique and said something like [paraphrasing]: "We have fought against and attacked the capitalists, but we didn't know how to combat capitalism. We can annihilate all the institutions of capitalism, or any other system of domination. We can annihilate private enterprise and the corporations that symbolize all of that, but if we don't combat our way of relating—which reproduces all these things—it seems like we are fighting an empty battle."

I think that's also one of the differences today. This day-to-day practice that we constantly talk about, the constant confrontation in our day-to-day lives, is a means to combat the old, while building alternatives. I think one of the most powerful things about *Enero Autonomo* was that we found ourselves sharing the present state of our current building efforts, as opposed to someone at a conference handing us a blueprint based on some theoretical framework, a sort of recipe of what to build. Instead, we were able to say, "We, who are living in this context, in this concrete reality, in this neighborhood where we're being hit in specific ways—we're doing things to resist all of this." This was the most powerful aspect of *Enero Autonomo*—this emergence of a climate of liberation, where no one was telling you what to do or how to act. Instead, we approached each other from the standpoint of experience.

SERGIO: If an earthquake struck and we weren't sure what rules should guide us, we could follow the rules of affect. If I like someone, I get the feeling that something can work, and this sentiment generates action. What I think has changed in terms of the new autonomy that is growing, is the person's previous obligation to relinquish the self. The self was dissolved in the massive collective of the traditional political parties of the left or the right. The individual ceased to exist. It seems to me that what we have going now is something akin to a recovery of the self. If the person can't feel affect, then there is a devaluation of the person. I don't want to call it individualism, because that can be confused with egotism, but there has to be an individual who is capable of thought, capable of feeling, capable of affect, capable of acting with consideration for others.

We shouldn't be concerned only with rational thought, but should also include those intuitive and affective qualities that help guide one's actions—albeit not exclusively, but they do help solve problems.

Trust is one of the most complex subjects for humanity, because no one really knows how it's generated or how it's destroyed. But, if I feel trust, and if what we're doing and saying makes sense...

CLAUDIA: Our chief enemy is fear. It amounts to an assault against everything that is being built, because fear, or suspicion of ulterior motives, begins to chip away at the trust we're creating.

NEKA: The thing is, everything depends on how far one wishes to go in creating a new society. If you begin with loving yourself, and if you can love those in your immediate surroundings, then you have the greatest potential for transformation. A life previously devoted to a single leader

Zanon worker and Hebe Bonafini, one of the founders of the Madres of the Plaza de Mayo.

now assumes a radical stance that is much more profound—it assumes a devotion that is much more profound. We have seen this in our day-to-day lives and in our day-to-day relationships. As we come together to work, or as we come together to carry out a joint project, we generate affective ties that strengthen common support for a project—the things that are fought for by the other person are the same things that I feel I must fight for. And so, it's as if things take on a different meaning. It's a completely different horizon, and that is something very new, very of the now.

Emilio, Tierra del Sur (a neighborhood assembly, occupied building, and community center)

The traditional leftist configuration is like a tree, where the central committee is the trunk. Next are the various branches, and the sub-commanders are the little leaves. Without the trunk, everyone would be lifeless and there would be no decision-making center, the flow of decisions would be unknown. On the other hand, the relations we are experiencing between different movements resemble web-like formations. It's like a network—a real network. There are articulations that exist not to pursue a single, consolidated, and unanimous objective, but rather there are relationships formed around concrete projects. For example, there are relationships for carrying out direct actions, there are relationships for expressing solidarity, there are relationships for exchanging products. Also in the between-group relationships, there is an attempt to reproduce a bit of the logic that exists within individual groups that are based on respect, based on mutual need, based on consensus and on respect for mutual agreements, and not on breaking these accords unilaterally.

Also, there are relationships based on affinity. There are autonomous assembly groups that come together on the basis of their affinity for being an assembly. This doesn't mean they attend marches under the banner of Autonomous Assemblies, nor do they petition on behalf of Autonomous Assemblies. Rather, they come together to work on concrete issues, and that constitutes an articulation where no single group leads, and where decisions are not made by a single group, nor is any group responsible for coming up with a line for the other. This is very interesting for so many reasons, including the new articulations that are beginning · for the exchange of products and many other things. This is where one begins to see the vision realized—the vision that we can function together as independent but interrelated communities on a large scale. It's a lie that this is something that can only work on a small scale, involving only two or three neighborhoods. This can spread from city to city, from nation to nation—it can occur on a global scale. We can form articulated webs in our personal relationships, as well as in our community relations. And, it is fantastic. It is one of the best flavors of the salad that constitutes the new movement. Yes, it is fascinating.

Paula and Gonzalo, HIJOS, (a collective of the children of those disappeared during the dictatorship)

PAULA: Our understanding of the idea of *el compañero* enables us to shield ourselves when we're up against a difficult situation—to come together with such great unity that we can withstand anything. We've taken some really hard hits. We were born of a rupture, and it happened to us again. We've endured all of this partly because of our profound political conviction, but humanism is the real key. We really believe that the only way we can achieve a revolutionary process—unleash a revolution—is by changing as human beings first. We try to build within ourselves that which we're trying to achieve for society. We believe that if we don't live our lives in the way we desire and seek to live, then we'll never achieve our goals.

GONZALO: Above all, what we have come to understand is what Che used to say: a revolutionary is moved by great feelings of love, and we must create this love between *compañeros*. Love is the link—what we're struggling for is of such great importance, it is only natural that we feel love among ourselves.

Compañeras, MTD Allen (an unemployed workers' movement)

COMPAÑERA 1: The thing that strengthens you is that your *compañeros* are always there with you. This is something quite beautiful that you won't find anywhere else—to be valued as a person—to know that you can speak, act, and make decisions. When we go out on the road blockade, it's the *piqueteros* who are in charge—that's us. We have, how should I put it, an inner strength that gives great joy, similar to the kind of power that makes one feel big.

I feel like I have achieved so much for myself and for my children, that it just makes me want to do more for them. My little girl who is only three years old, was chanting, "*Piqueteros Carajo!*" [Loosely translated as "*Piqueteros* and proud, damn it!"] It gives one such joy to know that the little ones know you're struggling for something that, in the future, will prevent them from tolerating domination. It's something that you have already started to instill in them—that they shouldn't let themselves be pushed around or moved out of the way.

A lot of children walk around chanting like my little girl. Susana's child, who's three, plays the side drum marvelously, and has been doing it for a little over a year. These young people are growing up immersed in an environment of *compañerismo*—in solidarity, in unity, with everything within reach.

COMPAÑERA 2: My little girl comes with me once in a while. She comes with me to the bakery. It's a big help for me to be here.

COMPAÑERA 3: I feel the desire to come here to be with the *compañeros*.

COMPAÑERA 4: Since being here, with the *compañeras*, we've developed great unity and affection.

COMPAÑERA 2: If you don't come, it's as if something is missing. It seems like being here gives you strength. If you're not feeling well, the assembly gives you strength, joy, and the desire to continue. When you get here, you forget everything else.

COMPAÑERA 5: We're building something different. It's like we're changing everyone's way of being. Those who come here to stay are really looking for the kind of change that's needed in society at large. To have unity, to have *compañeros*, to have direct expression, is to try to be more human—to put in plainly and in one word.

Neka, MTD Solano (an unemployed workers' movement)

We had to have a lot of patience and lots of affection as well, because this kind of progress can only happen on the basis of affect and affection. Otherwise, it would've been impossible. As we got to know one another, we came to understand that we're in this struggle together, and a strong and important affection grew and continues to grow. I believe that if there's one thing that supports this relationship toward the movement, it's affect. Sometimes we get mad at each other, but since we like each other, since we care for one another, we can move on.

dreams

Carina, Argentina Arde (alternative media and art collective)

What do I dream about? I don't know. It's funny, you know before I was dreaming only about the future, and now I'm dreaming in the present.

Alejandro, Assembly Colegiales (a neighborhood assembly)

Some of my dreams and some desires…

First, I think about what's happened in this country, something so atypical when we think about the phenomenon of the assemblies and *piqueteros*. It's something so new, so unusual, where many ideas that people didn't used to pay attention to are now not only prominent, but they're internalized. This process of social change happened differently in Argentina than in some other Latin American countries. One thing I dream is that we all continue advancing toward a Latin American unity—with each place maintaining their unique traits. Personally, my dream is to be able to participate in this process.

We may go through challenging or difficult times, but when I feel the stress of some of these challenges, I also still feel the effervescence coming from the movements and social change that we are creating—which is something that I never felt before. This all feels so extraordinary, and I don't want to be cut off from that. I really wish there was a way that this energy could continue projecting and enriching all other aspects of life.

I feel a real separation between my job and the movement's social practices. Something I'm learning is that I can't maintain such a separation inside myself. Before, I was the type of person who always thought about doing something else at work and saw my friends as outside of the workplace. People at work were more like my adversaries. Something I've been learning is to not see my workmates as opponents just because they're not in the movement. Now I'm learning to understand my co-workers, and to be more open to them.

Through participating in the assemblies, I have been able to change a lot. I hope to always continue changing, and to see life as more of a whole—which really isn't so contradictory.

Carlos G., Zanon (an occupied factory)

I have a wonderful dream. I dream we'll win this struggle with the factory. More than anything. This is my first dream, and it's a shared dream. We dream that this project we're undertaking becomes really viable.

My personal dream is to teach my son all the values I've learned: to never keep quiet, to fight for himself and others, and to know that what he thinks is important and valuable. So many of us were taught that if we thought differently from others our thoughts were bad, but I want him to learn to express his thoughts freely, to learn he is a person, living among all of us, and above all to teach him that there is always solidarity to be found. I want him to learn that we struggle now, and always, because we don't know what the future will hold.

I want for my son to understand that the craziness of these guys is still there, as is repression, and many of us could die or go to prison. But, as we say, it doesn't matter if we lose our lives if it's for something worth fighting for. Many people have lost their lives. And if that happens, I hope that he'll follow in his father's footsteps—knowing how to fight, and knowing why. When someone falls, as many have done before us, we want our sons to raise our banner and continue fighting. I don't want him to lose because of something politicians say—people who tell you one thing, pat you on the back, but stab you later—which is what politicians usually do. I hope that he fights for just reasons and is always aware that it's possible to improve himself. More than anything, I hope he fights for what he knows is right.

I'm talking so much about my baby Guillermo because he was born just a couple of months before this conflict began.

I want my son to understand and feel that he should continue fighting for what is just and not be tricked by lies. I hope my son will be a militant that fights for everyone. I want him to have a good education, to have everything I can give him. I hope he's always conscious, and never closes his eyes to the world, because in the past, many of us averted our eyes. I also hope that the generations that follow understand why we're fighting. We're not only fighting for ourselves, we're fighting for the entire working class. We are not only the Zanon workers, but workers all over who are organizing and demonstrating. We're fighting so no more workers fall, so they're no longer used as they are now. And if we lose, we'll remain recorded in history.

Toty, MTD la Matanza (an unemployed workers' movement)

I have dreamed, since I became involved in politics—in the union struggles, as a socialist—that a just, egalitarian society is possible. I've seen many things and identified the enemy, but today I believe that the process is more important than winning the struggle. People don't have to be prepared only to die for the cause, but to construct it—to live for the cause, which is more difficult. I dream that humanity can transform itself and the idea of losing, of dying, no longer seduces me. Quite the contrary. I believe it's more important to teach my children and grandchildren to keep fighting to make a better society, even if we don't achieve it now.

I've given everything and I believe in this dream of a different humanity. This is the motivation behind autonomy, *autogestión*, and this whole project we're living. This is truly a life project, and at the later stages of my political and personal growth, I'm coming to see the need to incorporate affective questions as central to everything we do. I have the happiness of knowing that other *compañeros* are also seeing this possibility. We're constructing with a happy passion. There's nothing sad about it for me. The autonomous groups are founded in love, laughing, and autonomy, and little by little, I'm learning this more. I like it a lot, though it's difficult to admit that in the neighborhood [laughs].

Guaraní community swimming on their retaken land

Claudia, lavaca.org (an alternative media collective)

This is a dream for me—to be with people where I can think, say, and do anything. This is an ideal moment in my life, and I believe I can let myself dream without limits. I have a great deal of confidence. I believe the worst has passed. I look at it as if things are advancing. Sometimes it feels as if we've arrived, sometimes it feels like it isn't so far off, and sometimes it seems like we'll never achieve it. This is reality—to be at the height of your dreams and confront reality all the time. For me, one of the most important things is collaborating and creating with people I want to be with, having togetherness.

Do I dream a particular thing? No, not really. I feel like I want to live this process—that is, to not dream.

Alberto, Clínica Medrano (a recuperated clinic)

My dreams have to do with this project and seeing it continue. I want the clinic not only to continue, but for it to give better service to everyone. If it were up to me, the clinic would give free medicine. That would be terrific. That would be my ultimate dream. Another aspiration is to coordinate all the recuperated workplaces, and for us to have everything necessary to resolve all the problems all workers have. I don't want to really say I dream of wages exactly, because we had salaries... But having money to be able to have a project that not only serves us, but serves others—those that have given so much, the sectors most unprotected, in that sense. Money is essential to making that happen. That's my main dream in relation to the clinic project.

As for a dream for the country, it's to have a more just country. I'd like to exist in a country that neither exploits nor is exploited, with equal rights for all—including healthcare, education, work, and housing. But as long as the government is for the huge monopolies and large corporations, we'll never have that. At least we could have a government that defends the interests of the workers.

Compañera, MTD Solano (an unemployed workers' movement)

I dream that this collective we're constructing never falls, and that we become better in every way. I hope to be free. Above all, I want my mind to be free.

Gisela and Nicolás, Elipsis-Video and Argentina Indymedia (an independent documentary group and an independent media collective)

NICOLÁS: At this moment in the world, there's a possibility of beginning a new way of being. And I believe, with the riches that exist—at least in this country—it's possible for everyone to live well. That would happen, in part, by assigning more value to the small aspects of solidarity. Not on the level of money, or how many things one can accumulate—not with the same parameters that have been used to value the merit of one person over another. But in a different way.

GISELA: What I would like is to begin from below to build an alternative society, so people can live in peace and have what they need without having so many challenges to that—simply living in peace. I hope for us to be able to recover this country, as people are pushing for. I hope that everyone participates and deliberates in assemblies, so that the decisions about the country seem fair to everyone.

I especially dream of there being work for everyone. Everyone has a right to work and the right to a home. I dream that we continue doing what's necessary in our country to recover our identity, our culture, so we feel we're in a new home.

Among other things—apart from my desire to change the country—I would like to recuperate all the land that has been sold, to begin to work it, and hold onto the tools we have. I want us to continue fighting for all of Latin America, which has the same problems as we do, and sometimes worse. I dream that all of Latin America will be able to live well and in peace, without being anyone's slave.

A Guaraní couple looking at their stolen land. They are in the process of taking it back.

Frederico, University of La Plata (student anti-capitalist collective)

As they say in the Leazama Sur assembly, they can't evict dreams. [Frederico is sitting outside the bank the assembly occupies, which is being threatened with eviction.] However, we have to work every day for these dreams to come true, because it doesn't happen with people saying, "I hope things will change." Hoping is waiting, and it isn't about waiting. It's about doing. If we don't do it, things aren't going to fall from the sky. We have to build them every day.

For me, my ultimate dream is to build a socialist society, without classes, without dominators or dominated, without oppressors or oppressed. Of course, that isn't something that just arrives from one day to the next, unless in a utopia. It's a horizon and something we walk towards. A dream is that all of us are able to bring forth the human potential we have within us—to develop our maximum potential. A dream that we can be critical subjects, lovers, feeling in harmony with people, nature, and with everything around us. And to be able to produce intellectually, as well as materially, in the service of society and not just for a few interests.

As Che said, "We are realists, we make the impossible," and we need to do this all the time.

Fabian, Grupo Alavio (an independent media collective)

What I would like is for my teenage son never to have to carry a weapon. That's what I'd like, but sadly, it probably won't be that way. For now, I have to carry a weapon to defend freedom.

How wonderful it would be if everything we want happened today. If there must be killing, that it would be my responsibility and not my son's. I hope that my son can dedicate himself to music, to think about… I don't know what, to learn whatever he wants, to do whatever he wants, and work in whatever he desires. And I would like for the children of my *compañeros* to have what I want for my son—to be able to develop their maximum potential.

Each of us must live in our own historical epoch and assume that responsibility. I hope that changes come quickly, at least so that the profound changes we are making can be felt by our children. The revolution is an eternal dream that never will end.

Gonzalo and Paula, HIJOS (a collective of the children of those disappeared during the dictatorship)

GONZALO: To dream, I believe you should always dream, because in dreams, you often find a respite. When there's such a difficult reality, dreams lift our spirits and to calm us.

In this country, everyone dreams, and now the time has come to wake up. This is a beautiful metaphor, because the dream lets us continue—the dream is like utopia. I believe that we have to learn how to continue when we are awake, and we must be awake to build new forms that will allow us to arrive at this utopia—this revolution we're seeking. I hope that we know how to build it—and this is more personal to me, but I hope that what we build is a revolutionary movement.

PAULA: It's difficult to answer the question "what is your dream?" If you mean dream, like an objective, I dream of the revolution. It's mystical to think about how we can get where we want to go. I dream that we recover our culture, that we recover the value of each other, and of merely being human. In this sense, it's mystical and objective at the same time. The revolution is a point of departure. We want to win back ourselves in this battle, and really construct new subjects necessary to construct a revolution.

Liliana, Brukman (an occupied factory)

My dream is that if we stop, our children and grandchildren will go on. I dream that things won't happen tomorrow like they have today. What to say? I'm forty-seven years old, I live in a poor neighborhood in an unfinished house. A house that I'll never finish, because they always threw me out of work—and the owners had the right to do that because I shut my mouth. My pain wasn't important. That I couldn't pay wasn't important. That's how I thought about things before. I believe I was blind, because I worked, and thought I deserved the wages I got. I believed the owners.

Children of the MTD San Telmo.

Now it's different. It's as if our minds woke up, and we don't believe the owners anymore. I believe this will help our children, grandchildren, and other young people that are still blind today. Through us, and our experience, they're opening their minds, and the same things won't happen tomorrow.

Vasco, MTD Allen (an unemployed workers' movement)

I'll answer the question of my dreams with a line from the song by Los Redonditos: "The future has arrived, the future is today." I believe we're living the future. That constant promise of capitalism was like a carrot held in front of the mule to keep it moving in the direction they want. What a lie! What sons of bitches! What pieces of absurdity they put in our drinks to choke us—the future as something to only hope for, and that's what will fulfill all our dreams. No. Like Los Redonditos, I believe the future has arrived, that the future is today. Happiness isn't something you can postpone until tomorrow—we must live with total fervor today. If we postpone our dreams or put off our aspirations, we're delegating, and we're subordinating—subordinating the evolution of things we are going to do, or allowing someone to finish the things we aspire to. In the end I believe every day must be lived. I believe that the rupture from the past is something permanent, and something that is part of our daily life. Freedom and the rupture are today.

Celeste, En Clave Roja (an anti-capitalist student group)

My biggest dream is for us to be able to return power to the true owners—the people who produce everything in the world. That's my greatest dream: to live in a society where no one exploits anyone else, where we subsist on our own work. My greatest dream is to live in a society where social classes don't exist, where there's no exploitation, where people are free—but truly free, not free like in a democracy or dictatorship. I dream of a society where people live well enough to be able to take advantage of all the beautiful things life has to offer—like art and culture—and are able to enjoy thousands of things that may seem small, but are things most people in the world can't enjoy. I dream of a world where, if someone wants to be a writer, they can be a writer. And whoever wants to be a ballet dancer can be a ballet dancer, instead of having to work from the age of nine. I dream of a society where children don't die of hunger, as happens in Argentina and all over the world. I know many people have these same dreams.

Right now, the whole region of Santa Fe is flooded, and this is a good example of what I'm talking about. Thousands of people died in Santa Fe—the government doesn't want to tell people that, but they did. Millions of people lost their homes and will never again have what they had, and the government has done nothing. In the capital, women from the Brukman factory, where fifty workers are locked out for taking over their workplace, are helping the families of Santa Fe. They've put sewing machines in the street, and once a week, they sew clothes for the people of Santa Fe. This is the sort of thing that is my dream.

I feel the best way one can be is not leftist, rightist, autonomist, or Trotskyist, but everything-ist. That's a really powerful image that I hold onto.

Daniela and Ariel, MTD Almirante Brown (an unemployed workers' movement)

DANIELA: I dream of a more just society, where the rights of all people are respected equally. More than anything, in the future, when I have children, I want a dignified future for them. That's why I'm in this struggle,

I believe dignity is something we must fight for. Overall, I want us to be able to live with dignity, work, justice, and equality.

ARIEL: I agree with Dani. I hope that, in the future, my children won't have to go out, cover their faces, and make a *piquete* to make the government and police treat my grandchildren with respect. I hope that things won't be like that, and that they'll have work and an education. I hope they won't have to go to the Ministry of Health to get what we have a right to, and especially that they won't have to use the threat of force to get their rights. I hope that the future arrives with a conscience. I hope that people with power will no longer steal and blame us, although I guess we'll always encounter resistance. I am going to continue fighting until I'm old, for my grandchildren.

DANIELA: The road is long...

ARIEL: The road is long...

DANIELA: And there are many bumps along the way.

Ezequiel, Asamblea Cid Campeador (a neighborhood assembly)

As far as dreams, I think of two things—on two plains. One is maybe a more utopian dream: that finally we can live in a different society, not so absurdly unjust and horrible like this one. That would be my highest dream, but I see it as a far-off one. I have other dreams—ones that are a bit closer—which are to live, or to generate conditions, so that in the present, we can see more of the things we're doing to create the far-off dream. These dreams are much more modest and small, and are perfectly realizable. A dream-come-true is this recent history we have—with people participating in assemblies. This is something that has come purely from us, without being imposed from the outside. We see it with people taking the reins of their own lives, without fear and with confidence. This is a dream come true in this movement.

Another dream is to be able to leave behind some of the most negative things from the old left—the old politics. For example, I want to be able to leave behind the mutual distrust we have that causes aggression, criticism, and negativity between us. After that dream would be the desire to experiment with different ways of doing things.

We have made many advances since the nineteenth and twentieth, but it seems to me that we're stagnating a bit now. I see this as the moment to mutate ourselves again and experiment with other things—maybe to fail, but to try. I see us as a little conservative within the movements—with less willingness to try, to experiment, to make mistakes. Other dreams might be, maybe, to find a context wherein we could propose this and to experiment. Maybe we'll find that context in the assemblies tomorrow, if not today. I believe it's better to try everything possible today, everyday, and in the present. It's frustrating to only have faraway dreams.

Mariana, MTD Allen (an unemployed workers' movement)

Above all, we want our children to be raised in an environment where everyone's equal, where they can get an education, where the MTD will be the force for the entire country, and where everything isn't politics. Some people already see this. I hope it'll become more widespread, so that people really understand that we're not just some group apart from society that blocks bridges and highways. I hope people see that we're fighting for what we believe is good for ourselves and our children. I hope we'll see equality in the future, and that people will have this human value, with the strength to struggle—with the strength not to allow themselves be repressed. Oh, I wish tomorrow would be like that.

Group of compañeras, MTD San Telmo (an unemployed workers' movement)

COMPAÑERA 1: We want something better for our children, to keep progressing, and to make this greater still. We have many dreams: to have the bakery, a bigger popular kitchen, a bigger snack bar. If that dream comes true, it'll be because, as a movement, we're all working together to move ahead and make it happen. My dream is to have a bakery that can provide enough for our popular kitchen. Now it functions, but only halfway. All of us dream. We still don't have an answer for our children at this moment. That's where we want to go.

COMPAÑERA 2: Yes, not to toddle like a baby.

COMPAÑERA 3: Yes, of course. A baby begins to crawl. We've already crawled, and now we're beginning to walk, but very slowly still...

COMPAÑERA 4: We want to walk faster...

COMPAÑERA 3: The dream is that, now that we've started to walk, we won't stop. Like a baby when he begins to walk, he doesn't want to stop anymore.

Martín K., Asamblea Colegiales (neighborhood assembly)

What a nice question. It creates a bit of fear though, because when you speak of desires, you become afraid that they won't come true if you say them out loud.

I dream of an existence that isn't regulated from the outside by moral imperatives, utilitarianism, nonscientific imperatives, but to have the right to just exist, and to play with existing. I dream of a kind of world where there's a place for desires, and help for those wishes. I believe there are many lovely wishes in this world. It's as if it were our responsibility to be able to dream of other worlds, and while making them, look for ways to make other worlds. We would have to be able to have more feelings, to have diversity, to have many worlds—not an island, not a continent. More than a continent, islands that are connected.

My wishes? If I had to reduce it to one thing...more happiness. I wish that poverty, all types of exclusion, and all sorts of misery would not exist, and, well, that would make me happier. I don't really have a problem with being poor, but beyond a certain material privation, there is the desire for a cultural, social, affective, and political territory. This is something that we don't have now, so I'd wish for a territory where nothing is forbidden, where everything is horizontal, and where there's no hierarchy.

Paola, Barrios de Pie (an unemployed workers' group)

The objective we have as a movement is to change this country. To create a just society where there aren't any popular kitchens. We say in the neighborhood that we don't want more popular kitchens. What we want is for each family to have enough money for food, to eat in their own home, to make enough money through dignified work. We don't want to have to go out and block a highway to demand 150 pesos, or so that we can go to school. The objective is that those things be normal.

That's the ideal. The little process of building every day—of breaking with old schemes, of fighting against this economic model, this system they want to impose in Argentina—this is hard, because sometimes you're trying to knock down a wall that's pretty tough to break. But I believe it's breaking.

Two years ago, no one thought we would be here—taking over and running this place in the center of Lomas, with popular assemblies and social organizations. I didn't imagine this. No one did. And today we're able to do it, and we keep holding on—we keep resisting. And who knows? Two years ago no one believed we could do all this.

Christian, Attac Autónomo (an anti-capitalist collective)

I want the country to be a little better. I'm not asking for us to be very rich, but I ask that no more children die of hunger. I ask for education, for respect for other people. I ask that we live in a little better society, and that, when I have children, I can give them security—at least that they won't ever live like I live sometimes—with the impotence I feel. There are many other things: to have better health, that people are conscious of a ton of things, that there is money for food in every home in the Argentine Republic, that we are a little better socially. That's all. I don't ask for all of us to be high class, to have a lot of money. No, I ask that we all have education, dignified work, health, the primordial values of being human. I wish this for everyone in the world. That's what we fight for every day, and I believe we're going to get it.

Neka, MTD Solano (an unemployed workers' movement)

My permanent wish is that every day there is a new reason to live. I don't like routines or rituals, or things always planned out. My dreams are related to this—to be able to be idealists, to imagine not having a capitalist system, and to convert oppression into love. I believe the dream is coming true, and I know we're able to create it. I don't want dreams where happiness is strangled or stagnant, where you can't have creativity or feeling. I guess this may place me with other dreamers—with those who are considered crazy.

Holding hands in the days of the popular rebellion.

index

Subject Index

Movement Index

This index locates the person and movement when they are the speaker, and not when that person or movement is mentioned in the general text.

MTDs—Unemployed Workers' Movements

Photo Credits

Carina Batagelj, Argentina Arde, 13, 196, 208, 239
Fernando, Argentina Indymedia, 6
Yuriria Pantoja Millán, 201
Olga Morales, 246
MTD Solano, 78, 99, 143, 212
Nicolás Pousthomis, Argentina Indymedia, 21, 44, 63, 79, 150, 251
Rulo, Argentina Indymedia, 3, 137, 164, 215
Sebastián, Argentian Indymedia, 231, 234
Zoe, self-portrait this page
Marina Sitrin, all others

Argentina Indymedia: <http://www.argentinaindymedia.org>
Argentina Arde: ardeprensa@hotmail.com
Nicolás Pousthomis: <http://www.sub.coop>

Friends of AK Press

AK Press is a worker-run co-operative that publishes and distributes radical books, visual and audio media, and other mind-altering material. We're a dozen people who work long hours for short money, because we believe in what we do. We're anarchists, which is reflected both in the books we publish and in the way we organize our business. All decisions at AK Press are made collectively—from what we publish to what we carry for distribution. All the work, from sweeping the floors to answering the phones, is shared equally.

Currently AK Press publishes about twenty titles per year. If we had the money, we would publish forty titles in the coming year. New works from new voices, as well as a growing mountain of classic titles that, unfortunately, are being left out of print.

All these projects can come out sooner with your help. With the Friends of AK Press program, you pay a minimum of $20 or £15 per month (of course, we welcome larger contributions), for a minimum three month period. All the money received goes directly into our publishing funds. In return, Friends automatically receive (for the duration of their membership), one free copy of every new AK Press title (books, dvds, and cds), as they appear. As well, Friends are entitled to a 10% discount on everything featured in our distribution catalog and website—thousands of titles from the hundreds of publishers we work with. We also have a program where groups or individuals can sponsor a whole book. Please contact us to finds out more. To become a Friend, go to: <http://wwwakpress.org>.

AK Press Recent and Recommended

DWIGHT E. ABBOTT—I Cried, You Didn't Listen
MARTHA ACKELSBERG—Free Women of Spain
MICHAEL ALBERT—Moving Forward: Program for a Participatory Economy
JOEL ANDREAS—Addicted to War: Why the U.S. Can't Kick Militarism
JOEL ANDREAS—Adicto a la Guerra: Por qué EEUU no puede librarse del militarismo
PAUL AVRICH—Anarchist Voices: An Oral History of Anarchism in America
PAUL AVRICH—The Modern School Movement
DAN BERGER—Outlaws of America: The Weather Underground and the Politics of Solidarity
STEPHEN BEST & ANTHONY J. NOCELLA, II—Igniting A Revolution
ALEXANDER BERKMAN—What is Anarchism?
biotic baking brigade—Pie Any Means Necessary: The Biotic Baking Brigade Cookbook
MURRAY BOOKCHIN—The Ecology of Freedom: The Emergence and Dissolution of Hierarchy
MAURICE BRINTON—For Workers' Power
MAT CALLAHAN—The Trouble With Music
CHRIS CARLSSON—Critical Mass: Bicycling's Defiant Celebration
JAMES CARR—Bad
NOAM CHOMSKY—Chomsky on Anarchism
NOAM CHOMSKY—Radical Priorities
WARD CHURCHILL—On the Justice of Roosting Chickens
CLASS WAR FEDERATION —Unfinished Business: The Politics of Class War
HARRY CLEAVER—Reading Capital Politically
ALEXANDER COCKBURN & JEFFREY ST. CLAIR—End Times: The Death of the Fourth Estate
DANIEL COHN-BENDIT & GABRIEL COHN-BENDIT—Obsolete Communism: The Left-Wing Alternative
HUNTER CUTTING & MAKANI THEMBA-NIXON: Talking the Walk
DARK STAR COLLECTIVE —Beneath the Paving Stones: Situationists and the Beach, May '68
DARK STAR COLLECTIVE —Quiet Rumours: An Anarcha-Feminist Reader
EG SMITH COLLECTIVE—Animal Ingredients A–Z (3rd edition)
VOLTAIRINE de CLEYRE—Voltarine de Cleyre Reader
HOWARD EHRLICH—Reinventing Anarchy, Again
YVES FREMION & VOLNY—Orgasms of History: 3000 Years of Spontaneous Revolt
LUIGI GALLEANI—Anarchy Will Be! The Selected Writings of Luigi Galleani
EMMA GOLDMAN—Vision on Fire: Emma Goldman on the Spanish Revolution

DANIEL GUÉRIN—No Gods No Masters
HELLO—2/15: The Day The World Said NO To War
GEORGY KATSIAFICAS—The Subversion of Politics
KATHY KELLY—Other Lands Have Dreams: From Baghdad to Pekin Prison
KATYA KOMISARUK—Beat the Heat: How to Handle Encounters With Law Enforcement
RICARDO FLORES MAGÓN—Dreams of Freedom: A Ricardo Flores Magón Reader
NESTOR MAKHNO—The Struggle Against The State & Other Essays
SUBCOMANDANTE MARCOS—¡Ya Basta! Ten Years of the Zapatista Uprising
MICHAEL NEUMANN—The Case Against Israel
CRAIG O'HARA—The Philosophy Of Punk
ANTON PANNEKOEK—Workers' Councils
ABEL PAZ—Durruti in the Spanish Revolution
RUDOLF ROCKER—Anarcho-Syndicalism
RAMOR RYAN—Clandestines: The Pirate Journals of an Irish Exile
RON SAKOLSKY & STEPHEN DUNIFER—Seizing the Airwaves: A Free Radio Handbook
ROY SAN FILIPPO—A New World In Our Hearts: 8 Years of Writings from the Love and Rage Revolutionary Anarchist Federation
STEVPHEN SHUKAITIS & DAVID GRAEBER—Constituent Imagination
VALERIE SOLANAS—Scum Manifesto
ANTONIO TELLEZ—Sabate: Guerilla Extraordinary
JOHN YATES—Controlled Flight Into Terrain
JOHN YATES—September Commando

CDs
MUMIA ABU JAMAL—175 Progress Drive
JELLO BIAFRA—In the Grip of Official Treason
NOAM CHOMSKY—Case Studies in Hypocrisy
NOAM CHOMSKY—The Imperial Presidency
WARD CHURCHILL—In A Pig's Eye: Reflections on the Police State, Repression, and Native America
ALEXANDER COCKBURN—Beating the Devil
ANGELA DAVIS—The Prison Industrial Complex
NORMAN FINKELSTEIN—An Issue of Justice: Origins of the Israel/Palestine Conflict
ROBERT FISK—War, Journalism, and the Middle East
FREEDOM ARCHIVES—Chile: Promise of Freedom
CASEY NEILL—Memory Against Forgetting
CHRISTIAN PARENTI—Taking Liberties

UTAH PHILLIPS—Starlight on the Rails box set
DAVID ROVICS—Behind the Barricades: Best of David Rovics
ARUNDHATI ROY—Come September
VARIOUS—Mob Action Against the State: Collected Speeches from the Bay Area Anarchist Bookfair
HOWARD ZINN—Artists in a Time of War
HOWARD ZINN—People's History Project box set

DVDs
NOAM CHOMSKY—Distorted Morality
NOAM CHOMSKY—Imperial Grand Strategy
STEVEN FISCHLER & JOEL SUCHER—Anarchism in America/Free Voice of Labor
ROZ PAYNE ARCHIVES—What We Want, What We Believe: The Black Panther Party Library
ARUNDHATI ROY—Instant Mix Imperial Democracy
HOWARD ZINN & ANTHONY ARNOVE—Readings From Voices of a People's History

ORDERING AND CONTACT INFORMATION

AK Press
674-A 23rd Street
Oakland, CA 94612-1163
USA

AK Press
PO Box 12766
Edinburgh EH8 9YE
Scotland

akpress@akpress.org
www.akpress.org

ak@akedin.demon.co.uk
www.akuk.com

For a dollar, a pound or a few IRCs, the same addresses would be delighted to provide you with the latest complete AK catalog, featuring several thousand books, pamphlets, zines, audio products and stylish apparel published & distributed by AK Press. Alternatively, check out our websites for the complete catalog, latest news and updates, events, and secure ordering.